Y/,←

THE PRESIDENTS AND UFOs

THE PRESIDENTS
AND UFOS

A Secret History from FDR to Obama

LARRY HOLCOMBE

St. Martin's Press ♞ New York

www.stmartins.com

Designed by Omar Chapa

Library of Congress Cataloging-in-Publication Data

Holcombe, Larry.
    The Presidents and UFOs : a secret history from FDR to Obama / Larry
Holcombe.
        pages cm
    ISBN 978-1-250-04051-0 (hardcover)
    ISBN 978-1-4668-3587-0 (e-book)
    1. Unidentified flying objects—Government policy—United States.
2. Government information—United States.   3. Presidents—United States.
4. Political leadership—United States.   I. Title.

    TL789.4.H648 2015
    001.942—dc23

                                                                    2014036368

St. Martin's Press books may be purchased for educational, business, or
promotional use. For information on bulk purchases, please contact the
Macmillan Corporate and Premium Sales Department at 1-800-221-7945,
extension 5442, or write to specialmarkets@macmillan.com.

First Edition: March 2015

10 9 8 7 6 5 4 3 2 1

This book is dedicated to my son Jeff, his wife, Lisa, and their children, Melissa, Jessica, Grace, Allison, Abigail, and Bret; and to my son Rob, his wife, Tracy, and their son, Lawrence. Alice and I have been blessed with these wonderful children and grandchildren.

Contents

Acknowledgments

There have been a number of people who have played important roles in the development of this project, however none more so than nuclear physicist Stanton T. Friedman, M.S. The reader will notice that throughout the book I cite Stan's work a number of times in endnotes or the bibliography. I do this because I trust his dedication to research and his thoroughness. But perhaps more than anything I admire his skepticism and his ability to unmask the fraud that does so much harm to the legitimate and scientific effort in unraveling the complex and compelling story of extraterrestrial visitation.

In the world of UFOlogy the difficulty and frustration in trying to unravel the truth will unfortunately cause even some of the respected and legitimate UFO researchers to occasionally play a little loose with facts or bend them just a bit to make a story work. In my years of following Stan's work I have never once found him to be guilty of this practice. He has followed in the footsteps of the late and outstanding UFO researcher and atmospheric physicist, Dr. James E. McDonald. Stan is a true gentleman who deserves the respect of all serious researchers into the UFO phenomenon.

Don Schmitt, another excellent UFOlogist, encouraged me to

pursue my interest in researching Bob Emenegger's background story in making the remarkable NBC documentary, *UFOs: Past, Present, and Future,* and played an instrumental role in the development of this book. Antonio Huneeus and Stephen Bassett were instrumental in my initial contact with Bob Emenegger to get the project moving ahead.

Special thanks go to Bob Emenegger, who listened and replied in detail to my many questions. Bob welcomed Alice and me into his home and guesthouse for an overnight stay to interview him. Bob is a delightful and gracious man whom Alice and I consider a friend.

Dr. Robert Wood and his son Ryan Wood have been valuable assets in my research for this book. Their insight into the authenticating process involving many leaked documents gave me a comfort level that allowed me to tread into some very sensitive areas. Their work in authenticating the Majestic documents and other related documents perhaps presents some of the most solid evidence in all of UFOlogy.

Thanks also to Nick Pope, former MoD officer who ran the department's UFO investigation program from 1991 to 1994. Nick's comments on the Milton Torres encounter added clarity to one of the more important UFO events in the 1950s.

Art Campbell took the time and expense to send me a number of documents and audio recordings of his investigation into the Holloman-Eisenhower UFO encounter. Art continues to work on the Plains of San Agustin crash; my thanks to this fine researcher.

Kathleen Marden took time from her busy book-tour schedule to assist me in the abduction chapter. There is a short bio of Kathy in chapter 13. Her work in the field of hypnosis, as told in her new book with coauthor, Denise Stoner, *The Alien Abduction Files,* is riveting and highly recommended.

Ann Druffel's help to understand the work and genius of

Dr. James E. McDonald cannot be overstated. Her book on McDonald, *Firestorm: Dr. James E. McDonald's Fight for UFO Science,* is also highly recommended.

Bob Salas and Dr. Robert Jacobs are also due thanks for their help with the Malmstrom UFO event and the Vandenberg AFB UFO filming event.

Leslie Kean and Stan Gordon were instrumental with their comments on the Kecksburg, Pennsylvania, UFO incident. Stan spent a lot of time in correcting my synopsis of the events involved in the Kecksburg UFO crash. Thanks also to Dr. Lynne Kitei for her most helpful comments on the Phoenix Lights case.

Early in my writing career there were two people who played an important role with my writing efforts—Madison Ready and Ann Everett. Madison, I understand, is about to have her first book published and Ann has two fun novels that are pure Texas sass.

I would also like to thank the directors and staff of the International UFO Museum and Research Center in Roswell, New Mexico, for their yearly invitation to attend as an author and speaker at the museum's celebration of the four-day Roswell UFO festival each July. It was at the 2011 festival that the idea for this book first took shape.

Col. John K. Wilson (USAF Ret.) spent many hours talking to his military and lobby contacts to help me with my research. John, who spent many hours in the right-hand seat of the great FB-111, is a true friend, a believer in this book, and a believer in the phenomenon.

Very special thanks go to my agent, Peter McGuigan, who saw worth in this project, encouraged me to expand my original idea for the book, and then helped me develop and polish my idea. Special thanks also to my editor at St. Martin's, Marc Resnick, who believed in the book and made it happen.

My brother, Calvin "Cal" Holcombe, also deserves special

thanks for his support. A true skeptic over the years, he has supported my effort in developing this book with his advice and encouragement. I'm a fortunate man to have him as my brother.

Finally, and most importantly, to my wife, Alice, whose quiet support is my strength. She has gallantly fought breast cancer and a stroke, and has overcome both. She continues to travel with me, support me, and make me proud. I'm a lucky man to have her enduring love.

Foreword

Larry Holcombe has provided a great deal of information about UFO sightings during the terms of all the U.S. presidents since Franklin Delano Roosevelt. It is clear that the government has not released all the information it has. Perhaps it would be useful to give some idea of the scope of the government's classified and intelligence activities to indicate why it is so difficult to dig more out of the government, and also to put out some ideas as to why aliens might want to visit Earth and why governments want to withhold information about the visitors. An alien studying Earth would quickly realize that the planet has a primitive society whose major activity is obviously tribal warfare. There are a host of air defense commands. Consider that during World War II we earthlings killed over fifty million of our own kind and destroyed 1,700 cities. We have spent a great deal of money developing weapons of mass destruction. Only two atomic bombs have been exploded on cities (Hiroshima and Nagasaki in 1945), when the U.S. was the only country to have atomic bombs.

The Soviet Union exploded their first atomic bomb in 1949 and, in total, we earthlings have since exploded two thousand nuclear weapons, including a number of very powerful fusion weapons, five hundred times as powerful as the Hiroshima device. Much effort has, of course, also gone into developing delivery systems such as long-range bombers and intercontinental ballistic missile systems and techniques for defending against them. Starting just before the beginning of World War II, radar was developed (mostly in secret) to monitor the skies and air defense systems to cover the planet. Since then, spy satellites and aircraft radar systems have also been widely deployed. Airborne craft coming here are treated as intruders whether from other countries or other planets. Shoot first, ask questions later is the rule. Are we warlike? The total military budget for 2014 has been estimated at $1 trillion.

Recent news articles in *The Washington Post* indicate that the black budget this year (not under congressional control) for intelligence activities for the U.S. will be $52.6 billion, with leading agencies the CIA, the NSA, and the NRO getting $14.7 billion, $10.8 billion, and $10.3 billion respectively. The NRO designs, builds, and operates the country's signals and imagery reconnaissance satellites. The NSA, as everybody knows, thanks to Mr. Snowden, intercepts foreign signals intelligence. Almost everything about these three is classified. Their data is born classified so it is almost impossible to obtain. Presidents don't see much of it. Motion picture and instrument data obtained by aircraft chasing UFOs are also born classified. Analyses of wreckage from saucers that crashed at Roswell, the Plains of San Agustin, and Aztec are all classified. The work is, of course, not published in the scientific literature. It is done in industry and at the several outstanding national labs such as Los Alamos, Oak Ridge, Hanford, Sandia, et cetera, not in academia. I doubt if presidents have a need to know for much of it, based on my working under security for fourteen years.

The strange thing is that UFO debunkers apparently believe that governments can't keep secrets. Astrophysicist Dr. Neil Tyson of the Hayden Planetarium, and the new host of the revitalized *Cosmos* TV series, claims the proof that no secrets can be kept is how much we know about President Clinton's genitalia! Dr. Seth Shostak of the SETI (Silly Effort to Investigate) community claims the proof secrets can't be kept is how bad a job FEMA did during Katrina and how poorly the Post Office is run! No mention is made of the black budget or the old Manhattan Project or the Stealth aircraft on which Lockheed spent $10 billion in secret over ten years. As Larry noted, Gen. Carroll Bolender clearly indicated that UFO sightings that could affect national security were treated separately from those that could not. The evaluation continued long after Blue Book was closed. Security was of great importance.

ETs have certainly long ago recognized that nuclear fusion produces almost all the energy being produced in all the stars. We have recognized that nuclear fission (atomic bomb energy source) can be used to power submarines and aircraft carriers and fission nuclear rockets such as Nerva, XE-1, and Phoebus. It has also been clear since the 1960s that, *if* we are willing to spend the money, fusion rockets can be developed to get us to the stars. They can exhaust charged particles having ten million times as much energy per particle as in a chemical rocket. Simply put, earthlings, with their war-related attitudes, are clearly a threat to the neighborhood. It makes sense to me that the members of the galactic federation would be very concerned about us taking our brand of friendship (*hostility*) out there. It also makes sense that all governments realize that it would be great to be able to duplicate alien-flight technology. The basic rule for security is that one can't tell one's friends without telling one's enemies. I still get people telling me "Can't they just tell *us*?" The answer is no. The work of Hastings and Salas proves that aliens are interested in our nuclear weapons technology. Earlier presidents knew how important it was that the fact that the Allies had broken the German and Japanese codes, a major triumph, could not be revealed because the codes would have immediately been changed, greatly reducing the Allies' secret advantage of being able to read the enemy's military communications.

For those who want proof that there is highly classified UFO data being withheld, I suggest looking at the 156 Top Secret Umbra NSA UFO Documents one can get using Freedom of Information. Everything is whited out except for a sentence per page. There are also heavily redacted Top Secret UMBRA CIA UFO documents. Most have just a few legible words. The NRO has, to the best of my knowledge, not even released any highly redacted documents. World War II greatly expanded the need for sophisticated technology. Why should the U.S. release technological data it has obtained from study of flying saucers (crashed or airborne) if potential enemies don't? Presidents after Truman and Eisenhower were not really involved with World War II Intelligence so vital to victory.

—STANTON T. FRIEDMAN, nuclear physicist, lecturer,
www.stantonfriedman.com, fsphys@bellaliant.net

IN MEMORY

Dr. Jesse Marcel Jr.

August 30, 1936–August 25, 2013

A gentleman—a gentle man—a hero to so many

Introduction

Maj. Donald Edward Keyhoe was a bulldog. In the formative years of UFO research from the late 1940s to the 1960s, and until the arrival in 1966 of Dr. James E. McDonald on the UFO scene, no single individual came close to Keyhoe in exposing Air Force deception and outright lies concerning the UFO phenomenon. There was nothing subtle about him. To say he was a thorn in the side of the Air Force would be a gross understatement; he was a true bulldog in ferreting out facts and unrelenting in his fight against Air Force UFO secrecy. Lie to Keyhoe and he was in your face.

Keyhoe was a retired Marine Corps aviator turned writer. He wrote for *True* magazine (among others), a top-rated, primarily men's magazine of that period. In 1949 he was called to New York by editor Ken W. Purdy, and given the task of writing an investigative story on the wave of UFO sightings that had been occurring for the past couple of years. Keyhoe, being a UFO skeptic, didn't want the job but Purdy convinced him to take it. He had high-level contacts in the Pentagon and military who Purdy felt would furnish Keyhoe with valuable background information.

For over a year he researched UFOs, at that time called flying saucers, and went from a skeptic to a true believer. However, it was still some time before he could bring himself to accept the theory that the saucers were extraterrestrial and the Air Force was withholding information from the public. On December 26, 1949, all his background research and resulting beliefs were finally published in *True*. The article caused a sensation with the public, a headache for the Air Force, and a bonanza for *True*. It is reported that the article, "Flying Saucers Are Real," remains one of the most widely read articles in magazine publishing history.

Keyhoe continued to pound on the Air Force to release the secret data it possessed on saucers while being slipped confidential data from his Pentagon contacts. He followed the article with several books over the next few years and continued blasting away at the Air Force brass and calling for congressional hearings after cofounding the National Investigations Committee on Aerial Phenomena in 1956.

My introduction to the phenomenon came in 1960 as a high school junior when I ran across two books by Keyhoe: *The Flying Saucers Are Real* and *Flying Saucers from Outer Space*. I was hooked by his passion and believability. Shortly after reading his books, it was advertised that he would debate an Air Force representative on the *Armstrong Circle Theatre* television program. I was sure Keyhoe would open the eyes of the world to the fact that the Air Force was covering up the existence of extraterrestrial advanced life visiting Earth. In the view of that naïve seventeen-year-old lad the world was about to grow up.

The night of the program I sat in front of the TV expecting to hear Keyhoe make statements that would result in banner headlines around the world by morning. Instead I saw a man sit meekly and quietly while an Air Force officer recited the same official Air Force line that UFOs were nothing more than misidentified conventional objects. I was stunned and confused. I couldn't understand how this man—allowed a chance to inform the world—could pass without taking the offensive. I was totally baffled.

A few minutes before the program ended, Keyhoe finally seemed to pull himself together and said he would make a statement about a subject that had not been revealed to the public. At that instant his sound was lost and it was impossible to understand what he said.

I was furious that network problems, so prevalent in the early days of television, would occur at such a critical time. The next morning I learned the truth. Keyhoe's sound had been cut off when he deviated from the prepared script the Air Force had imposed on the show's producer. The Air Force came in with a script and demanded it be followed. The producers caved in to the Air Force demands but Keyhoe balked and threatened to walk away from the show. After much discussion he agreed to go on. Keyhoe said in a later interview that he decided to go on because he thought he would be able to slip in a few comments before the show ended. The Air Force suspected just that and placed another officer in the control room to cut his sound if he deviated from the script.

The Air Force prevailed that night but lost in the long run. Many, including that naïve lad, now saw that Keyhoe was right. The Air Force and our government were covering up information concerning UFOs. Since that night in 1960 I have watched from the sidelines as the UFO story unfolded and the evidence mounted. I became a student of what is now referred to as UFOlogy. I did it as a silent avocation because, until recently, people who took the subject of UFOs seriously were considered by many to be unstable or worse. The government had started a campaign to cover up the phenomenon by debunking it and using disinformation as recommended by the Robertson Panel to the CIA in 1953.[1] The campaign was unwittingly bolstered by the huge fanatical fringe element that the CIA skillfully used to their advantage. The campaign worked well and the subject of UFOs went from a serious subject in the mind of the public to one of scorn and ridicule. Knowing this, I generally kept my views on UFOs to myself as I researched this fascinating subject for the next forty years.

In 2008, I was doing research on my first novel, *The Great River Disclosure*, with a plot based on the theory that the United States government is concealing an extraterrestrial presence. The desire for accuracy required me to study a great amount of UFO-related material that included declassified documents, leaked documents, news stories, articles, and TV documentaries. The majority of documentaries I watched on UFOs had both the advocates and the debunkers debate each side of the issue. In many cases the advocates were weak in their knowledge of the subject and factually incorrect. The debunkers had even less knowledge and had done little or no study on the subject. They built their opinions on the belief that what these craft were reported to do was impossible according to the laws of physics, so they couldn't exist. Their overblown egos and arrogance toward a subject about which they had no knowledge and had done no research were astounding. There were some good documentaries by the top researchers like Stanton T. Friedman, but they were rare.

While doing this research, I came across what I considered an extraordinary thirty-four-year-old UFO documentary, *UFOs: Past, Present, and Future*. The documentary, which aired on NBC in 1974, was extraordinary for several reasons. First, it was professionally produced using noted personalities such as Rod Serling, well known for his popular TV show, *The Twilight Zone,* as the host, and Burgess Meredith, José Ferrer, Jacques Vallée, and famed astronomer and UFO investigator, Dr. J. Allen Hynek, as narrators. Second, the documentary supported UFOs as being a real phenomenon and also the hypothesis that some are extraterrestrial. Third, except for the host and narrators, all participants were current or retired military or Department of Defense personnel. Fourth, and of greatest importance, the documentary felt official and that was remarkable. No looking through chain-link fences at old Air Force hangars or telephoto views into some secret facility. In this documentary, retired military officials and officers went on the record and talked about UFO encounters. They walked the halls of the Pentagon and talked about UFOs. Scenes were shot inside the very secure Holloman AFB, military flight crews were allowed to discuss UFO encounters, and there was no counterpoint. This documentary just could not have been made without military support and government approval. It is simply impossible to take camera and sound crews into the Pentagon or highly classified military installations without high-level government approval. I was mystified.

Upon further research I found that the writer of the documentary, Robert Emenegger, had spoken in recent years about the background of making the film. I located a video of his address to a Stephen Bassett X-Conference and some short video interviews. I found his shocking revelations about making the documentary to be more intriguing than the documentary itself.

Emenegger was a successful Los Angeles businessman working for Grey Advertising with such clients as Bank of America. He had numerous Hollywood connections and produced and directed a number of films, some for the Department of Defense. Due to his background and his personal connection (fraternity brother) to H. R. "Bob" Haldeman, President Nixon's chief of staff, the Nixon reelection campaign contacted him about joining the campaign as a media adviser. They asked him to develop a scientific documentary that would help bolster Nixon's image in the scientific arena. Emenegger, along with his partner, Allan Sandler, were directed to Norton AFB in San Bernardino, California, to confer with Air Force officials in selecting a scientific topic for the documentary. After some discussion about a number of topics, the two men were taken by an official of the facility to a "clean room" that was to-tally secure from electronic surveillance. In that room Emenegger was asked if he would like to do a documentary on UFOs. The question took him a back as his knowledge of UFOs until then was something only found in supermarket checkout counter tabloids. He and Sandler were advised that a landing had occurred in 1964 at Holloman AFB in New Mexico and some six hundred feet of film footage had been taken of the landing. The official, Paul Shartle, told Emenegger that the footage would be made available to him for the documentary. Although stunned, Emenegger and Sandler quickly decided to make a documentary of UFO history and use the film of the Holloman landing as the explosive finish.

Emenegger's story started to haunt me. For the first and only time the government appeared to have reversed its official position that all UFOs were of natural origin and actually endorsed the extraterrestrial theory. More shocking, this happened and everyone, even the best known of the UFO researchers, seemed to ignore what I considered to be a revelation.

In the spring of 2011 I was invited by the International UFO Museum and Research Center to attend the 2011 Roswell UFO festival as the author of *The Great River Disclosure*. At that four-day event, I had the opportunity to discuss my interest in the documentary and Emenegger with Stanton Friedman, Don Schmitt, Alejandro Rojas, and Antonio Huneeus. Schmitt and Friedman concurred that the story, for whatever reason, had slipped through the cracks and needed to be revived. Each person gave Bob Emenegger a thumbs-up as to his character and honesty. Stan Friedman, for one, has been known to shoot down many a phony, so thumbs-up from this group was all I needed to press on with an attempt to contact Bob Emenegger.

With the help of Antonio Huneeus and Stephen Bassett, I was

able to get a message through to Emenegger that resulted in an initial two-hour phone conversation. I found Bob to be an unassuming gentleman who views the issue of UFOs with great interest, wonder, and a little skepticism of some of the more outlandish tales that float around in the world of fringe UFOlogy. The more I got to know him, the more I was intrigued by his intellect, delighted at his wit, and completely comfortable with his total honesty. His story is fascinating and compelling.

THE BOB EMENEGGER STORY

It was while Richard Nixon was basking in the glory of his trip to open relations with China that the administration made contact with Bob Emenegger. Nixon's reelection was on the horizon and the Committee to Re-Elect the President (CRP) wanted a documentary made, a very special documentary, and needed someone on board who could handle the task. Nixon's chief of staff, Bob Haldeman, had been a fraternity brother of Emenegger's and knew he had become a successful advertising executive with Grey Advertising. Emenegger was apprehensive about becoming involved at such a high level in a political campaign with contacts that went all the way to the White House. He knew the project would require much of his time and stretch him thin when combined with his agency work. However, after giving it much thought, and discussing the issue with his wife, Margaret, he decided to at least go to the meeting to see what the CRP members had on their mind. It was a decision that would change his life forever.

The CRP meeting was held in Los Angeles and Emenegger was asked to come on board as a media consultant. He was told that the CRP wanted a documentary of what he was told would be some new, yet-to-be-selected scientific project. With the president riding high in the polls and a second term campaign on the horizon, it was felt that a scientific documentary, perhaps a documentary

revealing some yet-to-be-announced highly secret scientific program, would make a positive impact and help ensure Nixon's reelection. Emenegger found this to be an exciting project and accepted
the position.

Emenegger brought in Los Angeles film production studio
owner Allan Sandler to partner in the production. Emenegger had
partnered with Sandler in the past on a number of projects including Emenegger's advertisements for Bank of America and a number
of Department of Defense training films.

At that time there had been no mention of the UFO phenomenon as the subject of the documentary. In fact, they were directed
by their military contacts to fly to military bases and research facilities around the country to review a number of research projects
for consideration. In San Diego they saw dolphins being trained for
underwater demolition, in Georgia they saw dogs being trained
for reconnaissance, and at Wright-Patterson AFB in Dayton, Ohio,
they saw experiments with powerful lasers. It was not until they
attended a meeting at Norton Air Force Base in San Bernardino,
California, that the subject of UFOs was broached. In looking back,
Emenegger now wonders if these trips were merely diversions to
soften the impact of what they were about to learn.

In 1972, Norton AFB housed the Air Force Audiovisual Service in
the former SAGE Direction Center that closed in 1966. It was a
cubelike four-story building—environmentally controlled and
blast proof. It was in this structure that Air Force official Paul
Shartle, the audiovisual director at the Norton facility, met with
Emenegger and Sandler. The two men were directed to what they
were told was a "clean room"—meaning it was free of any outside
listening or viewing devices and totally soundproof. In fact this
room was so secure it was used by the CIA for training and other
agency purposes.

In this secure environment the subject of a documentary on UFOs finally surfaced. Shartle informed the two men that while most sightings were misidentification of conventional objects and, in many cases, top-secret aircraft being tested, the UFO phenomenon was real; the craft were extraterrestrial and the issue was highly classified. He continued to tell them that it had been decided by someone at very high levels to declassify some of the details of extraterrestrial UFOs through the use of a documentary. The film would end with an actual landing at Holloman AFB in 1964. Film crews at Holloman had taken six hundred feet of 16mm film showing the landing and subsequent meeting between the extraterrestrial occupants and Air Force officers. This film would be made available to the production for the explosive ending to the documentary. Shartle then warned them that their efforts in producing a UFO documentary should be concealed under their less exotic endeavors as there were people in the government who would not be happy with a government-supported UFO documentary, a documentary that disclosed UFOs as being extraterrestrial.

Emenegger and Sandler were stunned. Emenegger's personal knowledge of UFOs was what he had seen on the covers of news tabloids his wife brought home from the supermarket. Here was a government official giving them hard data on what could be considered the most important story in the history of mankind. How do you handle that revelation? Where do you start? Their heads were spinning and it slowly started to dawn on them that they were going to be the catalyst to reveal this historic story.

Emenegger understood that if he was to write the documentary for Sandler's studios to produce, they would need a quick education on UFOs. A trip to Washington was arranged to meet with Col. William Coleman, Air Force public information officer, at the Pentagon. It soon became clear to the two men that Paul Shartle's warning to be discreet in dealing with UFO issues should be heeded.

Emenegger said he and Sandler arrived at the Pentagon and were ushered into a small, sparsely furnished office. Three men, dressed in the obligatory dark business suits, started to interrogate Emenegger and Sandler as to the purpose of their visit. Then they began to warn them that they were dealing in a very sensitive area that could result in serious consequences. They were also warned that they could come in contact with information and hardware that they would not be authorized to hear or see. They were told that the smart thing for them to do would be to leave the Pentagon, return to the West Coast, and forget the project.

Sandler, who according to Emenegger was no shrinking violet, had had enough. He jumped to his feet and, pointing his finger at the men, told them they were there not on their own but had been directed there by the White House. He was fed up with being given the idiot's treatment and suggested that they call the White House and get the whole damn mess straightened out. At that point the situation changed dramatically and Emenegger and Sandler became VIPs who were instantly escorted to the office of Col. William Coleman.

Coleman was waiting for the two men outside his office and he started into a mini-version of what they had heard from the three men in the interrogation office. Then he ushered the men into his office and closed the door. Coleman explained there were people who held high office behind the documentary project, but there were others, high-level bureaucrats, who were adamantly against it. He warned that there would be conflicts from beginning to end, and when they came across highly restricted information they should do their best to ignore what they saw.

After this warning, Coleman told them of his own startling UFO encounter while flying a B-25 over the southeast U.S. some years before. Clearly Coleman had experienced a UFO sighting that had made a profound impact on him. The impact of observing a real UFO is described by many to be a life-changing experience. The skeptic seems to be the person most affected. They describe the experience as feeling as though their world has turned upside down, and this may have been the case with Colonel Coleman.

Emenegger and Sandler quickly understood they had stepped into a very black world of government secrets of the most sensitive nature. More important, they had become the pivot points between two powerful and opposing factions. It was now clear that Nixon, with his own UFO interest, as well as that of friend Jackie Gleason,[2] had directed his staff to get involved in some form of UFO disclosure. Nixon could see that adding a limited level of UFO disclosure to the list of his other major accomplishments would ensure his place as one of the most important presidents in history. Had it not been for Watergate there is no doubt he would have been correct.

After discussing general ideas for the documentary with Coleman, he decided that a meeting should be set up with Emenegger, Sandler, and Col. George Weinbrenner, head of the then Foreign Technology Division (FTD) at Wright-Patterson AFB. The FTD was responsible for studying and, as necessary, back-engineering foreign technology, be it of terrestrial or extraterrestrial origin.

The meeting took place in Weinbrenner's belowground office in the FTD. In one of our many conversations Emenegger told me that his meeting with Weinbrenner was beyond strange. He said: "Allan and I walked down this dimly lit corridor to Weinbrenner's office. It felt like being in some type of catacombs. I walked up to Weinbrenner's desk and asked, 'Colonel, what's the story about the UFO landing at Holloman Air Force Base?' Weinbrenner just looked at me for a few seconds then got out of his desk chair, went to a blackboard, and drew a picture of a jet fighter. He said: 'This is a Soviet Mig 25 and we don't know a damn thing about it. They know all about our latest fighters but we know little about theirs.' He continued on fussing over the disparity in aircraft knowledge between the U.S. and the Soviet Union and as he talked he walked to a bookcase and took out a book. Continuing to talk he opened the book to the cover page, which was written 'To my friend George Weinbrenner' and was signed by Allen Hynek. It was a book on UFOs."

Emenegger continued: "Weinbrenner talked on for a while then dismissed us by thanking us for coming. We left shaking our heads. We had not heard one word from Colonel Weinbrenner about UFOs or extraterrestrials but knew that the book was his way of confirming to us that it did in fact happen. I got to know George Weinbrenner well after that day and he opened many doors for us during the production of the documentary. However, every time we got on the subject of UFOs he would become vague and distant, but I considered him a friend. In 2010, not long before he passed away, I received an unexpected message from the husband of his caregiver. The message shook me to the core and I remember it as clearly as if I had just heard it an hour ago. The message was short and simple: 'Tell Bob the Air Force has five alien bodies stored in Utah.' "

I have discussed Colonel Weinbrenner with Bob Emenegger in depth and found that Emenegger stayed in touch with his old friend until just before his death. Emenegger said he was as clear of mind in their last conversation as he was at their first meeting. In researching Weinbrenner, I found his obituary from the San Antonio Sunset Funeral Home. In the funeral home guest book there was an entry from Robert Emenegger that read:

"I remember George very well when doing a TV special, *UFOs: Past, Present, and Future.* George was very helpful to us in this project and brought to us some of the past heads of Project Blue Book. . . . " I think it's clear that someone would have more than just a passing interest in a person to take the time to make an entry in his obituary guest book—someone close enough to be the recipient of a deathbed message. The message stating that Utah is the depository for the alien bodies also has some special meaning. I have for some years felt that Dugway Proving Ground with its 800,000-plus acres is a center for UFO artifacts and not Groom Lake or the famed Area 51. Dugway is more remote than the Nellis Range or Groom Lake and just as secure. Our government, as we shall see, is very good at disinformation and deception. Secretly encouraging speculation that UFO artifacts reside at Area 51 is perfect cover for Dugway to be the actual repository for these artifacts. Anyone who's read my 2009 novel, *The Great River Disclosure,* saw in the preface that Dugway, not Area 51 (Groom Lake), was the focus of my attention for UFO activity.

Weinbrenner proved to be invaluable in helping with the documentary, which featured scenes inside the Pentagon with Col. Bill Coleman; an interview with an Army helicopter pilot, Capt. Lawrence Coyne, and his flight crew who experienced a frightening UFO encounter; and access to Holloman AFB. It was Dr. J. Allen Hynek, who came on board with his background in the Air Force Project Blue Book, who educated Emenegger and Sandler and brought factual accuracy to the production.

With funding provided by Bankers Life and Trust owner John D. MacArthur, the crew hired, and the production about to begin, the entire project suffered a setback that almost derailed it. Emenegger was advised by his White House contact, Bill Caruthers, that use of the landing film had been withdrawn. A bewildered Emenegger asked for an explanation. He was simply told that opposition to the release of the footage was great and the increasing pressure from Watergate had made the administration back away from the project. He was told to proceed with production as planned but without the landing film at the end. In its place he could show a fictional landing and say this is what may happen in the future. Seeing Emenegger's distress, Caruthers added, "You may also say that perhaps this event has already occurred." That is exactly how Rod Serling (in the completed documentary) begins the future segment filmed at Holloman AFB.

THE DOCUMENTARY

The documentary opens with Rod Serling walking through what could be described as a cosmic tunnel as he speaks about man's place in the universe and how his existence came about. The scene shifts to a dramatization of a rather well-known Texas sighting by two men in a pickup truck that stalls when a UFO hovers overhead. The scene then shifts to Burgess Meredith and José Ferrer reading from biblical accounts of strange flying machines and encounters with strange beings thought to be angels or gods.

One of the most important segments of the documentary has newly retired Col. William Coleman walking the halls of the Pentagon as he explains the development of the 1948 Air Force report, *Estimate of the Situation,* written by personnel of the Air Force's Project Sign (forerunner to Project Grudge and then Blue Book). The document explained the reasons that Sign personnel, including its director, Capt. Robert R. Sneider, concluded that the extraterrestrial hypothesis was the best explanation for UFOs. As Coleman walks, he stops under a portrait of Gen. Hoyt Vandenberg. He explains that the report found its way up the chain of command, finally ending on Vandenberg's desk. The general wasn't happy with the report and batted it back down the chain of command due to what Vandenberg said was lack of physical evidence. All of the above is factual as related by Coleman in the documentary. In addition, Capt. Edward Ruppelt, the original director of Project Blue Book (as well as Project Grudge) wrote a book on Project Blue Book after retiring from the Air Force. In the book he covers the *Estimate of the Situation* issue in detail. Notably, Ruppelt's book was cleared by the Air Force.

There is an interesting side note to this story. In the 1980s, UFO researcher Kevin Randle talked with an unnamed Air Force colonel who told Randle that as a young lieutenant he worked on the report. There was a discussion of physical evidence in the report, specifically the metal recovered in New Mexico. He told Randle that Vandenberg had ordered that paragraph removed from the report and then said he was rejecting the report because of a lack of physical evidence.[3]

Unfortunately the document has never been found and is thought to have been destroyed. In Ann Druffel's excellent book on Dr. James E. McDonald's UFO research, *Firestorm*, there is an exchange between McDonald and Dr. J. Allen Hynek concerning the document. The author has granted me permission to reproduce an abridged version of that exchange from her book.[4]

> *The Congressional UFO hearing, held on July 29, 1968, went well, and the participants met that evening for cocktails and celebration in the DuPont Plaza, joined by some NICAP staff. Later that evening, Hynek privately conceded to McDonald that he had, indeed, seen the mysterious 1948 "Estimate of the Situation," a top-secret Air Force document, the existence of which UFOlogists had tried to prove since 1953. Donald E. Keyhoe and NICAP had tried for many years to procure a copy of it, for its existence had been confirmed to Keyhoe by Major Dewey Fournet, a NICAP Board member, and it was described in "The UFO Evidence."*
>
> *Intrigued by the fact that Hynek had actually seen this elusive document, McDonald asked why he'd never*

*come out publicly and admitted that "The Estimate of
the Situation" actually existed? Hynek squirmed, specu-
lating that the USAF never made the document official
after it found its way up the ladder to General Vandenberg. Therefore it never existed as an accepted Air Force
report. "However," repeated Hynek, "I've seen it somewhere along the line." (Druffel 2003, 78–79)*

Another compelling incident in the documentary was the story
of Capt. Lawrence Coyne and his helicopter flight crew and their
UFO experience. Coyne and his crew encountered a large bright
UFO over Mansfield, Ohio, on October 18, 1973. Expecting a collision with the UFO, the crew braced but the UFO hovered just
above the helicopter. Coyne tried to take the helicopter down in an
emergency descent but was instead pulled upward about fifteen
hundred feet before the UFO flashed off, leaving the crew extremely shaken. Col. Robert Friend, a former director of Project
Blue Book from 1958 to 1963, was allowed to interview the crew
in detail in the documentary.

There was a more bizarre event related by Colonel Friend that
was included two years later in a revised remake of the original
UFOs: Past, Present, and Future, named, *UFOs: It Has Begun.*
What follows is an abridged version of Colonel Friend's story.[5]

In July 1959, Friend was acting chief of Project Blue Book. As
such he was requested to fly to Washington, D.C., to evaluate a
discovery by Naval Intelligence. Arriving in D.C., Friend was met
by two Navy commanders and several CIA intelligence officers
headed by Arthur C. Lundahl, the highly regarded director of the
National Photographic Interpretation Center, who quickly began
to brief him on the reason for his trip.

Friend was told that in 1954 two naval officers had been dispatched to Maine at the request of a retired admiral who knew a

woman there who claimed to be in contact with extraterrestrials. This woman was a close friend of the admiral and the admiral's wife, and they obviously respected her enough to bring in Naval Intelligence. The officers met with the woman at her home and watched her go into a trance and start a communication with some space leader called AFFA. Through this woman, the alien advised that he was part of a group investigating atomic tests on Earth. The Navy officers then asked questions of this being through the woman that were far above her level of knowledge, including complicated astronomical questions. To their amazement the answers were quick and correct. This went on for a period of time and the officers were actually drawn into the event as participants.

After Friend was briefed, they went to a secret government office on the top floor of a building at Fifth and K Street NW. One of the commanders who had been involved in the experiment in Maine was able to go into a trance and start communication with AFFA. Friend saw the commander change; the muscles in his arms and neck became stressed. The commander started writing with a handwriting very different from his own. Among things AFFA said was that he was from the planet we call Uranus. He was asked if the officers could see his craft at some point. They were told they could see it now if they went to the windows. A brightly lit oval craft flashed into view. Later requests for radar confirmation from Andrews AFB and Washington National found that the area in which the craft appeared had been blacked out for some reason.

This story was so sensational, and involved Naval Intelligence, that an attempt was made in 1959 by naval personnel to locate the admiral. It was found that he was deceased but his wife verified their friendship with the woman, Frances Swan, and that Swan had continued contact with AFFA for a number of years.

I debated including this story in the book because of its

sensational nature, and decided to for several reasons. First, it was a part of the documentary and was proven to have had the support of the government. Second, it was told by an Air Force officer who headed the official Air Force investigation into the UFO phenomenon and was a firsthand witness to the event. Third, Colonel Friend (Major at the time) was well vetted and his background and his credentials were impeccable along with his work with the late Dr. J. Alan Hynek. Finally, Arthur Lundahl's involvement added tremendous legitimacy to the story. Lundahl didn't talk about the story, he didn't talk about his work at all; his record of involvement came from Colonel Friend.

Could this have been some sort of government disinformation, and if so, why? The story of the 1954 event is covered in an FBI memo dated August 8, 1954, and is included in the appendix.

The ending of the documentary is where the film footage from Norton AFB was to have been used to show the actual landing of a UFO at Holloman AFB, New Mexico. The segment, which is the "Future" portion, starts with Rod Serling at Holloman AFB stating, "This is what may occur at some future date . . . or perhaps it has already occurred." Film shows the inside of the Holloman's operation center, then moves to the control tower. We are told that three uncorrelated targets have been detected by radar approaching the base. Fighter jets are scrambled to meet, identify, and escort the craft to the base. The camera scans the desert and the far mountains from the tower. As the camera scans, we see a slight jump in the film as if some film had been inserted. It is at this point that a bright light is seen coming down toward the base and leveling out. This lasts only several seconds before the scene goes to animation and three disc-shaped objects are shown. One sets down on the runway and the other two remain hovering just above the craft. A door opens and a figure dressed somewhat like an ancient

Egyptian emerges. He is met by Air Force officials and we are told they will retire to a conference room for talks.

The controversial part of this segment is where the film scanning the horizon from the control tower jumps as if a segment had been spliced in. The segment lasts only several seconds but some claim that Emenegger told them they had gotten a few feet of the actual landing and were allowed to show the craft at a distance. I discussed this with him in his kitchen over coffee one morning and he denied that was the case. He said the light was the wheel light on a fighter landing at Holloman.

The ending of the film with the animation, in particular the artist's conception of the extraterrestrial, is somewhat disappointing. This is also a feeling shared with Bob Emenegger. Needless to say, if the actual film had been used, we most certainly would be living in a different world today.

I discussed my idea for a book on the background of making the documentary with Bob Emenegger; he seemed delighted and offered his assistance. After working on an outline for the book I presented my ideas to my agent for his suggestions. In these discussions the idea for developing a complete history of presidential involvement in the UFO issue evolved. Initially I was apprehensive for a number of reasons; chief among them is the fact that securing factual information from presidential records, especially classified information, is next to impossible. Factual UFO data that could be tied to presidents simply doesn't exist. Everything is rumor, or at least it was until Bob Emenegger entered the picture with his revelations that became the catalyst to bind presidential UFO history into one cohesive story. In an instant everything fell into place, and the pieces started to fit.

From time to time throughout the book I will revert to discussions of behind-the-scenes actions of researchers, congressional

leaders, and members of the scientific community who were involved in the very complicated UFO story. This may seem boring
to the casual observer who wants to read of sensational UFO events.
However, I think it is necessary for the casual observer to grasp
that the UFO issue was not just a subject that was embraced by
UFOlogists and believers, but also had deep respect by many in
Congress and in the scientific community.

What follows is the history of American presidents' involvement and handling of the greatest story in the history of mankind.
In telling this story the casual observer will be treated, for perhaps
the first time, to a general historical overview of the complete
modern UFO phenomenon.[6]

1

THE BEGINNING

THE ROOSEVELT AND TRUMAN ADMINISTRATIONS

BEGINNING THOUGHTS

The UFO/flying saucer phenomenon is a complex story with issues that run in many directions like the roots of a huge tree. The complexity of the story requires years of study to understand the true nature of the phenomenon. This fact makes it impossible for the casual observer to grasp the importance and enormity of the issue.

The subject is considered with varying levels of concern by every government around the world. It is a serious scientific subject that the United States government, for a number of reasons, has effectively debunked and ridiculed for the last sixty years. It is a phenomenon that is part of nature, a part of the universe. It is not a secret Department of Defense project, yet it is being handled by the government as if it were.

This book will examine the role the U.S. presidents played as this fascinating scientific saga began to unfold in the post–World War II era and the reasons for the extreme and continued secrecy. In telling the story of presidential involvement in UFO issues, the book will also educate the casual observer, the skeptic, and the agnostic about the very complex and complicated *big picture* of the UFO phenomenon in a simple and understandable manner. It will attempt to separate the wheat from the chaff of a complex subject that is riddled with inaccuracies, poor research, disinformation, a lack of logic, and blatant lies.

In discussing the UFO phenomenon with people I call the "casual observer," that is, people who have an interest in the subject but have not studied it in any depth, I am often asked what makes me so sure that UFOs actually exist? My reply is simple: There is a literal mountain of evidence that has accumulated for the last seventy-plus years that, when viewed as a whole, is indisputable that the UFO phenomenon is real and that objects or craft of unknown origin have the capability to fly in our atmosphere in a manner that defies known physical laws. This book will give snapshot versions of some major UFO events. By viewing the phenomenon using the presidential background for these events, we will show how the government has handled or mishandled the most important scientific subject in the history of mankind. The UFO events discussed in this book represent but a tiny fraction of legitimate UFO events that occurred over the last sixty-plus years. They were selected because of their quality, importance, and possible impact on national security.

Hopefully after the reader completes this work, he or she will at least have a flavor of the mountain of evidence proving UFOs exist and the government's continuing efforts to conceal this important scientific subject from the general population.

Before beginning this journey the reader is asked to consider the following:

1. In today's culture the abbreviation, "UFO" is generally understood to mean extraterrestrial spacecraft. The accurate definition of a UFO is a flying object that the observer is unable

to identify. Most UFOs are NOT extraterrestrial spacecraft but merely misidentification of some prosaic object or in many cases classified and experimental military aircraft. A true UFO as discussed in this book is an object that, when observed from a reasonable distance and perspective, defies conventional explanations. They appear to be intelligently controlled, and perform aerial maneuvers that defy the known laws of physics. They can hover and accelerate at tremendous speeds, both laterally and vertically, make flat right-angle turns, and stop instantly from incredible speeds. A UFO by definition does not have to be an extraterrestrial craft. It may well be, and it's my personal opinion that some are extraterrestrial. There is a huge accumulation of evidence that points in that direction, but as yet that has not been proven to be fact. In this book when referring to UFOs, the reference is to *true* UFOs and may also be referred to as UFOs/flying saucers.

2. UFOs exist: The accumulation of evidence is so great that no reasonable person can any longer deny their existence. To quote the Honorable Paul Heller, former Canadian minister of defense, "They are as real as the airplanes that fly over your head." (Heller, 2005)

3. The most common argument by skeptics and debunkers is that the government is unable to keep secrets. It is of utmost importance for the reader to understand that the government of the United States can and does keep secrets. The argument is that a story so big could not be kept secret for any length of time. That cry has been heard from the beginning of the UFO phenomenon. It is totally incorrect. The intelligence community and the military are accustomed and well qualified in keeping secrets that involve national security and military

hardware, and the darker the secret, the more secure it is. Political secrets are completely different; they rarely can be kept. For that reason politicians are almost never privy to black projects that involve national security or the military. The Manhattan Project is the perfect example. For ten years, over fifty thousand people worked on the development of the atomic bomb and no one in Congress knew they existed until they were dropped on Japan. It was eight days after the death of Franklin Roosevelt before Harry Truman knew they existed.

4. Finally, the reader is asked to understand the basic concept of UFO sightings. People who study and research these sightings agree that most sightings can usually be explained as something normal, natural, and terrestrial. This includes military black or secret projects. The number of true unexplained UFO sightings is generally thought to be in the area of 5 percent of all reported sightings, and for every reported sighting, either explainable or not, there are probably ten, and probably many more, that go unreported. This unfortunate fact will be discussed in the final chapter.

　　When researchers lecture on the UFO phenomenon, this fact is always pointed out to the audience. Though factual, I believe it gives a false understanding to the casual observer. Simply stated, if the casual observer hears that of all reported UFO sightings, 95 percent can be explained, then the normal thought process is that more study on the remaining 5 percent would explain those as well. I feel this approach dilutes the importance of what I consider 100 percent of legitimate UFO sightings made by competent trained observers of sightings as outlined in number one, above. With this in mind I believe UFO sightings should be viewed in two distinct groups. Group number one would be UFO sightings that when studied can be explained as something conventional. Group two would be high-quality sightings made by competent observers that when studied offer no conventional explanation.

In the fifty-plus years since Donald Keyhoe introduced me to flying saucers, the Air Force and the United States government have publicly stated that UFOs are simply misidentified natural or conventional objects. Officially they stated that these objects pose no threat to national security, even though reports of UFOs stalking airliners, causing many to take evasive action, have steadily increased. UFOs have been reported over major airports and military installations, especially nuclear installations. Reports from credible witnesses, such as pilots and police officers, have mounted. Some reports by multiple witnesses with trace evidence and radar backup were so startling and well documented that the attempted debunking explanations were more bizarre and unbelievable than the theory that they were extraterrestrial.[1] A few reports, such as Japan Airlines Flight 1628's UFO encounter over Alaska, slipped through the cracks and made world news before the U.S. government could cover up the story.

Finally, countries around the world started to see the folly in continued UFO secrecy. Many began to relax their internal UFO security and open their files. The release of previously highly classified files of UFO incidents by foreign governments, or files secured from the U.S. through the Freedom of Information Act (FOIA), freed many who were involved in the incidents and bound by their security clearance to tell their stories. The stories began coming in from very creditable people. Air Force Capt. Robert Salas, a launch control officer at an ICBM installation at Malmtrom Air Force Base, was one of these people. He related a fantastic story of a UFO hovering over the installation's front gate, shutting down all of their ready ICBMs. Stories also came from pilots such as Dr. Milton

Torres, USAF, stationed in England in the 1950s, who was ordered to shoot down a huge UFO (the size of an aircraft carrier according to Torres) orbiting over the English countryside before the craft shot away at over ten thousand miles per hour. Or Gen. Parviz Jafari of the Iranian air force who had a remarkable UFO encounter over Tehran in 1976 flying a U.S.-made F-4 Phantom. Countries around the globe—the U.K., Belgium, France (with their COMETA Report), Russia, Mexico, Brazil, Chile, Argentina, Australia, and many more—began to release tight UFO secrecy and open their files, while the U.S. was left standing alone in denial of a UFO presence that demanded scientific study.

THE ROOSEVELT YEARS

On the night before Halloween, October 30, 1938, the CBS radio network's *Mercury Theater on the Air* broadcast Orson Welles's adaptation of the H. G. Wells novel, *The War of the Worlds*. The show ran as a musical program interspersed with simulated bulletins about an invasion of Martians near the town of Grover's Mill, New Jersey. At the beginning, at intermission, and at the end of the broadcast the listening audience was told that the program was a work of fiction. Nevertheless a great number of people tuned in missing the disclaimer and thought the Earth was being attacked by invading aliens from Mars.

Although historical studies of this famous broadcast have shown that the ensuing panic caused by the broadcast was greatly overstated by the press, still hundreds of thousands of people were genuinely frightened by the show. There was widespread negative reaction resulting in lawsuits and some sanctions imposed on future broadcasts by CBS.

This broadcast and the thousands of newspaper articles that followed imprinted in the psyche of the population the notion that you can fool me once but not twice. Hence, as news reports of unknown flying objects started to appear in the press in the 1940s, the public was largely unimpressed. *The War of the Worlds* was no longer frightening, but a world at war was.

For the first half of the 1940s the population was consumed with the war effort and gave little thought to mysterious aerial craft or extraterrestrial life. This was not the case for our government and military. Recently leaked top-secret documents tell of the government's retrieval of extraterrestrial craft going back to 1941, and the ensuing deep involvement in efforts to unravel the mysteries of these visitors from other worlds.

Pilot Kenneth Arnold's Washington State sighting of a daisy chain of flying discs near Mount Rainier in 1947 is generally considered the beginning of the modern era of flying saucer/UFO encounters. However, in the mid-1990s, documents surfaced that indicate a crash and retrieval of an alien craft may have occurred near Cape Girardeau, Missouri, in the spring of 1941. The story first surfaced in a letter from Charlette Mann to UFO researcher Leonard Stringfield (Good, 2007). The letter recounted how her grandfather, William Huffman, a Baptist minister, had been summoned one spring evening in 1941 to the site of a plane crash some fifteen miles from Cape Girardeau. He was requested to offer prayers for injured or dead occupants of the plane. Arriving at the site, he discovered not a plane but a circular craft and three dead small humanoid occupants. Also present at the crash site were several police officers, firemen, and photographers. Huffman said a prayer for the dead creatures just before the military arrived and took control. All photographic film was confiscated by the military, who advised the group that what they witnessed was a matter of great national security. They were admonished to never speak of the event to anyone. Returning home, in a state of shock, Huffman related the event to his wife, then told her she must never repeat the story. Many years later when the grandmother was dying from cancer, Charlette Mann succeeded in getting her to tell the story, a story Charlette had heard whispered about within the family for many years.

Less than one year after the Cape Girardeau crash, the famous L.A. air raid took place. The event is important because it is the first indication of presidential involvement in the UFO issue. According to a leaked memo from Franklin D. Roosevelt to Gen. George C. Marshall, dated February 27, 1942, two days after the Los Angeles air raid (in reply to a memo from Marshall on the air raid), the president obviously makes reference to a previous crash retrieval.[2] The memo reads as follows:

> I have considered the disposition of the material in possession of the Army that may be of great significance toward the development of a super weapon of war. I disagree with the argument that such information should be shared with our ally the Soviet Union. Consultation with Dr. Bush and other scientists on the issue of finding practical uses for the atomic secrets learned from the study of celestial devices precludes any further discussion and I therefore authorize Dr. Bush to proceed with the project without further delay. The information is vital to the nation's superiority and must remain within the confines of state secrets. Any further discussion on the matter will be restricted to General Donavan, Dr. Bush, the secretary of war, and yourself. The challenge our nation faces is daunting and perilous in this undertaking and I have committed the resources of the government towards that end. You have my assurance that when circumstances are favorable and we are victorious, the Army will have the

fruits of research in exploring further applications of this new wonder.

FDR

This document, along with a number of others, was leaked to UFO researcher Tim Cooper in California. Cooper became interested in the Roswell incident and made inquiries about it to a number of retired military officers living near him. Apparently his inquiries resulted in the anonymous leaking of these documents. Cooper made contact with well-known UFO investigator and nuclear physicist Stanton T. Friedman, and sent him copies of the documents. Friedman, a staunch believer in an extraterrestrial presence, yet a skeptic when looking at startling new revelations, needed to check Cooper's credibility. He contacted friend and former McDonnell Douglas executive, Dr. Robert Wood, who was living in California, and asked Wood to check out Cooper. At McDonnell Douglas, Wood headed a team that quietly studied the UFO phenomenon using Friedman as a consultant. After retirement, Wood continued his investigation into UFO issues. Time spent checking out Cooper and reviewing the leaked documents resulted in Wood focusing his future efforts on the authentication of UFO-related documents. Of particular interest were the MJ-12 documents, which will be covered in later chapters.

Another leaked document, dated March 5, 1942, from George C. Marshall to the president states in part:

Regarding the air raid over Los Angeles it was learned by Army G2 that Rear Admiral Anderson has informed the War Department of a naval recovery of an unidentified airplane off the coast of California with no bearing on conventional explanation. Further it has been revealed that the Army Air Corps has also recovered a similar craft

*in the San Bernardino Mountains east of Los Angeles
which cannot be identified as conventional aircraft. This
Headquarters has come to the determination that the
mystery airplanes are in fact not earthly and according to
secret intelligence sources they are in all probability of
interplanetary origin. As a consequence I have issued orders to Army G2 that a special intelligence unit be created to further investigate the phenomenon and report
any significant connection between recent incidents and
those collected by the director of the office of Coordinator of Information.*

G. C. Marshall

These two documents continue to be studied by the Wood
team and at present carry a mid–high level of authenticity rating
on their Web site. If authentic, these two explosive documents reveal that the government knew of an extraterrestrial presence as
early as the spring of 1941. Roosevelt, in his memo, referred to
"celestial devices" in the "possession of the Army," which, by this
time line, would exclude the L.A. air raid recoveries. His reference
was probably to the Cape Girardeau recovery, or possibly a Louisiana recovery referred to in an FBI memo from J. Edgar Hoover.
In his memo, Hoover mentioned a disc recovered in "La" and lamented that it was "grabbed by the Army."

There is one other Roosevelt memo of special interest that is
under study for authentication: the Roosevelt memo to the Special
Committee on Non-Terrestrial Science and Technology. In this
memo he discussed "coming to grips with the reality that our
planet is not the only one harboring intelligent life in the universe."
He goes on to say that "we will take every advantage of such wonders that have come to us after we have won the war." These are

clearly references to recovered alien spacecraft and associated technology.

If these documents are genuine, the knowledge of the existence of an extraterrestrial presence goes back prior to the United States' entry into World War II, which makes President Roosevelt the first president to face this reality. How the president was able to deal with what is certainly the most startling discovery in the history of mankind while waging a worldwide war is not clear. It is clear that President Roosevelt understood the tremendous potential for a huge leap in technology that the newfound wonders offered. He also understood the huge leap in power they would give to those that possessed the secrets. He, along with those close to him, knew that these secrets must remain within the government. Under no circumstances should they be shared with any other country. Considering that the nation was on the verge of entering a great world war against strong enemies on opposite sides of the globe, any other position would have been measured criminal and impeachable.

As we move through the story of the presidents, we will see that these early words from President Roosevelt will resonate for decades to come, setting the stage for the greatest cover-up in the history of mankind. "The information is vital to the nation's superiority and must remain within the confines of state secrets." Roosevelt certainly understood the ramifications of the startling discovery of an extraterrestrial presence on Earth, but he didn't know their intentions. On the other hand, he knew well the intentions of the adversaries the country faced in Europe and Japan. He stated that these new and startling revelations must take second place to the waging of war against the Axis powers. They would be addressed after we were victorious, and when Roosevelt died they would fall directly into the lap of President Harry Truman.

THE TRUMAN YEARS

Harry Truman took the oath of office as president of the United States at 7:09 P.M. on April 12, 1945. Earlier that afternoon he had been summoned to the White House and taken to Mrs. Roosevelt's study. As reported in the *Reader's Digest Illustrated History of WWII*, Mrs. Roosevelt stepped forward and quietly said, "Harry, the president is dead." Truman, shocked, replied, "Is there anything I can do for you?" Mrs. Roosevelt said, "Is there anything we can do for you? For you are the one in trouble now."

That exchange, repeated many times by authors and historians, still doesn't convey the extent of the enormous vacuum that Harry Truman was about to enter. Truman, a former Midwestern farmer and failed haberdasher, who was viewed by many as a man of mediocrity, was about to attempt to fill the great void left by a man from wealth and privilege who many saw not only as larger than life but also as a savior. If these circumstances intimidated the new president, the intimidation didn't last long. On May 7, Germany surrendered and Truman proudly proclaimed May 8 V-E Day. In July he traveled to Potsdam to meet with British Prime Minister Winston Churchill and Joseph Stalin of the Soviet Union. On his way home from Potsdam, Truman gave the order to drop the first atomic bomb on Japan, and three days later to drop the second. He oversaw the rebuilding and recovery from the effects of the great world war. He initiated the Fair Deal that extended FDR's New Deal and the Truman Doctrine. His administration oversaw the Berlin Airlift that marked the beginning of the Cold War, the organization of the United Nations, the formation of NATO, the unification of the armed services, the beginning of the Korean War, and the firing of Gen. Douglas MacArthur.

It's clear Harry Truman faced, and would face in the future, national and world events that would change the course of history. Perhaps no other president has presided over such a time of enormous change. It was the birth of the atomic age coupled with the threat of the Cold War. The country—and the world—were growing up and Harry Truman, Midwestern haberdasher, was now leading the free world into an uncertain future. The momentous events listed above have been well chronicled by historians over the last sixty years. It now seems astonishing that the new president also had to address the possibility of the most monumental event in human history: the existence of an extraterrestrial presence of unknown purpose or origin. Truman had to deal with the fact that objects could violate the airspace of sovereign nations and fly into and out of our most sensitive areas while the military was powerless to stop the incursions. He had to deal with this knowledge while keeping it a closely guarded secret.

It is amazing that in the past sixty years no historian has added this important issue to the highlights of the Truman administration, considering the issue made headlines numbers of times. At one press conference Truman acknowledged that what were then called flying saucers were discussed at White House meetings. This is another example of the depth of the stigma of UFOs in academia. Scholars avoid any mention of the subject for fear that their work would not be considered credible.

Harry Truman was an honest, moral, and God-fearing man who was not afraid to make decisions and live with them. In World War I, Truman was an artillery captain who was highly thought of by the men under him. He was first elected to the U.S. Senate in 1934. During World War II he gained prominence as the head of a committee that exposed fraud in wartime contracts. He was not fearful or faint of heart, and he accepted challenges that were in the public interest. He was also feisty when crossed, had a taste for bourbon whiskey, and could have a salty tongue when necessary. After firing the general of the Army, Douglas MacArthur, and listening to his speech before a joint session of Congress on television,

Truman summed up the speech with little elegance. "With all the carrying on and the damn fool congressmen crying like a bunch of women, it was still one hundred percent bullshit" (Manchester 1979).

Truman had another attribute that served him well as president. He understood the need for security. He knew better than any other president, with the possible exception of Eisenhower, how to implement and maintain it. This was bolstered by the fact that he did not have a large ego that required constant inflation by excessive verbal discourse. For these reasons he may have been the perfect president to address the new phenomenon of flying saucers.

For the sake of clarity, a moment should be taken to address the terms "flying saucers" and "UFOs" and how they are used in this book. The term "flying saucer" originated when a newspaper reporter used it to describe what is commonly thought to be the first modern public knowledge of a UFO sighting. That was in June 1947 and made by Kenneth Arnold in Washington State. He described the objects he saw flying near Mount Rainier as looking like saucers skipping across water. The reporter used the term "flying saucer" in his article and the name stuck. In 1952 the broader term of "unidentified flying object" (UFO) was coined to cover the increasing number of different-shaped objects being reported. Discussing the Truman years in this book, the term "flying saucer" will be used, since it is the term used in that time period. In more recent years some UFOlogists, most notably well-known researcher Stanton T. Friedman, use "UFO" to describe all reported unknown objects, and "flying saucer" to distinguish extraterrestrial craft from terrestrial UFOs.

It is known that a number of well-reported flying saucer events took place during the Truman administration. However, memos and correspondence from or to the White House on the subject are difficult to find to the point of being all but nonexistent. One reason for this is Truman's excellent ability to maintain security. His correspondence and that of his assistants are vague, cryptic, and use an economy of words. The list of those inside the loop of knowledge concerning flying saucers who would have received memos was small; it included Secretary of State Gen. George C. Marshall, Gen. Nathan Twining, Gen. Hoyt Vandenberg, James Forrestal, and Dr. Vannevar Bush, to name a few. A good example of a vague memo is the well-known Truman-Forrestal Memo that read:

> *Dear Secretary Forrestal:*
>
> *As per our recent conversation on this matter, you are hereby authorized to proceed with all due caution upon your undertaking. Hereafter this matter shall only be referred to as Operation Majestic Twelve.*
>
> *It continues to be my opinion that any future considerations relative to the ultimate disposition of this matter should rest solely with the Office of the President following appropriate discussions with you, Dr. Bush and the Director of Central Intelligence. (See Appendix A.)*

The memorandum was on White House stationery, stamped "top secret eyes only" and signed by Truman.[3] The matter referenced in the memo was the investigation of flying saucers. It was established of a group of six high-ranking military officers and six highly esteemed scientists to study the flying saucer phenomenon. With high-security matters such as these, secure meetings covered the details, which were almost never put into print. The reason for this is that official documents live forever and can get into the wrong hands. Also, they are prepared by secretaries who, although holding a high-level security clearance, are nevertheless outside of the need to know. President Truman would not divulge his knowledge of a subject when asking for briefings on that particular subject from a person outside the circle of knowledge. He could be the consummate poker player in covering his knowledge and true feelings about a sensitive subject. This has led some UFO researchers to the belief that Truman's feelings about flying saucers were the same as his feelings toward MacArthur's speech to Congress. That is exactly how Truman wanted it.

Truman's Air Force aide, Gen. Robert Landry, tells of Truman's flying saucer interest in an oral history the general did for Columbia University. Landry explains how he was summoned to the Oval Office shortly after being appointed to the position and questioned by the president on his knowledge and thoughts on flying saucers. Truman went on to say that he hadn't given much serious thought to the subject. However, if there was any possible threat to national security, he wanted to be informed. He requested to be updated every three months with CIA information and sooner if new developments warranted such (Dolan 2002). Briefings were to be verbal, nothing written; again, the consummate poker player never revealing what he knew to Landry while looking for new intelligence

Truman was certainly briefed on the events and recoveries that took place during the Roosevelt administration. He knew that our best scientists were at work trying to unlock the secrets of these newly discovered wonders. He was not concerned with the technical aspect of these discoveries, knowing he would be informed of any resulting practical applications from the scientific study. His concern was in the broader area of the motives and intentions of these otherworldly visitors and what the future held. It was in this area that he required up-to-date intelligence while maintaining absolute security.

Starting in 1947 the country, and especially the Southwest, saw a surge in flying saucer sightings, especially around areas involved in nuclear or rocket testing. A number of persons who worked on those early projects have come forward in their later years to say that the sightings of mystery craft came to be expected at every test and were eventually all but ignored. From 1947 until early 1953, and the debunking initiatives of the Robertson Panel, there was a dramatic increase in sightings and press coverage. The Truman administration had to deal with some of the most dramatic sightings and encounters in all of UFOlogy, both behind the scenes and in public.

THE ROSWELL INCIDENT

The crash at Corona, New Mexico—about seventy miles from Roswell—is arguably the most important event in UFOlogy. It has been well covered by numerous books and television specials, so the event will not be covered in depth here. However, so much has been written about the incident that the very important basic facts can be overlooked and lost in the minutiae. For this reason, it is necessary to review some important factual details. In looking at these details the following facts should be kept in mind:

1. The Army outfit that recovered the crash debris was the 509th Bomb Wing stationed at Roswell Army Air Field. The 509th was the group that dropped both atomic bombs on Japan. It was the most elite bombing wing on earth.

2. The officer first sent to investigate the wreckage was Maj. Jesse Marcel, the chief intelligence officer for the 509th.

3. When the wreckage was retrieved and taken to Roswell Army Air Field, Col. William Blanchard, base commander, authorized the base public information officer, Walter Haut, to issue a press release stating that the base had recovered a "flying disc," as they were also called at the time.[4]

4. The press release created a worldwide uproar.

5. Debris from the crash was ordered to be loaded on a bomber and flown to Fort Worth Army Air Field, home of the Eighth Air Force, and commanded by Gen. Roger Ramey.

6. General Ramey's chief of staff, Col. Thomas Jefferson Dubose, got a call at Eighth Air Force headquarters from the deputy commander of the Strategic Air Command, Gen. Clements McMullen, at the Pentagon. McMullen told Dubose to kill the crashed "disc" story and send the crash debris to him in Washington, D.C. He would then put it on his personal plane and fly it to Wright Field in Dayton, Ohio, for investigation.

7. General Ramey quickly called a press conference to advise that Colonel Blanchard and Major Marcel had been mistaken and the debris found on the ranch was of a weather balloon and RAWIN radar reflectors.

The history of the official position of the Air Force in 1947 was that the recovered debris was that of a weather balloon and radar reflectors, and not a crashed disc as originally reported. With this cover story in place the Roswell incident all but dropped from view until 1978, when Stanton T. Friedman stumbled across Jesse Marcel (the officer first sent to investigate the wreckage) who was retired and living in Houma, Louisina. Marcel told Friedman that the material he found at the crash site was unlike anything he had seen before. There was tinfoil-like material that could be crushed in your hand but would return to smooth flatness when released. The material couldn't be torn, cut, or burned. There was also small beamlike material with strange marks that had the weight of balsa wood but that also couldn't be cut, broken, or burned. Nothing

Marcel saw looked faintly familiar. One would think that something would be recognizable to the chief intelligence officer of the only nuclear bomb wing in the U.S. if this was indeed a crash site of terrestrial equipment. The revelations he told Friedman resulted in several books written by Friedman and others, which revived the story and brought forth a number of firsthand witnesses—witnesses of quality who wanted to talk. The story grew and gained traction, forcing the Air Force in the mid-1990s to admit that the weather balloon was indeed a cover story, and what really crashed was a top-secret project called Project Mogul. The project was authentic and was an attempt by the U.S. to send electronic equipment aloft to listen for Soviet nuclear tests. This was accomplished by connecting radio equipment to a daisy chain of standard weather balloons and radar reflectors. There was nothing exotic or secret about the equipment, just plain vanilla weather balloons, radar reflectors made of balsa and foil, and radio equipment that (in those days) still used vacuum tubes. Admittedly there was some experimental equipment used to hold the balloons at a set altitude but nothing exotic.

We now have Air Force official story number three about what really happened outside of Roswell, New Mexico, in early July 1947. And once again the story has a number of holes. First, Gen. Nathan Twining, whose name is woven throughout the flying saucer issue during the Truman years, was found to have canceled a long-standing invitation from Boeing Aircraft in Seattle, Washington, to look over a new bomber prototype and then go fishing with friends over the Fourth of July holiday. He wrote his apologies saying that he was called to a matter of great national importance. Researcher Friedman found that Twining's day-to-day diary entries are blank for that time period, but he located General Twining's pilot, who allowed him to look at his flight log. The log showed that Twining flew from Wright Field on July 7 to Alamogordo, New

Mexico, and returned to Ohio on July 11. The evidence that Twining flew to New Mexico because of the Roswell incident is circumstantial, but when combined with his letters and memos written after this event (which are being authenticated by the Wood team), it makes an extremely strong circumstantial case.

The size of this story has now become enormous and it stays very much alive and continues to grow. It has not been conclusively proven that an extraterrestrial craft crashed near Roswell, New Mexico, in early July 1947. However, of greater importance, the Air Force, the military, and the government have not been able to prove that it didn't happen and they hold the evidence. When all the frivolity of this colossal story is stripped away, we are left with several important questions. Would General Twining cancel his long-standing trip to Seattle to view the mundane remains of a Project Mogul recovery? Would Gen. Clements McMullen order Project Mogul crash debris loaded into a bomber and flown to Washington when the nonclassified material could have been thrown into a dumpster (the project was classified, not the equipment)? Is it reasonable to think that the Roswell base commander and the chief intelligence officer of the most elite bomb wing in the Air Force (the only group capable of carrying and delivering atomic weapons) would not be able to recognize the remains of weather balloons, radar reflectors, and radio equipment, even experimental equipment?[5] Would Colonel Blanchard be severely reprimanded for authorizing the release of the saucer story? Actually, Blanchard went on to become a four-star general and assistant secretary of the Air Force and would have become secretary if he had not died of a heart attack at his Pentagon desk.

The Mogul balloon story was released by the Air Force in 1994 in a report called, *The Roswell Report: Fact vs. Fiction in the New Mexico Desert*. The thousand-page monster report, called the "phone book" by many, went into great detail about Project

Mogul but little about the actual Roswell incident. The Air Force stated that this would be their final official discussion of the Roswell incident. Two years later they issued another final official report, *The Roswell Report: Case Closed.*

The second publication came about primarily because there had been no discussion of alien bodies that had been reported by many over the years, and other points that the Air Force tried to clarify. First Lt. James McAndrew wrote a synopsis of balloon-research findings on Project Mogul that became the integral part of the Air Force publication. Lieutenant McAndrew did an outstanding job of giving the background on how Project Mogul originated, how it developed, the technical background of the project, the laboratories that developed it, the people involved, and so on. All of it was totally irrelevant and in some cases idiotic. The dissection of the idiocy of that report is left to others, but there is one important omission that needs to be noted. Of all the names he mentioned in the report in an effort to give it legitimacy, names that in most cases no one had heard of, he leaves out a key player: Col. Thomas Jefferson Dubose, later General Dubose, chief of staff to General Ramey. General Dubose is on record as saying he received the call from Gen. Clements McMullen, telling him to kill the disc story. General McMullen wanted to see it for himself and then put it on his personal plane and flew it to Wright Field in Ohio for investigation. Wright Field (later Wright-Patterson Air Force Base) had no interest in attempts to listen for Russian nuclear tests but it had a great interest in foreign-aircraft technology, whether it be terrestrial or extraterrestrial. As we shall see later, Wright-Patterson AFB would soon house the command of the Foreign Technology Division of the Air Force. It would become ground zero for the government's investigation into the UFO phenomena.

The question is why was General Dubose not mentioned in the report? The simple answer is he didn't fit the Air Force story and his character was such that he couldn't be coerced to change his story. In view of this, the Air Force chose to simply ignore him and pretend he didn't exist. The facts didn't fit so they were ignored.[6]

JESSE MARCEL AND JESSE MARCEL JR.

Although we are only covering the basics of the very complicated Roswell story, I believe it necessary to discuss the two most prominent players in the Roswell saga, father and son, Jesse Marcel and Jesse Marcel Jr.

On February 20, 1978, Stanton T. Friedman was in Baton Rouge, Louisiana, to lecture at LSU. While there, he was also interviewed on a local TV station. As he waited for the last interviewer, who was late, he chatted with the station manager. In the course of the conversation the manager said, "The person you should talk to is a ham radio buddy of mine, Jesse Marcel, who lives not far from here in Houma. He handled wreckage of one of those saucers you are interested in when he was in the military." The next day at the airport Friedman got Marcel's phone number and called him at his home in Houma, Louisiana.

There is little doubt that Marcel had been stewing for years over being forced to lie and being made to look like a fool over the Roswell cover-up—a cover-up the Air Force finally admitted in 1994 with yet another lie. Friedman's timing and luck in finding Marcel was spot on, and after thirty years of chewing on this injustice Marcel wanted to talk and tell his story. Unfortunately Marcel only lived for eight more years, but through Friedman and others he was able to get his story out in detail in spoken word and on video.

In a very condensed version, Marcel was sent by the 509th Bomb Group commander, Col. William Blanchard, to the Foster ranch some seventy miles from Roswell, to investigate strange debris brought into Roswell by the ranch foreman, Mac Brazel. What

Marcel found is described above but what has not been reported—
except in Jesse Marcel Jr.'s book, *The Roswell Legacy* (2008)—are
a couple of important facts. First, Marcel was, in his Army career,
schooled in radar and radar targets, including RAWIN radar targets
at Langley Air Force Base in Virginia. He was very familiar with
RAWIN targets and would recognize them immediately. Second, he
was a radio buff from an early age and even built a radio receiver
as a youngster. He went on to become an amateur radio operator
(ham) which requires an FCC license and sophisticated radio equipment. Both weather balloons and Project Mogul used RAWIN targets and radio equipment that contained vacuum tubes that would
have been easily recognizable to Major Marcel. These two points
are not known or are conveniently overlooked by Roswell critics.
This also disposes of another overused claim that Marcel initiated
his story for fame or financial gain. The fact is that Marcel initiated nothing; he was found by Stanton Friedman through hard
work and pure luck, and after thirty years of living a lie imposed
on him, he was ready to clear his name.

Jesse Marcel Jr. entered the picture when his dad returned to Roswell with some of the unusual debris in his car. It was late at night
and he stopped at his home in Roswell to show the material to his
wife and son, who were asleep. He spread the material out in the
kitchen for wife and son to see. Jesse Jr. clearly recalls the strange
material. A couple of days later, after returning home from taking
the debris to the Eighth Air Force headquarters in Fort Worth,
Marcel told his wife and son they were to forget what they saw
and never speak of it again. The lid had been clamped on the incident by the Army Air Force. Marcel never spoke of the matter again
in public until being contacted by Friedman.

  After his dad's death in 1986, Marcel Jr. started to speak on
the subject and advance the disclosure his dad had started eight

years prior. What many forget in telling the Roswell story is that Jesse Marcel Jr. was an M.D. specializing in ear, throat, and nose medicine, as well as a colonel in the Montana National Guard who flew helicopters and was called back to active duty in the Middle East at age sixty-seven.

In July 2013, my wife and I got to meet Jesse, his daughter, and son-in-law at the Roswell festival as speakers at the International UFO Museum and Research Center. Our tables were next to each other and we got a chance to chat during the four-day event. Unfortunately, two months later we lost Jesse to a heart attack while he was reading in his Montana home. Jesse Marcel Jr. was a patriot and a hero; he will be greatly missed by all in the UFO research community.

FRANKIE ROWE

While attending the 2013 Roswell UFO festival, an attractive older lady stopped by my table. She was using the help of a cane and as we chatted she seemed to know a lot about the Roswell event. My wife had not yet joined me and I asked this lady to come around and sit in the vacant chair as we talked. I soon found out she was Frankie Rowe, the daughter of one of the firemen, Dan Dwyer, who unofficially went to a reported crash site about thirty miles from Roswell. The fire department had been told to stand down by the military, who had taken charge.

I knew the basics of Frankie Rowe's background and was delighted to meet her and discuss details of her story. As with all flying saucer–related stories, Frankie's story is controversial and has its supporters and detractors. I take no side in the issue but simply report a story told by a very nice lady who claims to be a firsthand witness to certain parts of the Roswell incident.

In early July 1947, twelve-year-old Frankie Dwyer was in her home outside of Roswell when her father came in from his shift at the Roswell Fire Department. Frankie said he seemed out of sorts and started to relate a strange story to her and her mother.

The fire department had been alerted to a possible aircraft crash about thirty miles outside of town. Before they could respond, the military arrived and told them to stand down, as it would be handled by their fire-and-rescue people. Disregarding the military directive, Dwyer and several other firemen decided to go to the crash site. Upon arriving (it's not clear if the military had arrived at the site at this point) they saw a strange, damaged unknown craft with three dead and one living humanoids about four feet tall with large heads and frail bodies. The living being seemed to be in some sort of shock and walked back and forth among the bodies and the craft. Dwyer approached the being and the being looked at him and said, "You can't help me." Dwyer said this was not verbal but the words were clear in his head, and it confused him. This was before, as Frankie stated to me, anyone outside of science knew anything about the possibilities of mental telepathy. Shortly thereafter they were herded from the site by the military and sent away.

A week later Frankie was in Roswell having some dental surgery, and after the surgery she stopped by her father's fire station. A state police patrolman came by the station and said, "You won't believe what I've got from that crash site last week." He showed the firemen and Frankie pieces of the mysterious metal so often discussed in the Roswell incident. Frankie said she held a piece; it seemed to have no weight and when crumpled up in her hand it returned to its original flatness without any sign of creases or deformity. She said it had a burnished or pewter color.

Several days later men showed up at the Dwyer home stating they were from the government. Sitting at the Dwyers' kitchen table, they told Frankie and her mother that what they'd seen and heard involved the highest levels of national security and to never speak of what they knew of this event to anyone. If they did the consequences would be great and severe. The men became threatening and said the area was vast and desolate, people could be taken and never heard from again. Frankie recalls the men as intimidating and very scary. She also remembers the tears streaking down her mother's face as these men talked and wondering why her mother didn't take these men to task for their threats, why her mother didn't take up for her and protect her.

She now realizes that this was the military, and in 1947 the military, after winning World War II, was respected and viewed as all powerful. We have heard these stories over and over again from people who lived in this very desolate area of the high desert of New Mexico that just happened to be the center of our nation's most exotic research into advanced technology. Frankie went on to say that the men had also gotten to her father and what he saw and what he told them remained a family secret until Frankie came forward with her story many years later.

Is Frankie Rowe's story true and accurate? I'll pass no judgment on that except to say that she is a charming lady who seems sincere in telling her story. Testimony is just the word of the witness; it is admissible in courts but without physical backup and solid evidence it will always be subject to scrutiny and have its detractors. Whatever the case, Frankie Rowe's story is but another piece of the intriguing Roswell mystery.

In another case, there is a story the Air Force chose not to ignore but probably should have. It lends increased incredibility to their explanation for the Roswell incident. It is a story that also answers another question rarely asked or simply overlooked. What Brazel found, Major Marcel investigated, and the Air Force recovered was debris from something that crashed. Why did Colonel Blanchard authorize a press release stating that they had recovered a "flying disc" when what was found on the Foster ranch was nothing but "debris"? The next section explains that issue.

THE CRASH ON THE PLAINS OF SAN AGUSTIN

Research into the Roswell incident initially focused on the debris found by rancher Mac Brazel, foreman of the Foster ranch near Corona, New Mexico. However, a story told by state geologist Barney Barnett tells of another crash at the same time of the Corona crash. This crash was on the Plains of San Agustin, located about 70 miles west of Socorro, New Mexico, and 140 miles west of Corona. Barnett, along with a group of geology students from the East Coast studying in the area, stumbled on the wreckage. Unlike the Corona crash, this craft was relatively undamaged except for a rupture in the edge of the craft. According to Barnett, he and the students observed several small dead humanoid occupants outside the craft, and one that was still living. They appeared frail of stature and about three and a half to four feet in height. Since Jesse Marcel never mentioned that he saw bodies and since a number of eyewitnesses to the events at the Roswell Air Base speak of dead humanoid beings being brought there, the crash of a second craft seems to fit. Researcher Stanton T. Friedman believes that a collision of the two crafts may have occurred when their guidance systems were affected by the extremely strong radar systems used to track missile tests in that part of the country. The radars were left on at all times because their vacuum-tube circuits required a lengthy warm-up before they became operational.

As stated previously this subject has been covered extensively in other books and publications and will not be covered in depth here. What is important to understand in this matter is that the Air Force could have simply denied that there were any bodies of any kind in the New Mexico desert. Instead, in their 1997 report, they stated that what people actually saw was the retrieval of flight-test dummies that had been carried aloft to a hundred thousand feet in Skyhook-type balloons and dropped to research pilot ejection from aircraft at high altitudes. These tests actually did take place but there are several problems with the Air Force story. First, the dummies were human in size, about 175 pounds and six feet in height with normal features. Second, the tests didn't start until 1953—or six years after the Roswell incident. Friedman noted, "The Air Force had apparently invented time travel for crash-test dummies" (Friedman 2005).

In their attempt to explain the Roswell incident as debris from a secret U.S. project to spy on Soviet nuclear tests, the Air Force actually discredited their story and brought additional legitimacy to the theory that an extraterrestrial craft (or crafts) crashed in the New Mexico desert in 1947. The fact is if the retrieval in July 1947 was a crashed Mogul project, there would be substantial classified paperwork of such retrieval. Since the project has been declassified, then where is that paperwork? It is not in the thousand-plus-page report and the 1997 follow-up. On the other hand, if the retrievals were of an alien craft there would be substantial paperwork still classified and not about to be released.[7]

The Roswell incident was the first of a number of UFO cases that would confront the Truman presidency and establish the government's handling of all future UFO issues. With Truman's strong belief in maintaining security, the dictates he put in place relative to anything pertaining to the extraterrestrial subject would endure for years to come. It was during his presidency that the population viewed the flying saucer issue as real and of serious, even frightening, concern. Serious publications such as *Life* magazine published articles that leaned heavily toward the extraterrestrial hypothesis as the explanation for flying saucers. This was a concern for the Truman administration—and the more sensational the story and the wider the coverage, the greater the concern.

The Roswell incident and the three events that follow (along with many others not covered here) brought the saucer issue to a head. Government intervention was needed to defuse a situation that was headed toward hysteria.

THE THOMAS MANTELL CASE

The case of National Guard pilot Capt. Thomas Mantell was one of the most widely reported and unnerving UFO incidents in history. His death on January 7, 1948, while pursuing a strange flying object, spiked the public's awareness of UFOs and resulted in former Marine Corps pilot and UFO investigator Maj. Donald Keyhoe bringing pressure on the Air Force to disclose accurate information on the Mantell case and the UFO issue in general. The fact that a person had died in dramatic and very mysterious circumstances that were widely reported greatly increased the public's concern over this phenomenon.

Captain Mantell was a decorated World War II pilot who had recently left the Air Force and joined the Kentucky National Guard. On January 7, 1948, he and three other pilots were ferrying four F-51s (formerly P-51s) from Georgia to a base in Kentucky. Godman Army Air Field at Fort Knox, Kentucky, had received a report of a strange airborne object near Maysville, Kentucky, from the Kentucky State Police. Maysville was some ninety miles away and the police report said hundreds of people had seen the object moving toward Fort Knox. Reports were soon received from other areas, and a little before 2:00 P.M. personnel in the Godman tower sighted the object. It zoomed into view over the base. The base commander viewed the object through binoculars and said it appeared to have a red band at the bottom and a size of two hundred to three hundred feet in diameter. Another report from Lockbourne Air Force Base in Columbus, Ohio, said the object came within ten feet of the ground before rising rapidly to an altitude of approximately ten thousand feet at a speed over five hundred miles per hour.

Godman tower contacted flight leader Mantell and asked him to investigate the sighting. One pilot was low on fuel and continued on but the other three changed course to intercept the object that had been stationary for an hour and a half. The three planes reached about seventeen thousand feet when two of the pilots broke off due to lack of oxygen. Mantell continued on. He radioed the tower that he had spotted the object; it appeared to be metallic and was huge. His voice seemed strained. Mantell radioed in again, this time reporting the object was above him and had started climbing at about half his speed. He said, "I'll try to close in." Five minutes later he reported the object had increased its speed to about 360 miles per hour. Shortly after that transmission, the plane went out of control and crashed, killing Mantell.

An official Air Force investigation stated that Mantell probably blacked out from lack of oxygen while chasing the planet Venus. Although the crash caused by lack of oxygen remains extremely plausible, the theory that he was chasing the planet Venus is total idiocy. Venus at that time of day was all but invisible. A later report said that the sighting was probably a Skyhook balloon, which at that time was still classified secret. Although this is a more likely explanation, it still had problems. Skyhook balloons flew at the very high altitude of one hundred thousand feet and drifted with air currents. Mantell reported the object moving at half speed or two hundred miles per hour. Also, the reported sighting of the object was within ten feet of the ground before accelerating at a high rate of speed to twenty thousand feet which is not something a balloon can accomplish.

There are many unverified stories with this case as there are with most notable UFO sightings and encounters. It has been my belief from my own research that Mantell was probably looking at and chasing a secret Navy Skyhook balloon. However, the report from Lockbourne Air Base actually came several hours later and somewhat complicates the issue. The official Air Force position and the position of many respected UFOlogists is that the witnesses at the Lockbourne incident were looking at the planet Venus.[8] The more I worked on the Mantell case for this book, the more troubled I became with the story. I decided to dig out Donald Keyhoe's *The Flying Saucers Are Real* since he had researched the Mantell case in depth just after it occurred. In rereading the book I discovered some facts that made me question the balloon theory. First, Keyhoe had been a balloon pilot in the military, so he understood them. In the case of Skyhook balloons, they are inflated with a small amount of helium when launched. As the balloon ascends to higher altitudes, the gas expands and the balloon flattens out. This, of course, could give it the saucer appearance and is the reason it is widely accepted as what Mantell was chasing. Around a hundred thousand feet the gas bag would have swollen to about a hundred feet high and seventy feet in diameter. The instrument package under the balloon is released and comes down by parachute. The loss of weight allows the balloon to rise rapidly, where it finally explodes from expansion.

There are several problems with the Skyhook explanation uncovered by Keyhoe and verified by J. Allen Hynek. A number of reports, including from the men in the Godman tower, estimated the object to be 250 to 400 feet in diameter rather than the seventy feet of a Skyhook balloon. It was confirmed that the object was seen from areas 175 miles apart at the same time. This meant the object at one point had to be at least thirty miles high or higher. These calculations were confirmed by both Keyhoe and Hynek.

Within minutes after the Mantell crash, one of the F-51s was back in the air, refueled and with oxygen. The plane went to 33,000 feet and flew for a hundred miles but could find no trace of the object. The Air Force told Keyhoe the balloon probably dropped its instrument package and then exploded. Keyhoe felt it strange that this would occur in the few minutes the other plane was on the ground. Also, there was no sighting of a parachute or finding the instrument package. There are a number of other inconsistencies with the Mantell event, such as the object remaining stationary for an hour and a half and only starting to move when Mantell approached, that now leads me to reassess the Skyhook theory.[9]

This is an important story that deserves more study than the constraints of this book allow. What is important for the reader to understand is that it brought great pressure on the Air Force. It created a lot of internal strife among many high-ranking officers, as Mantell was highly regarded within the service. This high-profile case stoked the fires of public unrest with the official public position of the government and in turn brought more pressure to bear on the Truman White House and his military advisers.

THE FARMINGTON ARMADA

The sightings of flying saucers were reported frequently in the late 1940s and early 1950s, especially in New Mexico and the Four Corners area. Not many made headline news, but some did. This was the case with a sighting that became known as the Farmington Armada. For three days in the middle of March 1950, between 11:00 A.M. and noon, and again later in the afternoon, a number of flying saucers were seen above the small town of Farmington, New Mexico. The daylight sighting was seen by at least half the population of the town, which at the time probably numbered three thousand or less. Reports varied on the number of objects, from as few as several to as many as five hundred, as they darted about in formation and then flashed away at incredible speeds. A local engineer did a rough triangulation on one object. He said the height was approximately twenty thousand feet; the object's size was roughly that of two B-29 bombers, and it accelerated to a speed in excess of a thousand miles per hour.

The craft appeared to be silver in color, except for the largest of the group which acted as the leader. This craft appeared to be a red color. The objects flew at high speeds and would flip on edge at times, showing that they were saucer-shaped. One former B-29 tail gunner said that they flew in a manner that would be impossible for any known aircraft to duplicate.

The story made headline news, as it was only one hundred miles from the Los Alamos National Laboratory and White Sands where the first atomic bomb tests were conducted. It seems that the draw to this area were the nearby nuclear and missile test sites. Scientists at Los Alamos, Sandia, and White Sands had gotten almost nonchalant about saucers showing up at their tests, as we shall see later. What was different in this case was the number of saucers, their actions, and the number of private citizens who viewed them.

The next event of note also involved a large number of objects and it took place in a very sensitive area, but an area far east of New Mexico. The sighting took place in Washington, D.C., and the event changed the course of government involvement in the UFO issue forever.

THE WASHINGTON MERRY-GO-ROUND

No other UFO event has had the lasting impact on the government's handling of all UFO encounters than this remarkable event of July 1952 has. It stunned the government and the military and shocked the public, who demanded answers from their government.

It is important to keep in mind that in July 1952 the public still viewed flying saucers as a very real and legitimate phenomenon. The government, although not disclosing what it knew about the matter, had not yet engaged in a debunking and disinformation campaign and was in fact allowing some semiofficial statements to be made by senior officers.

On April 7, 1952, *Life* magazine, one of the most respected news and event publications in the United States, caused a national buzz when it published an article called "Have We Visitors from Space?" The article, written by H. B. Darrach Jr. and Robert Ginna, was a well-documented piece of investigative journalism on the phenomenon called flying saucers or unidentified flying objects. The truly remarkable aspect of this article is the cooperation of the Air Force, who opened their files on some bizarre cases and had a frank discussion on how the Air Force viewed the phenomenon.

Former head of Air Force Project Blue Book, Edward Ruppelt, stated that release of the information came from top Air Force personnel in the Pentagon. In this release of information Air Force officials gave the reporters the following startling information:

1. The Air Force maintained constant intelligence investigation of the objects.

2. Military aircraft were alerted to attempt interception and some were fitted with cameras and radar in an attempt to obtain factual data on the craft.

3. Operational units of the Air Force were alerted to report in detail any sighting of UFOs. Trained civilian watchers of the sky, pilots, scientists, weather observers, and so forth, were asked to make immediate reports to the Air Technical Intelligence Center at Wright-Patterson AFB.

4. The Air Force invited all citizens to make reports of any sighting to their closest Air Force base. (This may have been the reason the Air Force was so open with their information.)

5. The Air Force concluded by saying that there was no reason
   to believe that the objects were the result of a foreign power
   or a clear and present danger to the United States.

The *Life* article continued on with ten case studies and the
evaluation of those studies. It concluded by suggesting that the extraterrestrial hypothesis presented the most likely explanation for
the phenomenon.

Although important and shocking in 1952, the conclusion
reached by the journalists is not the subject of greatest importance in this discussion. What the article validates is that going
back to 1947 and the famous Kenneth Arnold sighting at Mount
Rainier, Washington, the public and the media in general took
the subject of flying saucers very seriously. This article and the
July 1952 Washington, D.C., event would prove to be the zenith
of the public's acceptance of the great importance of UFO phenomena. The Washington merry-go-round (as the event was ladled
by the media) and the resulting reaction to the public's outcry
would result in clamping the lid on any government knowledge
of the issue and a debunking and disinformation campaign that
continues today.

Three months after the *Life* magazine article was published,
Washington, D.C., became the site of one of the most startling
UFO events in history. On two successive weekend nights, July
19–20 and July 26–27, 1952, the sky over D.C., including the restricted airspace over the Capitol and the White House, was flown
over by unknown objects and tracked on radar at Washington National Airport and Andrews AFB. The events of July 19 started at
11:40 P.M. and continued until 5:30 A.M. the following morning.
The first sighting on July 26 was made at 8:15 P.M. and continued
until dawn the next morning. Albert Chop, Air Force and Pentagon spokesman, was alerted and he called for Air Force jets to be

scrambled on the night of the nineteenth, but the objects would disappear when the jets arrived, then reappear when the jets returned to base. On the twenty-sixth, the objects stayed and seemed to play cat and mouse with the fighters by hovering and then flashing away at speeds estimated to be in excess of seven thousand miles per hour.

The objects were seen by thousands of people in the area. They were photographed and reported around the world. People and politicians alike wanted answers and were exerting heavy pressure on the Air Force for them. At ten o'clock in the morning on the twenty-seventh, General Landry, at the direction of President Truman, called the Pentagon and requested information on the prior night's events. Hysteria was building rapidly and the president wanted to defuse the situation before it ballooned out of hand. As a result, on July 29 Air Force generals John Samford and Roger Ramey held a news conference in an attempt to calm public anxiety over the events. It was the largest Air Force news conference since World War I and it achieved the desired results. General Sanford explained that the lights were simply the misidentification of stars and the radar returns were from temperature inversions. The public and the press accepted this explanation. However, on the inside the explanation was criticized. The radar operators were furious that they had been made to appear as incompetents who couldn't distinguish a return between a temperature inversion and a hard target. Respected atmospheric physicist Dr. James E. McDonald, from the University of Arizona, felt the explanation ridiculous and physically impossible. Even Air Force Project Blue Book director, Capt. Edward J. Ruppelt, took issue with the explanation in his book *The Report on Unidentified Flying Objects,* after retiring from the Air Force.

THE ROBERTSON PANEL

Although the mounting hysteria from the sensational Washington sightings had been quelled by the news conference, there remained an uneasy feeling that another major sighting could reignite public panic. In the twilight of the Truman administration, the newly formed CIA convened a panel of noted scientists to review the UFO issue and report their findings and recommendations to the CIA. The Robertson Panel, as it became known, was classified at the time, and met for four days of two daily sessions each to review a number of UFO cases. One notable case was the review of film taken by a naval officer in Tremonton, Utah. This film showed a number of luminous rapidly moving objects. The Naval Photographic Interpretation Center (NPIC), headed by famed photographic interpreter, Arthur Charles Lundahl (to be discussed in chapter 3), studied the film for over one thousand hours. Their expert witnesses testified to the panel that the objects were not balloons, planes, or birds. The objects were self-luminous and of solid structure. Although there were no experts in photographic interpretation on the panel, the panel nevertheless rejected the lab's finding and officially ruled that the objects were birds.

Dr. J. Allen Hynek, who was working as a consultant for the Air Force's Project Blue Book at the time, attended as a junior member of the panel. He later wrote that it became clear to him that the panel seemed predisposed to debunk all UFO sightings, and in fact, their secret report to the CIA (called the Durant Report and now declassified), recommended a concerted government effort to debunk and discredit UFO sightings. In addition the panel recommended secretly *watching* civilian UFO investigatory groups.

After the Washington merry-go-round, most in the Air Force fell in step with the official Air Force line to discredit UFO sightings. One who did not was Albert Chop, the former head of the Air Force public information office and newly retired. At the time,

Donald Keyhoe had just come out with his book *Flying Saucers from Outer Space,* which was very critical of the Air Force and their handling of the entire UFO issue. In short, it was giving the Air Force fits. Ruppelt pretty much fell in line with the Air Force, but Chop was another story. He had been in the Washington tower and watched the events unfold. In late October 1953, he was found by the press in California and asked his opinion on the UFO issue. Chop was forthright with his talk to the press. He defended Keyhoe, he criticized Blue Book, and he stated:

> *There is too much unexplained. Granting the reliability of the observers, one draws the conclusion that they are faster than anything on earth, are controlled, can hover and go to thousands of miles per hour in a split second. Where they come from we don't know. But they are here, have been since one was first seen over Sweden in 1945, and are probably from somewhere else. With no earthly explanation, what else is there to think, if I believe in the creditability of the person reporting.* (Swords and Powell 2012, 211)

Al Chop summed up the situation and discord within the Air Force beautifully at that time.

Another peek into Air Force thinking and policy in 1952 is found in the book, *Legerdemain,* by James J. Heaphey (2008). In 1952 Jim Heaphey was a young Air Force officer assigned to Nouasseur AFB in French Morocco. His cover job was the base newspaper editor but he worked undercover to spy on the French and feed information to the Moroccan nationalists. Truman wanted the French out because it was felt that if we helped the nationalists we would gain their favor and keep them from siding with the Soviets and in turn lose important air bases.

The only person on the base who knew Heaphey was an undercover agent was General Jackman, the base commander. In October 1952, while privately meeting in the general's office and discussing an operation, there was an interesting change of subject by the general. Heaphey recounts the exchange as follows:

"What do you know about the Air Force Blue Book?"

"It's a record of unidentified flying objects," I said.

"We've had our first UFO reports here at Nouasseur, both during the past week. A KC-97 crew said they saw a circular light making passes at them. A few days later an F-86 pilot—you might know him, Bob Johnson—says he chased an object for 30 seconds at 530 mph but couldn't catch it. He said it was about the size of a fighter without wings, tanks or trails."

"Where do I fit in?" I asked.

He explained to me that the Air Force had an official explanation for all UFO sightings. According to that policy, UFO sightings were to be one or a combination of the following: a mild form of mass hysteria, an attempt by an individual to gain publicity, a form of psychopathology, or misidentification of various conventional objects.

"Your job is to interview the witnesses, I have them all quarantined in the security barracks on the strip, and write a report for Blue Book that conforms to Air Force explanations."

"What happens to the witnesses?" I asked.

"None of your business," he said flatly.

Actually I could guess the answer. They would be sent to Project Blue Book Headquarters, Wright-Patterson Air Force base in Dayton, Ohio, for debriefing. While the pilots would be debriefed, the real purpose in bringing witnesses to Wright-Patterson was to brief them on Air Force policy and to warn them about publicizing their UFO sightings. What was important to General Jackman was to keep it all as quiet as possible. (Heaphey 2008, 22)

While not a startling story in itself, it does indicate that by 1952, and a little more than two months before the Robertson Panel, the Air Force had the word out to all base commanders around the world to dummy up UFO sightings before sending on to Blue Book.

I met Jim Heaphey at a book conference held at a local resort where we were both speaking. My first novel, *The Great River Disclosure*, based on the government UFO cover-up, had just been released and that was the subject of my talk. Jim wanted to impress on me that my book was more fact than fiction. He said the extraterrestrial hypothesis (ETH) was the accepted norm but quietly spoken of in that time period within the Air Force in Europe.

The lid was now on and the great modern UFO cover-up was firmly in place, as the Truman administration turned the executive branch of government over to the incoming Eisenhower administration. Harry Truman, a stickler for guarding government secrets, a man known for dressing down congressmen for loose talk, would be succeeded by another man equally noted for his stewardship in guarding state secrets.

In an interesting footnote to the Truman years and his attitude toward UFO secrets, Art Campbell, UFO researcher, former educator, and NICAP investigator, tells of returning to his hometown of Independence, Missouri, and meeting the retired Truman in an Independence museum along with two Secret Service agents. Truman in his early years had been friends with Campbell's family and they reminisced a bit and laughed about Truman playing piano at a family member's wedding. When Truman asked Campbell what he was now doing, and why he was in Independence, Campbell told him he investigated UFOs and was speaking that night to a group at a local hotel. At that point Truman's whole demeanor became icy and the conversation ended. On that same evening Truman was addressing a group in the same hotel as Campbell. Campbell noticed that one of the Secret Service agents came into his meeting and stood at the back through his entire talk, no doubt at the direction of Truman. This is but another indication of Truman's deep interest and concern with the subject.

THOUGHTS AND CONCLUSIONS

The Truman years were very troubling for the government and the military, but particularly for the Air Force as they were charged with guarding our sovereign airspace. We know now that within the higher levels of the Air Force there were three schools of thought: Those who felt UFOs had a natural explanation, those who thought they were Soviet platforms developed with the help of their captured Germans to deliver yet-to-be-developed atomic weapons (we had atomic weapons but not the proper platforms to deliver them), and those who felt UFOs were extraterrestrial craft. We can now eliminate the second school of thought as Dr. Stefan Possony did in 1952.[10]

What is important to consider is the number of high-ranking and senior Air Force investigators who we know from the record in the pre–Robertson Panel era felt the extraterrestrial hypothesis was the logical explanation for UFO events. As early as 1948 most of the Air Force Project Sign group studying UFOs felt that the ET hypothesis was the only reasonable conclusion for the phenomenon. Serious consideration was being given to author the *estimate of the situation* to give to their superiors in the chain of command.

They had held off developing the *Estimate* over concern as to how it would be received. Then on July 24, 1948, the Chiles/Whitted event occurred.[11] This pushed them over the top and sometime in the late fall of 1948 the *Estimate* was released to the chain of command and stated that the unexplained UFO sightings were most likely extraterrestrial craft. The explosive result of the release of this document is discussed in a later chapter. However, it was the demise of Project Sign and the start of the Air Force's housekeeping effort, Project Grudge.

Within the Pentagon, from 1949 through 1952, the amount of confusion and incompetence was almost incomprehensible to this writer as I researched that time period. Project Sign was in shambles and replaced by the debunking Project Grudge. Much to the chagrin of the Air Force, the Navy was quietly taking the issue seriously and unloaded a couple of bombshells that badly rattled the Air Force and its debunking efforts.

In the desert of New Mexico there was no debunking. Many of the top scientists—LaPaz, Neef, Rees, Kaplan, Bradbery, Reines, and Teller—were dealing not only with flying discs but green fireballs that seemed interested in Los Alamos and Sandia. Clyde Tombaugh, the discoverer of Pluto, sitting in the backyard of his Las Cruces home with his wife and mother enjoying the clear, star-filled night, saw a number of rectangular lights that he said, "Defied any explanation of known phenomena."[12] He had also seen saucers and the green fireballs, as had most of his colleagues. This became a matter that all of the Los Alamos and Sandia scientists took seriously and reported to the Pentagon where, unknown to them, they were received by persons with a debunking mentality.

In April 1949 the Navy's top secret Project Mogul team, headed by Dr. Charles Moore, launched a Project Mogul balloon train, tracking it with a theodolite. While tracking the balloon train they noticed something else: a saucer that moved radically while rising at high speed until it disappeared at what the scientists estimated to be three hundred thousand feet. Dr. Moore, highly respected in the field of object-tracking, stated, "We did see an object under almost ideal observational conditions, which we cannot explain nor rationalize, but we do not claim that it was necessarily a flying disc or space ship."

When Moore heard how the Air Force tried to debunk his report, he followed with another statement that is a snapshot of the New Mexico scientists' feelings toward the current Air Force/ Pentagon position on the flying saucer issue.

> *It appears from reading the report analysis that the Air Forces have been more interested in disproving or casting doubt on all unidentified object observations rather than any attempt to evaluate or explore them. It is believed that if some object, extra-terrestrial in origin, actually be observed, this group would spend more time disproving its existence than investigating it.*[13]

The disagreement within the Air Force over the origin of the phenomena continued to grow into 1952. Most of the researchers from Project Sign, Project Grudge, and later from Project Blue Book embraced the ET hypothesis including Gen. William Garland, who had seen a UFO, while other officials outside of the research held the theory that there was a terrestrial explanation.

The question must be asked why so many high-ranking officers and officials disagreed over the UFO phenomenon if the Air Force, from as early as 1941, had in its possession alien craft and living and dead occupants. The answer is speculation, but reasonable speculation.

If Truman authorized the very secret Majestic-12 (MJ-12)

group, as seems likely, those in the loop of knowledge would be small and carefully controlled. It made no difference how many stars an officer had on his shoulder; if he was not in the "need to know" he didn't know, and this included Sign, Grudge, and Blue Book personnel. Those on the outside or not in the need-to-know loop would have no knowledge that a very small group of high-ranking government and military personnel and a few eminent scientists had possession of and were studying extraterrestrial craft and biological entities. The group of eminent scientists knew that something very unusual was going on but remained outside the loop of insiders. Edward Teller most certainly was on the inside but could not share his knowledge with fellow scientists. If it appears that a very few insiders, including several high-ranking Air Force officers, were letting the Air Force twist in the wind, that would seem to be a reasonable assessment of the situation.

This internal Air Force disagreement worked in favor of those in the loop of knowledge to help conceal from the public the secrets this group possessed. Let the researchers continue to gather data that the MJ-12 group could use while developing a disinformation program to offset anything made public by Sign, Grudge, and Blue Book research. General Vandenberg's knocking down the *Estimate of the Situation* in 1948 and the Sanford-Ramey press conference in July 1952 after the Washington, D.C., sightings were prime examples of this policy. A parallel can be drawn between the work of Majestic 12 on the UFO issue and the Manhattan Project's development of the atomic bomb.

The next eight years saw a continuation of the policies relating to UFO secrets under the Eisenhower administration. The world was growing up rapidly while the U.S. and the Soviet Union were locked in a missile and a space race and living under the frightening policy of mutual assured destruction. The U.S. continued with its post–World War II policy of maintaining the highest level of classification on UFO issues. Documents and statements by a number of both civilian and military personnel now indicate that Eisenhower may have been involved in some truly astounding UFO-related matters that still remain highly classified. However, the status quo would remain until a young former senator from Massachusetts moved into the White House and attempted changes that may well have had tragic results.

2

FIRST CONTACT?

THE EISENHOWER ADMINISTRATION—SHIFTING
THE PARADIGM OF POWER

On December 7, 1941, newly appointed Brig. Gen. Dwight D. Eisenhower, Third Army Chief of Staff, was taking a nap in his quarters at Fort Sam Houston when his executive, Lt. Ernest "Tex" Lee, called with the news of Pearl Harbor. Five days later he was standing in front of Gen. George C. Marshall in Washington, D.C., and his life would be changed forever.

Marshall's original charge to Eisenhower was the handling of the Philippines and in particular, Gen. Douglas MacArthur. Within five months Eisenhower had 107 officers working under him in the newly formed Operations Division. Crucial to all his work was intelligence and he found the Intelligence Division (G2) woefully inadequate (Ambrose 1983, 145). It was during this period that his understanding for the need of proper intelligence developed, and in hand with that the need to secure that intelligence.

In June 1942, Marshall appointed Eisenhower to command the European Theater of Operations and Eisenhower moved to London. From that date until January 1961, Eisenhower would be a world figure and the guardian of some of the most highly classified issues of those times. It is almost certain that he was in the loop of knowledge of the Manhattan Project after becoming supreme allied commander. His strict enforcement of security issues is well known and he relieved a number of officers, some his friends, for violating security codes during Overlord planning.[1]

It's difficult to pinpoint the exact date that Eisenhower became aware of mysterious aerial craft that would in years to come be called flying saucers and UFOs. It is reasonable to believe that if the memos between Marshall and Roosevelt on the L.A. air raid from chapter 1 are factual, then Marshall would have shared that intelligence with one of his most senior and trusted commanders, a man who would soon become supreme allied commander. It is also reasonable to think that Eisenhower would have been kept abreast of the puzzling foo fighter mystery reported by bomber crews and fighter pilots from both war theaters.

The recent release of Ministry of Defence documents in the U.K. included a letter from an unnamed scientist sent to the MoD in 1999 requesting information on a UFO cover-up authorized by Winston Churchill in the late stages of World War II. In the letter, the scientist said his grandfather was a member of the RAF and one of Churchill's bodyguards. The grandfather had stated that he was present at a meeting where Churchill and Eisenhower discussed an encounter an RAF Mosquito bomber-reconnaissance aircraft had with a UFO near the English coastline. After being briefed on the event, Churchill is reported to have told Eisenhower: "This event should be immediately classified as it would create mass panic amongst the general population and destroy one's belief in the church."[2] Regardless of when he found out, by the end of the war, Eisenhower was a member of a very small group of people who knew that the airspace of countries around the world was being invaded by aerial craft of unknown origin.

•   •   •

Dwight David Eisenhower was inaugurated as the thirty-fourth president of the United States on a chilly January 20, 1953. However, the air chill couldn't match the chill that existed between the president and the president-elect. It has been reported in a number of publications that in 1945 Truman had told Eisenhower, probably at the Potsdam Conference, that he would help Eisenhower get anything he wanted, including the presidency. This would prove to be the high point in the relationship between the two men. Although Truman appointed Eisenhower chief of staff in November 1945, their relationship would never resemble the Truman-Marshall relationship. With Truman, Eisenhower's relations were correct but formal. They never established an intimacy nor did they work closely together (Ambrose 1983, 443).

There is another remarkable event that accelerated the deterioration of the Truman-Eisenhower relationship. In 1947 Truman called Eisenhower to his office, where according to Eisenhower, he made a remarkable offer. If Eisenhower would accept the Democratic nomination, Truman said he would be willing to run as the vice presidential candidate on the same ticket. The general wanted nothing to do with the Democratic Party; his answer was an emphatic no (Ambrose 1983, 460). Truman was not a man who would have taken that type of rebuff gracefully and it marked the beginning of the decline of the relationship between the two men.

On February 7, 1948, Eisenhower turned over the Office of Army Chief of Staff to Omar Bradley, and he and Mamie soon headed to New York City in a new Chrysler paid for in cash. Now, except for his $15,000-per-year Army salary, he was broke. However, in the two years he was chief of staff he had amassed a cadre of wealthy friends who offered a number of lucrative positions. He finally settled on an offer to become president of Columbia University. He also became a member of the Augusta National Golf

Club and a member of what he called the "gang" of some of America's wealthiest men. It was this group who started to put pressure on him to run for the presidency. Eisenhower did not want to run, did not want to be president, and fought the idea at every turn. His desire was to retire from Columbia after a few years, play golf, and fish.

The stories of his evolution from flat-out refusal to some consideration and finally to his acceptance to run for president have been well detailed by his biographers and will not be covered here. It is interesting to note a major turning point that occurred in February 1952. Famed aviator Jacqueline Cochran and the wife of wealthy industrialist Floyd Odlum flew to Paris where Eisenhower and Mamie were staying after Truman had directed him to take over command of NATO. Cochran brought a two-hour film of a huge Madison Square Garden rally for Eisenhower. The enormity and the passion of the rally seemed to do the trick, and he soon entered the presidential race.

The heat of the campaign began to increase the frosty relationship between Truman and Eisenhower. By the time Eisenhower was elected the relationship between the two was barely civil. It is safe to assume that Truman did not go out of his way to brief the incoming president on any subject, including the UFO issue. That issue would be in the hands of old friend and wartime chief of staff, then CIA director, Gen. Walter Bedell Smith and, if the leaked Eisenhower Briefing Document is to be believed, Adm. Roscoe H. Hillenkoetter.

Even with the frosty relationship between the two presidents, the Truman-Eisenhower years could be called the golden years of UFO history. Some of the strangest events in UFO lore come from this time period. Many, like the Washington merry-go-round, are backed up by hard evidence but others are more anecdotal in nature.

To properly understand the Eisenhower years it is necessary to jump forward to December 1984. This is when a roll of undeveloped 35 mm film showed up in the mailbox of film director Jaime Shandera who was working on a UFO documentary and had asked Stanton T. Friedman to come on board as a consultant. They needed script help and Friedman recommended friend and UFO researcher Bill Moore, who had written and directed plays. Moore and Shandera, both now in California, became friends and began to work together on UFO projects and consult with Friedman back east. Shandera told Moore about the film that was mailed in an envelope without a return address and postmarked Albuquerque, New Mexico. When the film was developed there were photographs of eight pages of documents marked "Top Secret/Majic, Eyes Only, Briefing Document: Operation Majestic 12, Prepared for President-Elect Dwight D. Eisenhower," and dated November 18, 1952 (see Appendix B).

In quick summary, the documents told of a craft of suspected extraterrestrial origin that crashed near Roswell, New Mexico, in July 1947 and the recovery of four humanoid occupants. The document was prepared by Adm. Roscoe H. Hillenkoetter, the former director of the CIA, who was listed as the briefing officer, with the title of MJ-1, of a top-secret group called Majestic 12. Officially it was noted as being a *preliminary* briefing for the president-elect.

Moore and Shandera contacted Friedman and told him about the documents on the film. Friedman, although excited over this finding, advised that they should move with caution and do whatever necessary to verify the authenticity of the documents on the film. He knew that this could possibly be disinformation used to discredit UFO research. If they went public and then had someone claim they'd authored the phony documents, it would be a major discrediting embarrassment.

THE MAJESTIC DOCUMENTS

The term "Majestic documents" refers to top-secret documents concerning extraterrestrial craft and entities that were surreptitiously leaked to various UFO researchers over a period of years starting in December 1984. Since these documents are so important to the casual observer's understanding of presidential involvement in UFO issues, some time should be devoted here to chronicling and detailing the background of these documents.

The first MJ-12 documents showed up in the mailbox of Jaime Shandera in December 1984 as outlined above. In addition to the Eisenhower Briefing Document (EBD), the last page was a simple memo from President Truman to Secretary of Defense James Forrestal, dated September 24, 1947, authorizing Forrestal to proceed with Operation Majestic-12 with advice from noted scientist Dr. Vannevar Bush and the director of Central Intelligence (Friedman 2005, 22).

Operation Majestic-12 was a top-secret group of twelve men: high-ranking military personnel and noted scientists.

They are as follows:

Dr. Vannevar Bush[3]	Adm. Roscoe
Dr. Detlev Bronk	Hillenkoetter[4]
Dr. Lloyd Berkner	Secretary of Defense
Dr. Jerome Hunsaker	James Forrestal
Dr. Donald Menzel	Gen. Nathan Twining
Gordon Gray	Gen. Hoyt Vandenberg
Sidney Souers	Gen. Robert Montague

The second set of MJ-12 documents showed up in early July 1985 when Shandera and Moore flew to Washington to review some recently declassified files in the National Archives. In the review of these files, Shandera discovered a carbon copy of a memo from presidential assistant, Robert Cutler, to Gen. Nathan Twining dated July 14, 1954. The importance of this brief memo is that the subject was shown as "SUBJECT: NSC/MJ-12 Special Studies Project." The memo was simply changing the timing of this special meeting, but the importance is that it listed MJ-12 as being a legitimate operation. In the world of Majestic-12 documents this has become known as the Cutler-Twining Memo (see Appendix C).

In 1992, three additional MJ-12 documents surfaced in the possession of UFO researcher Tim Cooper of California. One of the documents dated February 1948 was from director of Central Intelligence Hillenkoetter to President Truman on developing summaries of "Majic" material for the president. A second document was a memorandum for the president from Secretary of State George C. Marshall concerning a briefing General Twining was to give the president and the necessity to keep the information top secret. The third document was a memo from the president to General Twining directing him to go to New Mexico to appraise the "unidentified objects" being kept there. I will not include these documents as my confidence in their authenticity is suspect, and one is almost certainly bogus.[5] I am not saying that Cooper is the author of the documents, only that they were passed on to him from an unknown source.

The fact that bogus documents would appear in the mix of legitimate documents should be expected in something as controversial as this issue. However, they should in no way diminish the importance or reflect negatively on what are believed to be legitimate documents. What causes individuals to fabricate lies and deceptive information on a subject of such major importance is left to the psychiatrist.

In late 1994, researcher and aviation expert Don Berliner received unexposed film in much the same manner as Jamie Shandera did exactly ten years before. This film, when exposed, showed twenty-two pages of a manual titled "Special Operations Manual: Extraterrestrial Entities and Technology, Recovery, and Disposal." This remarkable, and, if authentic, explosive document known as SOM 1-01, gives detailed instructions to highly classified Majestic-12 units on how to recognize, recover, store, and dispose of extraterrestrial craft and entities (see Appendix D).

It goes without saying that this document created a firestorm of controversy among skeptics and believers. Former McDonnell Douglas executive Dr. Robert Wood and his son Ryan have devoted considerable time and effort to authenticate the SOM 1-01, as they have with all of the Majestic Documents. Determining the authenticity of original documents with today's sophisticated equipment by testing ink, paper age, watermarks, and so forth is relatively easy. However, in the case of SOM 1-01 there were only photographs of the manual. In this case the expert trying to authenticate the documents must rely on other things, such as type style, printing equipment, and in particular the writing style for the period in question.

As stated earlier the manual has its critics. Most recently Dr. John B. Alexander wrote a book titled *UFOs: Myths, Conspiracies, and Realities*. In this controversial work, Alexander supports the theory that UFOs exist, but he sees no indication that the government is involved in any cover-up of UFO knowledge. His position is that he held a top-secret clearance and knew many others who did and he can find no one who has any knowledge of a secret group of people involved in UFO research. Dr. Alexander seems to feel that the government and the intelligence community, after over sixty years, are still as dumb as the proverbial stump when it comes to UFO issues.[6]

In reading Dr. Alexander's book he addresses SOM 1-01 by saying that most UFO researchers regard the manual as a total hoax. He included UFO researcher Don Berliner, the man who received the film, in this group. He further stated that both Bob and Ryan Wood spent considerable time attempting to authenticate the manual and have come to a different conclusion. They feel certain the manual was written in 1954. However, Alexander goes on to say that this does not make it a real UFO document. Alexander said Bob Wood told him that he believes the manual was created at the time indicated but was a piece of disinformation to fool Soviet spies into thinking our experimental aircraft, such as the U-2, were extraterrestrial flying saucers.

This statement didn't ring true and I sent an e-mail to both Bob and Ryan Wood. I received a reply from both stating that they have complete confidence in the authenticity of the document and that it was intended for exactly the purpose stated in the manual. Bob Wood wrote me that what he actually told Alexander was that *critics* would probably say it was for Soviet disinformation, and Bob Wood emphatically added that that was not his belief.

Words mean things and when they are taken out of context they can easily distort people's understanding of a subject as complicated and complex as this. It is something we see over and over as UFOlogists take the words of others and bend them to support their own theories. It's an unfortunate fact that adds skepticism to an issue that suffers from believability.

To say that the Truman and Eisenhower administrations were the golden years of UFOlogy is certainly accurate. It was in these years that U.S. policy toward the UFO issue was molded. It must be understood that the UFO events listed during the Truman presidency were not some obscure sightings known only to a handful of people. These events made headlines around the world and the population demanded answers from a baffled government.

In looking back, the challenges faced by President Truman and his administration now seem incomprehensible. Truman had to face what no president had to face before: the possibility that extraterrestrial beings were invading the nation's airspace and its people were helpless to stop them. This was taking place while he led a worldwide effort to heal the scars of war. The problem was compounded by the fact that the president presided over a government whose psyche had been worn thin by the abrasion of war. More than fifty million people had perished and once-great cities now lay in ruins. The possibility that extraterrestrial beings were invading the airspace of countries around the world could not be revealed. The psyche of the population was at that time too fragile to handle such revelations from a government ignorant of their origin or purpose.

Truman demanded answers from his military leaders and the matter received the highest level of classification. Thus began the greatest cover-up in the history of mankind. A cover-up started with good and just intentions at a fragile time in history.

The baton of secrets, the knowledge of the possibility that we were being visited by extraterrestrials, was passed to President Eisenhower. It was a time of great change—a time Secretary of State Dean Acheson called the Creation. Later, as the country and the world started to face the atomic age, the cover-up should have slowly been lifted. However, by then too much had transpired in the attempt to maintain security. Too many laws had been broken and too much power had been amassed by a select few. The immensity of the issue had grown exponentially and the need for safeguards to guard against abuse and corruption of the fantastic secrets being uncovered was not anticipated. The keepers of the secrets grew in number with agendas that did not always reflect the ideas of the Truman and Eisenhower administrations.

President Eisenhower took office at a time when the secrets were starting to be unlocked. He saw the evolution as scientists were brought into the loop of knowledge. He was becoming increasingly troubled with the rapid changes taking place and spoke of it in his farewell speech warning of the increasing power of the military-industrial complex. In the eight years of the Eisenhower presidency tremendous strides were made in understanding the UFO phenomenon, as was the increase in extreme security. It is probable that Eisenhower was at the center of this phenomenon for his eight years in office and perhaps, as some believe, was part the first official contact with beings from other worlds.

THE HOLLOMAN AIR FORCE BASE STORY

There is perhaps no stranger story in all of UFOlogy than the rumored meeting between President Eisenhower and extraterrestrials at Holloman Air Force Base sometime around February 11, 1955. There is also the reported meeting between Ike and extraterrestrials at Edwards Air Force Base in February 1954. The president's brief unexpected absence from his Palm Springs vacation in the latter has been explained as a chipped tooth requiring dental attention. This explanation is backed by the Eisenhower library archivists, although the dentist is deceased and dental records of this visit have not surfaced.

What seems illogical is that people, primarily some UFO researchers, find it unusual that the president was out of the public view from somewhere around 8:00 P.M. until he showed up at church the next morning. This seems a perfectly normal time frame for a president on vacation to be out of public view. What seems unusual and unnecessary was for Press Secretary James Haggerty to announce to the press that Eisenhower had chipped a tooth while eating fried chicken and required some emergency dental work that night. The story had little news value.

The president's diary for Saturday, February 20, 1954, shows that he played golf in the morning and had a private lunch at the golf club with nine other men, including Samuel Goldwin. Later that evening, somewhere between 8:00 and 10:00 P.M., the president is said to have chipped a tooth and needed dental attention. The diary stated that the president and Mrs. Eisenhower attended church services the next morning at 9:30 A.M. and then hosted a large reception for over one hundred guests at 8:30 P.M. at the Smoke Tree Club. The following morning he played a round of golf with a foursome that included Ben Hogan. To say that the president played golf on Saturday, then had lunch with some buddies knowing that that night he would be hustled off to meet with extraterrestrial visitors, be back the next morning for church, host a huge reception that evening, and then play a round of golf the next morning is . . . well, a pill that's just a bit too large to swallow. The facts of this alleged 1954 meeting with aliens just don't hold up to logical examination.

Of greater difficulty to explain is the president's 1955 quail-hunting trip to Georgia and the Holloman UFO story. In an effort to unravel the facts and myths of this bizarre story and get to whatever facts exist, I contacted the Eisenhower presidential center in Abilene, Kansas, to search their archives.

The president's diary shows that he flew from Washington, D.C., to Georgia on Thursday, February 10, 1955, arriving at Millstone Plantation at 4:30 P.M. and went quail hunting until 6:30 P.M. The diary then states that the president went quail hunting with Secretary Humphrey and Mr. Clifford Roberts from 9:20 A.M. to 11:30 A.M. the next morning. After that, the president didn't schedule any activity until Saturday, February 12, 1955, at 4:10 P.M. It is also possible that the diary for the eleventh could have been deliberately *adjusted* and the president didn't go quail hunting the morning of the eleventh as the diary states. In any case the president was out of the public eye for about forty-two hours. Unfortunately those are the only hard facts relating to this event that I found from the library.

To dig deeper into the story I turned to UFO researcher and educator Art Campbell. Art has spent much time in researching the Holloman story and has focused his efforts on that event and the 1947 saucer crash on the Plains of San Agustin that occurred around the same time of the famous Roswell incident. I knew that Art had several first- and secondhand witnesses to the event and he graciously agreed to pass on his data to me.

The first witness was an airman named William Kirklin, who in 1955 was approximately twenty-one years old. Kirklin had been assigned to Holloman AFB in the spring of 1954 where he was placed at the Aero Medical Research Laboratory and later to the base hospital.

Holloman AFB was, and remains, a very secure base. Located about ten miles west of Alamogordo, New Mexico, just east of the White Sands National Monument, and about fifty miles south of the Trinity site, where the first atomic bomb was exploded, Holloman sits in an area where some of the nation's most sensitive military experiments were carried out. It is also this area, and a corridor that runs northwest to the Four Corners area, that became a hotbed of UFO activity in the 1940s and 50s. Some old-timers who worked at various government installations in New Mexico said that saucer sightings became so common during various tests that they were expected and virtually ignored.

In 2006, Art Campbell interviewed the former airman at the Eisenhower museum and library in Abilene, Kansas. The information below is based on that interview and abridged for brevity.

Airman Kirklin graduated from basic training in 1953 and when assigned to Holloman in early 1954, he was required to get a secret security clearance. This is unusual for a low-ranking airman on most bases and indicates the high level of security that existed at Holloman in the early 1950s. Also, it was well known by both military and civilian personnel who worked at Holloman that you didn't talk about what you saw on base.

In February 1955, the word was out that President Eisenhower would visit the base. Kirklin was asked by his commanding officer at the hospital if he would like to be part of the welcoming parade. This was not a parade in the true sense but simply a military honor guard to welcome visiting dignitaries. Kirklin declined and his CO said fine, you'll be on duty at the hospital. It was soon revealed that there would be no parade and no ceremonies whatsoever and personnel were told to forget whatever they heard about a presidential visit to Holloman.

On the morning of February 11, Kirklin was on duty at the hospital when a coworker, Airman Dorsey, asked him if he had seen the disc hovering over the flight line. Kirklin thought Dorsey was talking about something like a discus used in sports. "What do you mean 'hovering'?" Kirklin asked. "It was just hovering about twenty feet off the ground. It must be remote controlled," Dorsey replied. Kirkland was still thinking of something the size of a dinner plate. "How big was the thing?" Kirklin asked. "Oh about twenty to thirty feet across I guess." Kirkland was stunned. "What was it made from, could you tell?" "It looked like some kind of shiny metal, like stainless steel or aluminum. Why don't you go take a look, it's probably still out there?" Kirklin asked for permission to leave the hospital but permission was refused until his break. By the time he was able to go outside on break the object had gone.

After his shift he was walking to his quarters behind two Air Force officers who were talking about Eisenhower's visit that day. Kirklin remembers their discussion in detail.

First officer: "Did you see the president's plane?"

Second officer: "Yeah, that Connie [Lockheed Super Constellation] is a big bird. Came in on the active runway but didn't taxi off, just turned around and shut down, closed the runway."

First officer: "We were told to shut down the radars."

Second officer: "Why?"

First officer: "Don't know. Rumor is radar fouls them up and that is what brought one down at Roswell some years ago."

Second officer: "Do think the ones today were the same from Palmdale last year?"

First officer: "Could be. I heard there were three and one landed at the monument [White Sands National Monument] but I only saw two. One set down on the runway in front of the Connie and the other hovered above it like it was protecting it. After a few minutes someone left the plane, walked to the disc, a door of some sort opened and the person went inside. He stayed about forty-five minutes then went back to the Connie."

Second officer: "Was it the president?"

First office: "That's what I thought but it was on the far runway and I didn't have binoculars."

At that point Kirklin stepped up behind them and asked, "Are you talking about the president?"

One of the officers turned to Kirklin and said, "It's not important" and covering their name badges they hurried off. Kirklin did see their wings and knew they were pilots.

Later Kirklin was in his quarters when someone called him out to see the president's plane that had just taken off. The plane flew over his head and then through the no-fly area over the base housing. Later that evening he saw lights on in the flight surgeon's office. Since one of his responsibilities was to see that those offices were secure, he went there to check. In the office he saw his direct superior, a captain, talking with a lieutenant colonel, discussing the fact that Eisenhower had been on base earlier and spoken very briefly to two or three groups of base military personnel. Kirklin asked why the president was on base and what he spoke about. He was simply told the visit and talk was classified.

Kirklin is a credible witness, who, after retiring from the Air Force, worked for a number of military contractors such as North American Aviation, Motorola, Lockheed Missiles and Space, and NASA. The record certifies that he was stationed at Holloman during the time period that Eisenhower is alleged to have made a secret visit to the base. In UFOlogy there are a number of credible witnesses to alleged UFO events, but added credibility comes with the existence of multiple witnesses. In this event there are at least two more.

In 2007, a Nebraska resident was interviewed and videotaped by researcher Art Campbell. She told him of a personal letter she had, written by her mother some years before that had information on the Holloman incident. The lady's father, an electrician, had worked at Holloman AFB in the 1950s and had told his family of an experience he'd had while working at the base. The story, often told within the family, became known as "The Fireman's Story." The story always fascinated the family members and now with her dad's advancing age the lady asked her mom to get her dad to put the story into a letter for posterity.

The mother and father lived in another state and the mother sent an occasional letter to bring the daughter up to date on how she and her husband were doing.

I had originally included a transcript taken from a recording of the daughter reading her dad's story that he recited to his wife for the letter. The recording was sent to me by Art Campbell. Unfortunately I have been unable to locate her to gain permission to include the story in her own words so I have included an abridged version of the story below. It should be noted that a video of her reading the letter can be seen on the Internet by searching "Art Campbell X Conference."

Sometime in early 1955 this lady's father was working at Holloman AFB in New Mexico. There was a rumor circulating around the base that President Eisenhower would be flying in for an unofficial visit. Base personnel were told there would be no formal greeting and if they saw the president not to wave, gawk, or what have you, but just go about work as usual.

The electricians went to work on the day the president was to arrive and heard his Constellation, now known as Air Force One, lining up to land. They expected to see the president's plane taxi to the tarmac but it shut down on the runway. Since this was very unusual, some of the electricians said one of them should climb one of the tall electrical poles and see what was happening. Since the father had his climbers on he was elected to go up the pole.

He said he started climbing with the sun to his back, a safety rule, and as he got to the top he saw men tarring a hangar roof pointing to the flight line and starting to run. He also noticed his own crew had jumped in their truck and were heading away. When he turned to see what the excitement was about he saw a silver disc, like two pie pans, coming toward him. He hit the ground in a flash and started running toward the electrical building. He stopped once and saw that this strange craft had also stopped. It was just hovering in the air. Once he got to the electrical building they all had a good laugh and told him he came down that pole faster than a fireman.

There was an unwritten rule that workers at Holloman didn't talk about what they saw there. However, as the years passed this story was told by the father to his family and it became known as "The Fireman's Story."

The father often wondered why we didn't use this technology in later conflicts but came to realize that the reason Eisenhower was there was because it wasn't our technology.

The simplicity of this first-person account of events on February 11, 1955, at Holloman AFB certainly adds believability to this strange story. It's clear that for a long time the father thought he'd seen some secret military craft. It wasn't until many years later when the Eisenhower extraterrestrial story became known did he realize what he had seen.

The last story is also a simple story that adds additional support to the Eisenhower visit.

Staff Sgt. Dave Wyckoff is an extraordinary man. He joined the Army Air Corps in 1943 as a tail gunner on B-29s. He flew forty-three missions over Japan and received a Bronze Star and two Purple Hearts. During the Korean War he was a loadmaster supervising cargo deliveries and remained in the Air Force until his discharge on February 22, 1955.

His last delivery before his discharge was from Vacaville AFB in Indiana to Holloman AFB, arriving in the evening of February 10, 1955. The next morning the cargo crew reported to the flight line for departure. They were advised that President Eisenhower was arriving and the base was closed to all other air traffic and would remain closed until the president departed later that afternoon.

Wyckoff saw the president's Constellation land but paid no further attention to the plane or his arrival on base. At some point, possibly while dining in the base mess, he was asked if he wanted to hear the president address a group. He said sure and was given clearance to hear the president speak. According to Wyckoff, Eisenhower only spoke for a couple of minutes but he enjoyed the chance to see him.

Eisenhower departed Holloman around 4:00 P.M. that afternoon and Wyckoff sometime after 5:00 P.M.

These three vignettes present strong evidence that President Eisenhower did make a secret visit Holloman while bird hunting in Georgia in February 1955. What is less evident is that he made contact with extraterrestrials during the visit. It is almost certain that the Secret Service would not allow the president to exit his plane alone, walk across the runway, and enter an alien spacecraft. Could Eisenhower have overruled his security detail? That's certainly possible but still improbable. If there had been prior contact and this trip was simply for the president to tour this otherworldly craft in a secure location, he most surely wouldn't have been alone. Certainly he would have been escorted to the craft by an agent or two even if they didn't enter. However, it is still beyond the pale to believe that the president of the United States would enter an alien spacecraft alone and run the risk of being whisked off into space in a craft that we had no defense against. Maybe it wasn't Eisenhower but rather Vice President Nixon, or Secretary of State John Foster Dulles. This, of course, is all speculation.

Perhaps a more reasonable explanation is that the craft was really constructed in the U.S. using back-engineered alien technology. That could have been what Pat Sorenson's dad saw and it would have been something that the president would like to have inspected. The problem with that theory is that if the U.S. had technology that advanced in 1955, it would have most certainly been revealed before now.

Whatever the truth it is one of the most fascinating stories in UFOlogy, and with the number of reliable witnesses, it's almost certain the president's plane was at Holloman AFB on that date.

The story told by Bob Kirklin brings to mind a story told to me many years ago while a senior in high school. I had just read Maj. Donald Keyhoe's books on UFOs the year before and, as stated earlier, was fascinated with the subject. Then, watching the Air Force attack Keyhoe on the *Armstrong Circle Theatre*, I became a believer in an Air Force cover-up. This was post–Robinson Panel and the government had been successful in ridiculing and debunking the UFO subject in the eyes of the public.

At the time I had an older friend who ran a service station in the little village of Sandston, Virginia, my hometown. Doug was a great fellow and, at thirty-two, was about fourteen years my senior, and a carbon copy of Will Stockdale (Andy Griffith) in the movie *No Time for Sergeants*. He was raised on an old tobacco farm deep in the backwoods of Southside Virginia and could probably knock out a bull with one punch. After enlisting in the Air Force, there was a substantial list of fellow airmen who suffered a broken jaw after making fun of this Southside Virginian who they perceived to be a hillbilly.

In the early 50s, Air Force Gen. Curtis LeMay, at the suggestion of Emilio "Mel" Bruno (a former national AAU wrestling champ), established a judo training program to train pilots in the craft. The problem was they didn't have any instructors. Gen. Thomas Power took over the program and requested twenty-four men to be sent to the Kodokan Institute in Tokyo for training to become judo instructors. When Doug's CO saw the request for airmen to train in judo he knew he had just the man. Doug was in this group and became a judo instructor for pilots at Biggs AFB in El Paso, Texas.

Some years later I mentioned to Doug that I had read several books on flying saucers and was fascinated by the subject. Expecting Doug to blast me for believing in something he viewed as silly junk, I was shocked by his reply. He said he knew that flying saucers were real and not from Earth but it was not something he talked about. He told me that many of pilots he instructed in judo at Biggs had told him chilling stories about encounters with saucers. I remember him saying that these pilots were brave guys who had been truly shaken by things they saw in the sky and told him that nothing made by humans could perform like the saucers they'd encountered. Doug also spoke of one pilot who told him he'd flown debris from a crashed saucer in New Mexico to Wright-Patterson AFB. Since this was almost fifty years ago, my memory of this discussion is less than perfect, but I still remember the basics and how this man, born and raised on a tobacco farm in the backwoods of Southside Virginia, believed in a subject that most scientists of the day couldn't get their arms around. Doug died in his late forties from lung cancer caused by asbestos from a project he worked on as an electrician in New York City. He had never smoked.

The case has been made that pilots flying in the post–World War II 40s and 50s in New Mexico and the Southwest were well accustomed to seeing flying objects that defied the conventional, as were scientists and personnel who worked at White Sands, Sandia, Los Alamos, Oak Ridge, and the Skyhook facility at General Mills. I think this story goes to reinforce the conversation Bob Kirklin overheard while walking behind two pilots at Holloman on February 11, 1955.

There is one more side note to this story. After the Roswell incident reemerged in the 1980s, I was bothered by the fact that I had felt that Roswell, New Mexico, for years—before the 1980s— was an important area in the UFO phenomenon. But I couldn't put my finger on why, going back to the 1960s, I had associated Roswell with UFOs, long before the story broke. I thought that Keyhoe must have mentioned Roswell in one of his books, but I reread the books and found no mention of Roswell. I was baffled to the point that it was starting to bother me . . . to eat at me to find the answer as I researched this book. When I started editing the completed manuscript, the fog started to lift and I began to remember discussions I'd had with my friend Doug Locke, mentioned above. He was not only instructing pilots in judo from Biggs AFB but pilots from other bases in the Southwest. With Roswell Army Airfield less than two hundred miles from Biggs, they were almost in each other's backyard.

I now recall—although fifty-two years have passed and my memory of discussions I had when I was eighteen is at best hazy—

that Doug specifically mentioned pilots from Roswell who had told him the Air Force had recovered alien craft and bodies and Roswell was where they were taken. I recall that the pilots believed the atomic tests in New Mexico had something to do with the saucers.

I also remember that, although I believed in the Keyhoe school of flying saucer sightings, I was skeptical about stories of recovered crashed saucers and dead aliens. In any case it placed Roswell in my mind as a center of UFO issues on par with Wright-Patterson AFB.

I wish I could recall details of the conversations but fifty-two years is a long time. I met Doug in 1959; at the time he was about thirty-one and had enlisted in the Air Force after high school. Considering basic training, advanced training, and the special judo instructor training he received, this would put him at Biggs AFB in a late 40s to 1950s time frame. I believe he served four years, from 1946 to 1950. He left the Air Force in 1950.

THE MILTON TORRES ENCOUNTER

On May 20, 1957, 1st Lt. Milton Torres, then twenty-five years old, was on alert at RAF Manston in Kent, U.K. He was attached to the 406th Air Expeditionary Wing of the 514th Fighter Interceptor Squadron flying F-86D jets. Torres was one of two pilots on five-minute alert in the alert shack at the end of the runway. Around 11:00 P.M., Torres and his fellow pilot were scrambled to their jets and both were in the air in less than the required five minutes. After airborne he was briefed that radar was tracking an uncorrelated target alternating between orbiting and then becoming stationary in the East Anglia area of England. Torres requested authentication; when it was received, he was ordered to go to afterburner and climb to thirty-two thousand feet. Ground control asked

Torres and his wingman for any visual identification but Torres advised ground that he was in "the soup" and visual sighting was impossible.

Torres's F-86D was equipped with twenty-four Mk 40 FFAR rockets, each with the punch of a 75 mm artillery shell. He was vectored toward the target and his onboard radar picked up the bogie. According to Torres the return was so strong "it was burning a hole in the radar" and "it had the proportions of an aircraft carrier." Torres continued, "The return on the radar was so strong that it could not be overlooked by the fire control system on the F-86 . . . The larger the aircraft the easier the lock on. This blip almost locked itself . . . it was the best target that I ever remember locking on to. I had locked on in just a few seconds, and I locked on at exactly fifteen miles, the maximum range for lock on."[7]

Torres asked for instructions and the word came back to fire all his rockets at the target. In Torres's mind he had just received his death warrant. Whatever was out there was far beyond the technology of his fighter or of anything he had ever encountered. There was little question in his mind that he had locked on to something truly extraordinary and that firing on this object would result in he and his craft being vaporized.

Now locked on and preparing to fire, Torres noticed the object start to move. In one sweep of the scope the object was gone from both Torres's cockpit radar and ground radar. It was estimated that the object went from stationary to over ten thousand miles per hour almost instantly.

Now with no target, Torres and his wingman were ordered to return to base. Upon landing the pilots were told the incident was classified and to speak with no one about it until a debriefing the following day. The next day Torres was ushered into a room where a man in civilian dress showed him his government ID and debriefed him on the events of the attempted intercept of the previous night. He was told never to speak of the event to anyone, including his family. He was told that discussion of the incident would be considered a breach of national security and would end his military career and future flying status.

Milton Torres went on to gain a bachelor's degree in engineering and became a range control officer at Cape Canaveral. He flew over two hundred combat missions in Vietnam and was awarded the Distinguished Flying Cross before retiring from the Air Force in 1971. After retiring, he earned a Ph.D. in mechanical engineering and became a college professor. During that time he never spoke of the incident over East Anglia in 1957. It was an incident he thought of daily but it was a secret he thought he would take to his grave.

Several years ago, when the Ministry of Defence (MoD) in the U.K. started releasing its UFO files, a transcript of Torres's UFO encounter was included in those files. This effectively declassified the event and allowed Milton Torres to finally tell the story he had concealed for so long. Since the story was detailed in the MoD documents it was impossible for debunkers to attack it. However, skeptics and debunkers did attempt to come up with a conventional explanation. In his book *Mirage Men*, author Mark Pilkington offers a theory that the radar returns were actually false returns created by "traveling wave tubes" referred to as "spoofing."

The firing of twenty-four rockets over the English countryside at a nontarget that was part of a military experiment made little sense to me. With this in mind, I contacted Nick Pope, a former MoD officer who ran the department's UFO investigation program from 1991 to 1994. I explained my skepticism of the wave tube theory. Nick was kind enough to reply and allow me to quote him. His reply follows:

I can't go into too many details on this, as the capabilities of military radars and the effectiveness of countermeasures such as "spoofing" are classified. However, for a number of reasons, Mark Pilkington's assessment of the Milton Torres case is unlikely to be correct. First of all, the point about spoofing is that one wants to generate a radar return that looks like an aircraft. Creating a radar return the size of an aircraft carrier is singularly unhelpful, because it is more than likely that it will be assessed as a spurious return (e.g., one caused by anomalous propagation) and thus ignored. Moreover, while the theory might look attractive to skeptical UFOlogists, it doesn't add up when viewed from the military perspective. Had this been a radar spoofing trial I have no doubt that someone would have said to Torres that he had been involved in an exercise, the details of which were classified, and that he was not to discuss it. Allowing him to believe the incident was real made it much more likely that he would discuss it. Furthermore, unless one believes the weapons had been disabled, it would be extremely dangerous to generate a situation where, by all accounts, Torres came very close to opening fire. Having worked for the U.K. Ministry of Defence for twenty-one years (and spent three years on their UFO project) and having spent some considerable time with Milton Torres after his story was released, I do not believe the radar spoofing theory fits the facts here. Nothing I've seen in MoD's UFO files (publicly released or withheld) supports the theory either.

Nick is still covered by his MoD security clearance and as such is limited in discussions and details of various events. However, it is clear from his statement that he believes that Milton Torres was ordered to fire on a very real target. Special attention should be directed to the last two sentences in Nick's note to me.

I watched Dr. Torres tell his story about the events of May 20, 1957, to Stephen Bassett's X Conference at the National Press Club. I saw his emotional closing and how he was comforted by his son as he recalled the encounter that almost cost him his life, an encounter he was forced to conceal for so many years. I listened to him plead for our government to disclose what is known about the UFO issue and free others to tell the many stories they have had to conceal for so many years. Dr. Milton Torres is a hero.[8]

As the Eisenhower administration drew to a close, indications are that he saw the control over the UFO issue moving from the White House to the intelligence community and the military-industrial complex. Many feel his warning in his farewell speech to the nation concerning the growing power of the military-industrial complex was rooted in the UFO issue.

Eisenhower biographer Stephen Ambrose makes it clear that as Army chief of staff Eisenhower believed, perhaps beyond reason, that U.S.-Soviet relations could be one of friendly active cooperation. He remained optimistic even as Soviet actions proved to others that relations were becoming adversarial. Eisenhower was an optimist who considered the Soviets friends and allies. This was what brought about the breakup of the long-standing deep friendship he had with George Patton, who considered the Russians our real enemy. As with all optimists, when their optimism is crushed they are also crushed. This could have played a role in his distress over the shift in power over the UFO issue.

In writing this book, I believe that this was a pivotal point in the development of a paradigm shift in power from the executive branch of government, as Truman had directed, to the ever-expanding intelligence community in concert with the military-industrial complex during the Eisenhower administration. This shift in power was fueled by Cold War concerns, and the discovery and research into the "wondrous secrets" that Roosevelt spoke of, combined with money and the resulting power amassed in developing Cold War weapons. It was a snowball rolling down a hill, ever gaining size, that Eisenhower was unable to stop.

When Eisenhower met with John Kennedy in a transition meeting, the subject of UFOs was certain to have been discussed. One must believe that his concern of the shift of UFO information research away from the executive branch to the intelligence and military-industrial community was passed on to Kennedy. It is not unreasonable to believe that Kennedy took this to heart and it played a role in his attempt to have the executive branch regain control over the top-secret UFO issue. It is no secret that Kennedy and CIA director Allen Dulles were not on friendly terms, as Kennedy attempted to put National Security Advisor McGeorge Bundy in a position to draw power, and in particular control of top-secret UFO issues, back to the executive branch.

FLYING SAUCERS FROM OUTER SPACE

Starting in 1953 three publications had an enormous impact on the Air Force and its handling of the UFO issue. The first of these publications, Maj. Donald Keyhoe's *Flying Saucers from Outer Space,* hit the bookstores and shook the Air Force to its foundation. This was due in part because Air Force public information office Chief Al Chop, who had become a believer in the extraterrestrial hypothesis (ETH), wrote a strong official letter (see Appendix J) on Air Force stationery in support of the book and the ETH which was reproduced on the back cover of the book, much to the surprise of Chop and the Air Force. Chop had been present in the Washington National radar room the second night of the Washington merry-go-round and knew, as did everyone in the room, that they were tracking solid targets. Chop confirmed that all the cases Keyhoe cited in the book were legitimate cases from official Air Force files. The book caused fits up and down the Air Force chain of command and there was much finger-pointing on how Keyhoe had gotten the detailed file information. Keyhoe, in fact, had gotten much of his information before a policy was put in place to restrict release of flying saucer files to him. The CIA also entered the picture and admonished the Air Force for releasing case files to private citizens.

Then once again the Air Force shot itself in the foot. Air Force congressional liaison Gen. Joe Kelly stated that "All information on sightings of aerial phenomena, including our conclusions, is unclassified and available to the public." This of course was a total lie and as soon as Keyhoe heard it he was at the Pentagon asking for additional reports. When he was turned down he asked why and was simply told that General Kelly had made a mistake. Keyhoe was furious and demanded a retraction from Kelly. Unfortunately for Kelly he continued to make mistakes and within short order he was out of sight and a new Pentagon spokesman took over.

The impact that Keyhoe's book had on people worldwide cannot be overstated. Important cases were on the rise around the world and the Air Force was in the crosshairs. The Air Force blamed Keyhoe's book, newspapers, magazines, and the media in general for the rise in sightings. They did have an ace up their sleeve called *Blue Book Special Report 14*, then in the final stages of completion.

AIR FORCE *PROJECT BLUE BOOK SPECIAL REPORT 14*

In late 1951, Ed Ruppelt met with the Battelle Memorial Institute, a respected think tank in Columbus, Ohio. The Air Force wanted a more scientific study of the UFO issue for increased credibility. By 1954, Battelle had made a massive study that covered some 3,200 cases. Because of the size and scope of the study, it won't be covered in detail here but there are several important issues to touch on.

Of the 3,200 case studies detailed statistics were established: knowns, unknowns, the quality of each, number of witnesses, educational background, and so forth. The final report stated that 22 percent were deemed unknown. What was surprising was that the higher the quality of the sighting, and the better educated the witness or witnesses, the more likely it was to be classified as unknown. Thirty-five percent of excellent cases were listed as unknown and only 18 percent of the poor cases were listed as unknown. This was a shock to the Air Force, skeptics, and debunkers. The ace up the Air Force sleeve was starting to fall out and something needed to be done. The Air Force reverted to a tried and proven tactic when in trouble: lie.

In October 1955, *Special Report 14* was released with much hoopla and a statement by Air Force Secretary Donald Quarles. As usual the media read Quarles's statement but ignored the report. The media can be given a small pass on this because the report was all but unavailable.

Quarles said, among other things, that the report listed the unknowns at 3 percent, not 22 percent as stated in the report, and gave the impression that with better information they could all be explained. The press hailed the demise of the UFO phenomenon and that would have probably ended the issue for years to come except for Congressman John Moss who wanted to know why the highly revered *SR 14* was so hard to get. This started a two-year struggle within the Air Force. They stated they didn't have the money to mass print such a huge study (probably true). They also knew if they were to release the report en masse it would need to be somewhat "sanitized" and reduced in size.

Then, in 1956, the Air Force took another hit.

THE REPORT ON UNIDENTIFIED FLYING OBJECTS

Blue Book insider Edward Ruppelt's *The Report on Unidentified Flying Objects* hit the bookstores in 1956. Here was the man himself, the former head of Blue Book, with the real inside story. Although the book is carefully written and doesn't blast the Air Force, it is factual and converted many skeptics. Combined with Al Chop's letter in Keyhoe's book, Keyhoe attacking Congress for hearings, and a film company acquiring the rights to the Tremonton and Great Falls UFO footage for a UFO documentary built around Al Chop, the Air Force had taken a nuclear hit.

NICAP and Keyhoe were now the enemy to the Air Force and they tried to stop the hemorrhaging by bring out big guns like Gen. Jimmy Doolittle, then chairman of the NACA (forerunner to NASA), who denied that UFOs were spaceships. Keyhoe, not to be outdone, had his own big guns in Adm. Delmar Fahrney, former chief of the Navy's Guided Missile Program, and the biggest gun of all, Adm. Roscoe Hillenkoetter, former director of the newly formed CIA. The war was on and it raged on for years as unexplained sightings increased. The infighting was intense; Dr. J. Allen Hynek moved from the Air Force side and started to embrace the ETH. Dr. James E. McDonald in the 1960s entered the fray that lasted until the arrival of the very flawed *Condon Report* in 1969, to be discussed in chapter 7.

THOUGHTS AND REFLECTIONS: 1940–1960

It was discussed earlier that it was correct and proper for President Truman to clamp a lid of secrecy on the flying saucer issue post–World War II. The postwar population was simply too fragile to face the frightening fact that strange and unknown craft could violate our sovereign airspace at will and the most powerful military force on the planet was incapable of stopping these incursions.

If people take a few moments to reflect on the role of the United States government, and all democratic governments of the world, it is clear that it is to govern the will of the majority and to maintain a military for the protection of the citizens. The actions then of Truman and Eisenhower in concealing the flying saucer phenomenon were responsible and justifiable. However, the government is a political establishment and in itself is not structured for scientific research. Historically, scientific advances have come from within the private scientific community. In the United States that changed in 1942 with the start of the Manhattan Project operating under the Army Corps of Engineers. From that came the Atomic Energy Commission followed by the Nuclear Regulatory Commission, and finally the Department of Energy.[8]

From these government agencies came such notable facilities as the Oak Ridge National Laboratory, Sandia National Laboratories, Lawrence Livermore National Laboratory, and the Los Alamos National Laboratory, to name just a few. Also Operation Paperclip, where German scientists were brought secretly into the U.S. to assist in developing our space program, should not be overlooked. So the U.S. government, a political entity, now became deeply involved in scientific research.

These government facilities are funded by the government but run by scientists. Scientists in general are independent minded and, to a certain degree, tend to follow their own beliefs and may reject or ignore government dictates. It is not a stretch to believe that as research into highly classified projects advanced, the depth of their scientific findings were not always passed on, at least in total, to the government and the military in particular, but were concealed within in-house operations. Joining in this research were defense contractors who had perhaps a greater ability to operate at a higher level of security than the government scientists.

After World War II we had a rapid rise of government-funded scientific research facilities. Defense contractors were brought in to work in conjunction with government-run research to aid in their research and develop systems based on the findings and results of this research.

Now let's hypothesize that in this work on nuclear energy, rockets, satellites, advanced aircraft, and so forth, the government comes into possession of extraterrestrial artifacts. These artifacts are turned over to their government labs and various defense contractors for evaluation and, if possible, back engineering. Let's say that XYZ Aircraft Company was given some strange lightweight metal that would withstand enormous heat and had fantastic strength. XYZ scientists ran tests for months and finally reported to their superiors that this material most certainly was not something produced on Earth, but they had discovered how to duplicate it. The question is how would these fantastic discoveries be handled by corporate executives? Would the person in charge at XYZ pick up the phone and call Washington or would they tell the subordinates that this is internal classified information and it stays within the company? Of course this very simplistic hypothesis brings up many questions, the least of which is violation of federal laws, since XYZ was working under contract with the government for this research. However, in the rarefied air of multibillion-dollar contracts, rules in many cases don't apply.

The great scientific advances made post–World War II during the Truman-Eisenhower years established the breeding ground for domestic clandestine activities that was fed by research into the "new wonders" referred to by FDR. The great military-industrial complex was being formed. Those in the need to know were moving from the executive branch of government into special-interest dark groups deep within the military and industry. A great floodgate of money opened to fund the space race starting late in the Eisenhower administration. A new president took office in 1961 with a warning from his predecessor to stop this shift in power, and it may have cost him his life.

3

THE GREAT CONSPIRACY THEORY
THE KENNEDY ADMINISTRATION

The tragedy ending the Kennedy administration makes this a most difficult chapter to write. Conspiracy theories have swirled around the assassination since the day his life ended in Dallas, Texas, on November 22, 1963. Some are absurd to the extreme but some are supported by facts and worthy of consideration and research. One theory involves Kennedy's interest in the UFO phenomenon. In writing this book, I have given much thought of how best to handle Kennedy's involvement with the UFO phenomenon and the possible role it may have played in his assassination. The emotional issues and the scars left from that horrific day make this a subject of extreme delicacy. However, facts exist that tie the president to the UFO issue and may have played a role in his assassination. For this reason no serious work can ignore or overlook them. They will be presented here and the readers can arrive at their own conclusions.

In 1961 a young new president took office proclaiming "that the torch had been passed to a new generation." Indeed, John F. Kennedy had new ideas, and some of those ideas were not popular with established government bureaucrats and the leaders of the mushrooming military-industrial complex. As stated in the last chapter, Kennedy most certainly had been influenced by Eisenhower with his concern over the erosion of power from the executive branch on the very secret UFO issue. Kennedy was no admirer of CIA director Allen Dulles because of the Bay of Pigs fiasco, and he relieved him from his position in September 1961. Kennedy is reported to have said he wanted to "splinter the CIA into a thousand pieces and scatter it to the wind," but that is hearsay. This in itself would not make him a popular figure within the agency, if true.

It has also been stated that Kennedy planned to strip some power and responsibility from the CIA and place it with the newly formed Defense Intelligence Agency (DIA) under the direction of Secretary of Defense Robert McNamara. This was not only troubling to the CIA but it met strong resistance from the military-intelligence community. It should be remembered that in the short period since its inception, the CIA had amassed great power and was almost autonomous in its operation. Contrary to what some historical revisionists have said, Kennedy and McNamara were not popular within the intelligence community.

The longtime head of CIA counterintelligence, James Jesus Angleton, was named by Allen Dulles in 1954 to the position and he held it until his forced resignation in 1974. Although Angleton was very close to Dulles and had access to him at any time, he was highly respected in his field and not fired by Kennedy when he fired Dulles and several other senior CIA officials. As we shall see, Angleton will be a major player in this story.

Kennedy, as a member of the Harvard Board of Overseers, had an established relationship with Dr. Donald H. Menzel, Harvard astronomer and professor. Menzel was also an active and leading UFO debunker who we now know led a double life. In secret he held a top-secret ultra-security clearance in the government. He is known to have been deeply involved in the CIA and the NSA. His name appears on leaked documents as a member of the UFO control group Majestic 12 as noted in chapter 2.[1] Menzel, as we shall see, played a role in the Kennedy administration, most certainly as an adviser on the UFO issue.

Official documents between Kennedy and the CIA clearly indicate his desire for joint space exploration with the Soviet Union and the sharing of research data. He also requested UFO data from the CIA. Kennedy had a great concern that UFOs could be mistaken by the U.S. or the Soviet Union as a nuclear attack, and it is believed he discussed this issue with Khrushchev.

There is an unconfirmed report that in February 1961 there was a frightening event that took place within NATO headquarters. About fifty objects were picked up on radar flying at ten thousand feet from the Soviet Union to Europe at high speed. Everyone went on red alert but in a few minutes the objects disappeared over the Norwegian Sea. The U.S. realized they were not Soviet and the Soviets understood they were not from the U.S. Such a scare, if true, would certainly give pause to the new president and a desire to establish some failsafe arrangement with the Soviets.

Sharing our space secrets with the Soviet Union and working with them on space exploration did not sit well with the intelligence community or the military. If you combine that with Kennedy's requests for top-secret UFO data from the CIA for possible public disclosure, an explosive environment developed between the intelligence community and the administration.

If we are to believe information found in the Burned Memo, to be covered later in this chapter, then this explosive environment *may* have led to the assassination of John F. Kennedy. To better understand this story line it is necessary to know the background of the major participants.

DONALD HOWARD MENZEL

Donald Menzel was born April 11, 1901, in Florence, Colorado, and at a very early age developed a deep interest in science and mathematics. He was a graduate of the University of Denver with a degree in chemistry. He received a second degree in astronomy from Princeton University and a Ph.D. in astrophysics. After teaching at several universities, he eventually moved to Harvard. During World War II Menzel joined the Navy as a lieutenant commander, heading up a division of intelligence. He returned to Harvard after the war, eventually becoming director of the Harvard College Observatory. Menzel retired from Harvard in 1971 but remained active in government work as a consultant.

This brief biography does not begin to examine the depth of his work, accomplishments, and the many honors he received throughout his career. In addition to his work in astronomy he publically had a great interest in the UFO issue . . . as a staunch skeptic and debunker. He authored three books debunking UFOs as prosaic phenomena such as clouds or airplanes.

As well researched as his writings on astronomy and other scientific subjects were reviewed and received by his peers, his writings and discussions on the UFO phenomenon were seen by many as underresearched, weak, elementary, and unfitting of his academic background. In his appearance before the 1968 U.S. House of Representatives Committee on Science and Astronautics Symposium on UFOs his address was torn to threads by the well-researched address by Dr. James E. McDonald, senior physicist in atmospheric physics at the University of Colorado. In 1969, at a meeting of the American Association for the Advancement of Science in Boston, one observer said that Menzel appeared close to cardiac arrest as Dr. McDonald's address rendered Dr. Menzel's address as academically void, elementary, and unworthy of a man with his credentials and background (Friedman 1996, 27).

Why would an academic giant like Menzel put himself in such a position? The answer may lie in Stanton T. Friedman's discovery of his double life. Perhaps Dr. Menzel, with his academic background in astronomy and his secret background work for the NSA and CIA in radio wave propagation and cryptography, would be the perfect point to carry the debunking agenda for the Majestic 12 group of which he was listed as a member in MJ-12 documents. His unscientific views that were exposed by Dr. McDonald's testimony would indicate a debunking agenda that by necessity had to ignore serious scientific study. When the pieces of the Menzel puzzle are put together, we see a man who proclaimed to the world, using weak theories and in some cases made-up nonsense, that all UFO sightings were merely misidentified natural phenomena. In his secret life the evidence indicates he was, from the beginning, deeply involved in UFO research as a member of MJ-12.

In his book, *Top Secret/Majic,* Friedman tells of locating a man who worked at Engineering Research Associates in Minnesota after the war. The company was involved in code breaking and was started at the suggestion of then Secretary of the Navy James Forrestal. Menzel was employed as a consultant to the company and had a working relationship with this man. The man told Friedman that he remembered one summer Menzel dropped his consulting work and hurried off on what he told the man was a very highly classified project. Friedman asked the man if he remembered the date. After thinking for a few moments the man said he thought it was 1947. Also, it is known from Menzel's travel notebook that he made frequent trips to New Mexico in a period from 1947 to 1949.

What then would make Menzel a player for the government in the study of a crashed saucer? People who actually saw the debris from the Roswell crash said that the small lightweight I-beams contained a pinkish grouping of symbols similar to hieroglyphics but were totally unfamiliar. With Menzel's background in cryptography and his high level of security clearance, he fit the picture nicely. Menzel secretly held some of the nation's highest security clearances while doing wartime work for the government. Then, after the war with a background in astronomy, physics, and cryptography, he is brought into the select loop of scientists and high-ranking military officers to study the flying saucer issue. As a member of MJ-12, he takes the point in the UFO cover-up with disinformation and public debunking.

There is an interesting side story to the Menzel issue. Friedman said that when he first saw Menzel's name as one of the original MJ-12 group members, he knew the documents must be bogus because of Menzel's intense public debunking of UFOs. It was not until Friedman spent many hours of research, requiring great expense and approval of many people, did he learn of Menzel's secret background. If the MJ-12 documents are bogus they had to have been prepared by someone on the inside with great knowledge of the events in question. You have to ask why they would include Menzel on the list as a group member. The odds of someone like Friedman spending the time and money to dig into Menzel's background were extremely slim. So why put a man's name on a bogus document that would most likely discredit it from the start? If discrediting the document was the purpose in including Menzel, it's still an odd choice since he had a secret background that the originator would know could possibly be uncovered and tie him to MJ-12, as Friedman did. The use of Menzel's name by someone preparing a bogus document makes little sense from any direction one wants to look, and lends credibility to its authenticity.

One final point: The closeness of the JFK-Menzel relationship is revealed in an August 22, 1962, letter from Menzel to JFK. The letter concerns the Sugar Grove Radio Telescope. The salutation is to "Jack" rather than Mr. President, and is signed "Donald." To address a sitting president by his first name would be an indication of something far deeper than a casual relationship. Some may find this a small point. I don't. I find it highly unusual and an indication of an extremely close relationship, a relationship that would allow Menzel to brief the president on MJ-12 operations.

JAMES JESUS ANGLETON

In his service at the CIA as chief of counterintelligence he was a shadowy figure who was all but unknown to rank-and-file agency personnel. To the few who did know of him most cared not to cross his path or feared him. Angleton, in his position as head of counterintelligence, had direct access to the DCI's office at any time.

If we are to believe that assassinations were carried out by the CIA during the time Angleton was chief of counterintelligence, they most certainly came across his desk. His history of counterintelligence work going back to World War II is far too extensive to be covered here but the respect he had within the field of counterintelligence, both foreign and domestic, is legendary. He was known to be both brilliant and paranoid as he became increasingly convinced that the CIA was being compromised by the KGB while working under his close friends, Directors Richard Helms and Allen Dulles.

Since the primary function of counterintelligence is protecting secrets and preventing penetration into those secrets, Angleton's job as it applied to the MJ-12 group was as the chief guardian of those secrets. Although not a member of MJ-12, he would have worked on the periphery. If the group or some members of the group felt that measures needed to be undertaken to guard those secrets, Angleton would have been in operational control.

This in no way is to imply that Angleton ordered the Kennedy assassination but it is almost certain that Dulles and Angleton were disturbed by Kennedy's requests to receive UFO information.

Going back to the late 1940s and early 1950s, Angleton was greatly troubled by the increased flying saucer incursions into U.S. airspace. Records seem to indicate he held deep religious concerns about the subject and held a belief that the knowledge the U.S. possessed of these phenomena must remain a highly guarded secret.

In his book, *Oswald and the CIA* (1995), John Newman stated:

> *In my view, whoever Oswald's direct handler, or handlers were, we must now consider the possibility that Angleton was probably their general manager. No one else in the agency had the access, the authority, and the diabolically ingenious mind to manage this sophisticated plot. . . . Whoever those who were ultimately responsible for the decision to kill Kennedy were, their reach extended into the national intelligence apparatus to such a degree that they could call upon a person who knew its inner secrets and workings so well that he could design a failsafe mechanism into the fabric of the plot. The only person who could insure [sic] that a national security cover-up of an apparent counterintelligence nightmare was the head of counterintelligence.*

ARTHUR CHARLES LUNDAHL

Art Lundahl is legendary in photo interpretation within the government. He headed up the team reviewing the Tremonton UFO film for the Robertson Panel in 1953 (discussed in chapter 1) and developed a great interest in UFOs. Although the panel disagreed with his findings and said the objects in the Tremonton film were birds, Lundahl knew that was an absurd cover-up and became convinced UFOs were extraterrestrial craft. In 1960 he became the director of the National Photographic Interpretation Center. His interest in UFOs became intense during the 1960s and he amassed a huge library of UFO-related books.

What is of particular interest here is that Lundahl is known to have been an adviser to John F. Kennedy and gained hero status for his work on the Cuban Missile Crisis. One cannot but help connect dots between Menzel and Lundahl discussing the UFO issue with JFK. In fact Lundahl and his deep interest in the UFO subject adds additional credibility to Menzel being a UFO researcher and member of MJ-12.

In 1999, Tim Cooper, a UFO researcher, received a remarkable document mailed from the Fort Meade Maryland Freedom of Information Office (see Appendix E). Cooper had been bombarding the government with FOIA requests for UFO documents and in all probability the FOIA office at Fort Meade wanted to send Cooper something to get him off their back. They had an old document from the early 1960s that most likely seemed unimportant; it was declassified and sent to Cooper. The importance of what was stamped on the cover by the Air Force in 1961 was not realized by the declassification personnel.

The document was a 355-page manuscript written by Vernon Bowen in the early 1950s and is a discussion of the flying saucer phenomenon. Bowen had a keen interest in the saucer issue and sent his completed manuscript to the Air Force in 1961 for their review. The manuscript is a rather remarkable piece of detailed journalistic work on flying saucers for that time period, so remarkable that when received by the Air Force it was immediately classified as top secret and Bowen never saw it again.

What is most remarkable about the manuscript is what the

Air Force did to the title page when received from Bowen (see Appendix E). Stamped in red ink is the following: "THE HIGHEST CLASSIFICATION FOR THIS DOCUMENT IS TOP SECRET/ MAJIC NOFORN DISSEM. FOR US 'EYES ONLY.' " EXEMPT FROM DECLASSIFICATION ORADA. 'SPECIAL HANDLING REQUIRED-NOT RELEASABLE TO FOREIGN NATIONALS.' " What makes this truly remarkable is that it is an original, allowing for forensic examination, and it authenticates the existence of Majestic 12 with the top secret Majic classification. In addition to the title page, there are a number of pages that have notes in the margins from Air Force personnel who reviewed the manuscript.

Tim Cooper sent the manuscript to the Woods, who began the authenticating process. First, Speckin Forensic Laboratories performed thin-layer chromatography on the red ink from the front-page stamp and found that it was from 1961, the year Bowen sent it to the Air Force. Dr. Wood contacted the Bowen family and found that Vernon Bowen had passed away in the 1970s. However, he was able to talk with Bowen's son, who verified that his dad did in fact write the manuscript. As to the question of why Bowen felt it necessary to send it to the Air Force, the answer is that Bowen was a patriot. Nowhere in the book is he critical of the Air Force; in fact he speaks highly of them. He simply wanted their approval of his manuscript before he attempted to have it published.

As far as the notes, a number of government officials looked the manuscript over and made notes in the borders, some of which today have special meaning. One reviewer of the manuscript in 1962 made a handwritten note in the border that referenced the very secret "Project Moon Dust." All the notes in the manuscript are fascinating but of particular relevance is that well-known New York columnist Dorothy Kilgallen stated in her column that a Harvard professor was telling his students he could prove that there are people on other planets. The notes in the border say such things as "what is DM doing" and another, with an arrow pointing to the Kilgallen statement in the manuscript, says, "I hope DM will keep his big mouth shut." These are all obvious references to Dr. Donald Menzel. He was known to have had an ego that would be in character to let him debunk UFOs but still let the secret knowledge he possessed leak out in his classroom discussions (see Appendix E).

Kilgallen had mentioned UFOs and extraterrestrial life in her column in the past. In a 1955 column she wrote, "British scientists and airmen, after examining the wreckage of one mysterious flying ship, are convinced these strange aerial objects are not optical illusions or Soviet inventions, but are flying saucers that originate on another planet. The source of my information is a British official of cabinet rank who prefers to remain unidentified." Information from various sources has said the source of the information was given to Kilgallen by Lord Mountbatten at a cocktail party he hosted. It is no secret that Mountbatten had a very deep interest in UFOs as, it is reported, does Prince Phillip.

THE BURNED MEMO

In June 1999, Tim Cooper received documents from someone who claimed in the cover letter to be a retired CIA counterintelligence officer (see Appendix F). This person stated that the documents were ordered destroyed by the Nixon administration but were retrieved before being destroyed. The envelope was postmarked McLean, Virginia, with a CIA zip code. The first document, which has burn marks, is known as the "Burned Memo" and is from MJ-1, who was the director of the CIA, to MJ-2 through MJ-7. The pertinent part of the memo states that "Lancer," JFK's code name, was making inquiries about their activities and that could not be allowed. At the bottom is an acknowledgment signature "Fritz" for J.J.A. who would be James Jesus Angleton, who ran the counterintelligence operation for the CIA. The person who sent the documents said in the cover letter that he worked for Angleton. Included also were eight tabbed pages marked A through H. The most chilling is page H, which is marked "Top Secret/MJ-12" and in essence says that when conditions become nonconductive for growth in our environment and Washington cannot be influenced any further . . . it should be "wet." "Wet" is a code word for assassination reportedly coined by the Soviet KGB. It's not a stretch to think that our own intelligence agencies would adopt this code word.

The Wood team gives these documents their highest rating of authenticity (see Appendix G).

DR. ROBERT WOOD AND RYAN WOOD

From the 1940s forward, this book has documented the government's intention and actions to keep knowledge of UFOs and an extraterrestrial presence a closely guarded state secret. Documentation of what the government knew about the phenomena was primarily from documents leaked to researchers by government insiders. This situation improved somewhat with the implementation of the Freedom of Information Act (FOIA), signed into law in 1966. It has been amended a number of times since then by executive orders that both weakened and strengthened the law. In more recent years the advent of encrypted electronic communication has all but eliminated the government paper trail. However, from the 1940s to the 1970s we have a rich accumulation of leaked and FOIA documents to help piece together the truth about an extraterrestrial presence that the government so closely guards.

In the case of leaked documents it is necessary to accurately and scientifically study these documents to authenticate them. This is also true of FOIA documents that may have been prepared by counterintelligence officers for purposes of disinformation.

The Wood team has been mentioned in this work previously as being involved in document authentication. I believe it's important for the reader to understand their background to better understand their competency in authenticating documents discussed in this book. It is also of critical importance to understand why different documents carry different levels of confidence in their authenticity and how they arrived at the levels of confidence.

Dr. Robert Wood has a bachelor of science in aeronautical engineering from the University of Colorado and a Ph.D. in physics from Cornell. He had a forty-three-year career at McDonnell Douglas managing a number of highly technical research and development projects. His career work included the Nike Zeus missile program, sophisticated radar systems, and a number of other highly classified projects. Later in his career at McDonnell Douglas, he was asked to head up an investigation into the UFO issue. McDonnell Douglas's interest was simple business logic; they saw the phenomenon as real and they wanted intelligence on the subject before their competitor Lockheed got it. Wood became fascinated with the subject, hired a number of consultants, including Stanton Friedman, and personally studied the subject in depth.

After his retirement from McDonnell Douglas, with the help of his son Ryan, who is now the CEO of an aerospace company, he started research into the authentication of UFO-related documents. Their work has become a major factor in the work of UFOlogists' investigation into the phenomena. It cannot be understated as to how much time and money they have spent in the authentication process and in hiring professionals certified to authenticate documents.

Their Web site www.majesticdocuments.com gives a complete history of their work, the documents they control, and the quality of their research. Their help has been a huge resource in the development of this book.

SUMMARY

As a patriot, to accuse ranking personnel within major government agencies of unspeakable crimes is not something that one takes lightly. The fact is that the government is made up of mostly loyal patriotic citizens. Sometimes people in power can make bad decisions, that's forgivable, but as in any endeavor bad people can come to positions of power or good people can be corrupted by great power and money. Is this the case with the assassination of John F. Kennedy? Let's now look at the facts.

1. Dr. Donald H. Menzel did lead a double life, as exposed by Stanton T. Friedman. He was a noted scientist, astronomer, professor, and ardent UFO debunker in his public life. In his secret life he held an extremely high security clearance; did highly classified work for a number of government intelligence agencies; is listed as an original member of the above top-secret group, Majestic 12; and was on a first-name basis with and an adviser to President John F. Kennedy.

2. It is known that on November 12, 1963, President Kennedy sent a letter to the director of the CIA requesting UFO data for NASA and the White House. He also wanted to set up a program with the Soviet Union for joint cooperation in space exploration. As documents seem to indicate, this most likely did not sit well with the keepers of the secrets. Also the depth of his relationship with Dr. Donald Menzel has only recently become known.

3. Vernon Bowen's *Encyclopedia of Flying Saucers* gives credibility to the existence of the above top-secret group

MJ-12. The border notations also give added credibility that Donald Menzel was an MJ-12 member, as well pulling columnist Dorothy Kilgallen into the Kennedy assassination picture.

4. The Burned Memo exists and is in the possession of Dr. Robert Wood. It is an original document that underwent forensic testing for authentication. This document and the related tabs carry the highest level of authenticity on the Wood Web site www.majestic-documents.com. Certainly these documents have had their skeptics and debunkers, but as of now all attempts to debunk them have not succeeded.

5. Columnist Dorothy Kilgallen had an interest in UFOs or flying saucers and most likely received inside information on the U.K. investigation into the matter from Lord Mountbatten. Her flying saucer columns were noted by Vernon Bowen in his manuscript when she mentioned a Harvard professor claiming to his students that he could prove life existed on other planets. From border notes in the manuscript, this most certainly was Donald Menzel and would indicate she had access to Menzel. After the Kennedy assassination, Kilgallen wrote an article stating that in a future article she was going to blow the lid off the assassination story. Within a few days she was found dead, fully clothed, sitting on her bed at her home in Manhattan. The coroner's report was that she died of a mixture of drugs and alcohol. The death still remains mysterious.

The question of whether Oswald acted alone or if there were other shooters involved in an assassination conspiracy is not relevant to this discussion. The question is one of motive and if his assassination was planned and directed by agents within the government to preserve the secrets of a very dark operation. It's an uncomfortable question but in light of the above facts, one that needs to be asked. It's up to the reader to decide if these dots are connectable. Hopefully, it will encourage additional research.

4

LEADER FOR SPACE
THE JOHNSON ADMINISTRATION

Lyndon Baines Johnson and space go back to his days as Senate majority leader when he became appalled at the advances the Soviets had made in space exploration and the fact that they had beaten the U.S. in placing an artificial satellite in orbit. His concern was that the Soviets would soon threaten the security of the United States from space. This concern and his Senate leadership and his influence helped pass the 1958 National Aeronautics and Space Act establishing the civilian space agency NASA. Johnson brought NASA to Houston, where the space center is named for him, and NASA was his charge during the Kennedy administration.

A number of some of the most important UFO cases occurred during his time as vice president and president. These include the Kecksburg incident, the Malmstrom ICBM shutdown, the great Northeast blackout of 1965, and the Lonnie Zamora case. However, there is a side story that is little known and probably played an important role in the U.S. approach to the entire space issue.

After World War II, the Rand Corporation was bringing pressure on the government to get seriously involved in spy satellite research. In 1953, the Air Force combined all of its various satellite projects into one and in 1956 Lockheed got a production contract for what was known as WS-117L. This program worried President Eisenhower for diplomatic reasons, so he held up the program. The Soviets were screaming about our so-called weather balloons (actually Skyhook balloons) that were floating over their territory. These objections would escalate if we put satellites in orbit over the Soviet Union. They would consider them spy satellites, which of course was exactly what the first balloons were meant to be.

On October 4, 1957, the Soviets probably made a misstep and launched Sputnik 1, a little ball of a satellite that did nothing more than beep. Secretly Eisenhower was ecstatic because it opened the door for the U.S. program of spy satellites to move forward. If the Soviets put a satellite into orbit, how could they condemn us for doing the same? In public, Eisenhower showed little emotion, declaring that we were not in a space race with the Soviets or anyone else.

Lyndon Johnson had other ideas. He saw great political gain in claiming that the Soviets were about to take control of space. Democratic strategist George Reedy told Johnson that whoever had control of space would dominate the world. Johnson took the bit and was off like a racehorse. Johnson set up and chaired the on Preparedness Investigating Subcommittee. Johnson talked about a space race and the media picked it up. As Johnson hammered on with talk about the necessity of controlling space it was also picked up by scholars. Whether Eisenhower liked it or not, the space race was on and money started to flow into NASA. It was money that all but had Lyndon Johnson's name on it.

Although Johnson ran for the presidency 1960, that prize went to John F. Kennedy, who then picked Johnson to run as his vice president. Once president, Kennedy put Johnson in control of the space program. It was a job that Johnson loved and one he took seriously. The space race was on and Johnson was heading the charge.

After the Kennedy assassination in 1963 and Johnson became president, the race for space continued. However, there were dark days ahead. The escalating cost of the Vietnam War began to take its toll, and the man who had started the race for space ended it. In 1967, after conferring with the Soviet Union, the Outer Space Treaty was signed, calling for the elimination of expensive space projects and developments.[1]

The involvement that LBJ had in the UFO issue is murky at best. As previously discussed, the power of the presidency over UFO issues had been eroding and taken over by the intelligence community, the military, and the military-industrial complex. It is not a stretch to believe that if the U.S. government was in possession of miraculous extraterrestrial equipment and was beginning to unlock just a minimal amount of secrets from this hardware, those secrets needed to be concealed at all costs. Those mentioned above would become less and less inclined to pass the findings on to the executive branch, as originally directed by President Truman. This shift in power, I believe, is one of the most important aspects of the entire and complex UFO story. Although it is pure speculation, one can see that Johnson's political interference in early space projects could have sent up a red flag to those who now had possession of these secrets and felt it was necessary to remove politicians from the circle of those in the need to know. It is this speculation that makes the connection of the assassination of JFK to the UFO issue even more compelling.

DR. JAMES E. McDONALD

In six short years, starting during the Johnson administration and running into the Nixon administration, one of the most important figures in UFO research made a lasting impact on UFOlogy and brought scientific legitimacy to the phenomenon.

To many UFO researchers (including the author) Dr. McDonald was a true hero in the area of UFO research. He was brilliant, analytical in his research, open-minded and yet skeptical, and had a roving and intensely curious mind. With an endless quest for knowledge, his breakthrough research into the UFO phenomenon is still being studied today. His head-butting with another well-known UFO researcher, Dr. J. Allen Hynek, is legendary in UFO research circles.

Dr. McDonald was the senior physicist at the Institute for Atmospheric Physics and a professor in the Department of Meteorology at the University of Arizona in Tucson. I won't go into a lengthy biography of McDonald here but refer readers to the excellent book on his UFO research background in *Firestorm: Dr. James E. McDonald's Fight for UFO Science* by author Ann Druffel.[2]

When McDonald first became interested in the UFO phenomenon is not clear, but probably dates back to 1958 when several sightings of unusual aerial objects were brought to his attention. In 1954, just after coming to Tucson, McDonald and four of his academic colleagues saw a strange aluminum-colored object they couldn't identify. He made a report to the Air Force, but received no response. What is clear is that between 1966 and his tragic death in 1971 a scientist of impeccable national and international reputation dared to openly study, braving criticism from some of his peers, one of the greatest riddles of our age: unidentified flying objects. With his high-level contacts in government, the military services, and the scientific establishment, he seemed on the verge of unlocking much of the mystery that has puzzled the world since 1947 (Druffel 2003, 1).

It's interesting to note that for many of the years McDonald researched UFOs he was reluctant to acknowledge that the government was concealing UFO information. He referred to the government's reluctance to acknowledge the depth of the UFO issue and the very real possibility that they were extraterrestrial as the "the government foul-up." It was only late in his research did he realize and accept the probability that the government was in fact concealing UFO information. In an interesting exchange between McDonald and Dr. Robert Wood of McDonnell Douglas, told to author Ann Druffel in an interview with Wood in 1997, the change in McDonald's belief of "the government foul-up" to a government cover-up is clearly indicated.

Wood had a stopover in Tucson and McDonald met him at the airport bar for a beer. After a bit of conversation McDonald began to confide in Wood.

"Bob," said McDonald, "I think I've got the answer."

"To what?" asked Wood.

"I found out what's behind it," said McDonald. Wood realized from the change in his manner that McDonald had found out something very important about the UFO phenomenon. "What is it, Jim?" he inquired.

"I just can't tell you right now, all I can tell you is that I think I'm hot on the trail." He paused for a moment then added, "You won't believe it! I've got to pin it down a little bit more, and then it'll come out."

"And that was it," says Wood. "I just don't remember the details of the rest of the conversation, but I do know that part really stuck in my mind. I can speculate now that I know what I know, about what he might have meant. I think he found the trail to the classified work . . . and some documentation that made it pretty clear that there was a cover-up going on, that this was the most classified program in the country.

"The thing that would have made him say, 'you wouldn't believe it'—the first thing that was 'unbelievable' in that era—is that we had in fact recovered a craft." (Druffel 2003, 492)

Druffel states in *Firestorm* that Wood was referring to the Roswell event and the recovery of one, and most probably two, extraterrestrial craft. She notes that McDonald did not mention the foul-up versus cover-up question in the conversation.

From 1965 to 1970, McDonald studied cases, interviewed hundreds of witnesses, appeared before Congress and numerous scientific panels, and conferences—all the while tearing to shreds the ill-founded opinions of some of his scientific peers who tried to debunk the UFO phenomenon. In general McDonald was a kind, soft-spoken, gentle man, very much in love with his wife, Betsy, and their children. However, he could become enraged when he felt peers he was close to were off track or not being responsible in their work. Famed UFO researcher Dr. Jacques Vallée recounts being in the office of Dr. J. Allen Hynek when McDonald stood before Hynek, pounding on his desk and in raised voice saying, "You should have spoken out years ago."[3]

Dr. McDonald was dedicated to his research and a perfectionist in his work. In the last six years of his life he was consumed by his UFO research and then to his opposition to the development of supersonic transport (SST), which he felt would harm the atmosphere. In speaking before a congressional hearing on the SST on March 2, 1971, McDonald's known interest and research into UFOs was ridiculed by a congressman on the committee. It was a situation he had never encountered and it deeply depressed him.

His consumption of these projects kept him away from his family for extended periods of time with research, meetings, and speaking engagements. In late March, his beloved Betsy (Bets, his pet name for her) told him that the loneliness of his inattention had taken its toll and she had become involved with a younger man. She asked McDonald for a divorce.

His failure to bring true scientific research into the UFO issue, the ridicule he encountered, and the divorce broke him. He carefully planned his suicide. The first attempt failed but left him partially blind. The second attempt succeeded and the world lost a pioneer and true giant in the field of UFO research.

Although Johnson's UFO background is murky, we do have some fascinating tidbits. It appears from various sources that he was hounded by two well-known UFO researchers, Dr. James E. McDonald, and Maj. Donald Kehoe. Dr. McDonald badgered Johnson when a university study was announced for UFO research. The study's behind-the-scenes purpose was to take the heat off the Air Force. McDonald became extremely active and vocal, insisting that UFOs were real and the university project must be properly researched. After the research study was awarded to the University of Colorado and Edward Condon, Maj. Donald Keyhoe sent a four-page letter to Johnson (see Appendix H) blasting Condon's bias about the subject and his disgust over how research was being conducted.

It is reported that LBJ was so disturbed by McDonald's badgering that he asked his vice president to intervene by using Humphrey's aerospace adviser, Frank Rand, to do a secret in-house study of UFOs to "get McDonald off my back."[4] Rand brought in

Art Lundahl and Kelly Johnson, of Lockheed Skunk Works, as well as several other scientists who were convinced that UFOs existed. It is said that the study concluded that UFOs were most likely off-planet devices (Swords and Powell 2012, 308).

I have not been able to find solid proof that this study was made or how it would help Johnson "get McDonald off my back," but it seems certain the James McDonald never saw or knew about the study. Author and UFO researcher Ann Druffel had access to all of James E. McDonald's papers and no mention of his knowledge of the Johnson study was in her fine book on McDonald, *Firestorm* (2003).

With Johnson's early involvement with space and later with the space program, there can be no doubt that he had a deep interest in the UFO issue. However, Johnson, like FDR, became consumed with a war—the Vietnam War. That, combined with the shift in influence from the executive branch to the intelligence and military-industrial community, probably diminished Johnson's participation in UFO issues, but it did nothing to stop UFO incidents during his presidency.

THE LONNIE ZAMORA—SOCORRO, NEW MEXICO, SIGHTING

The Zamora incident is considered by many UFOlogists as one of the most important UFO events in modern times. It was studied by some of the most respected researchers in UFOlogy, including Dr. J. Allen Hynek and Dr. James E. McDonald. After almost fifty years it remains unexplained and controversial.

The incident began at 5:45 P.M. on April 24, 1964. Thirty-one-year-old police officer Lonnie Zamora was on patrol when he spotted a car speeding through the town of Socorro, New Mexico. Zamora started to pursue the car out of town and in this pursuit he heard a loud roar and saw a flame in the sky. Breaking off the chase, he turned to investigate what he thought may have been the explosion of a dynamite shack. Driving to the crest of a steep hill, he spotted a shiny egg-shaped object a couple of hundred yards away. At first he thought it was an overturned car, and noticed some "little people" standing next to it. As he drove to within a couple of hundred yards he noted the little people seemed startled as he approached and what he thought was an overturned car he now realized was some strange egg-shaped craft.

The terrain blocked his view for a few seconds but when the object was again in view, he noticed that the figures were out of sight. He stopped, and as he started to get out of the car, the craft came to life and lifted into the air with a roar, emitting blue flame from the bottom. Startled, Zamora knocked off his glasses, which fell to the ground broken.

The roar and flame now ceased and the craft became totally silent as it moved laterally about twenty feet above the ground, leaving burning mesquite in its wake. Zamora watched the craft rapidly gain speed until it was out of sight and then called for backup, which arrived within several minutes. The mesquite was still burning when the backup arrived and the two men examined the landing site. The craft had been sitting on some type of legs, and indents in the sand from the legs were noted. Also in this area there was what appeared to be melted lavalike rock.

Many articles and books have been written on this important case, which remains unexplained today. The importance of the event in this book is twofold. First, it involved substantial research by Dr. James E. McDonald and Dr. J. Allen Hynek, who both studied it in detail. Second, the event occurred in 1964 and received worldwide news coverage. As such it is sure to have reached the desk of the president. However, research at the Johnson library has turned up no information on Johnson's knowledge of the event. Since many sensitive documents in the library remain classified and redacted from pertinent files, this is not surprising. I have filed FOIA requests for the president's daily CIA briefings for that specific time period.

I find this case troublesome because the circumstances seem to present two conflicting viewpoints of UFO sightings.

First, Zamora described a loud noise and flame coming from the craft. This goes against most other reliable UFO sightings that describe little if no noise from the craft and no flame or smoke.[5] This would indicate to me some sort of government test of a terrestrial craft such as the Lunar Lander.[6] This is an area of the United States where tests of experimental government devices were many and frequent.

The conflicting view is that experimental tests were not done by a couple of pilots jumping into a craft and taking off by themselves. That's not the way tests were conducted. There would have been chasing aircraft in the air with the experimental craft flying chase, either fixed-wing or rotary-wing craft, as the test dictated. The test would have also been done in an area not accessible to the public and closely monitored by radar.

So we have conflicting views. One hypothesis could be that the Socorro event was perhaps a different craft other than the typical saucer, with different visitors. Most UFOlogists believe that there are several different species, perhaps many, from different parts of the universe that visit Earth. The small "Grays" seem to be the most prevalent and seem to have a benevolent connection with humans.[7] It is possible that some race of extraterrestrials not familiar with Earth dropped in for a quick look in their strange craft and were spotted by Zamora.

Whatever the case it is almost certain that this was not an experimental craft of the United States government. Several years ago some new information surfaced claiming that the event was a hoax engineered by some college students. At first look it seemed plausible, but under closer examination the story fell apart. The theory involved a rear-projection device, balloons, and firecrackers, none of which fit what Zamora and other witnesses observed. Also, it should be remembered that the event was investigated and studied by Dr. J. Allen Hynek, Dr. James E. McDonald, the military, the FBI, and Project Blue Book. It's not reasonable to believe that this group of experts would not have uncovered or at least suspected a hoax. The case remains a mystery.

THE VANDENBERG AFB/BIG SUR UFO FILMING— SEPTEMBER 1964

This is another incident that I believe is of major importance but has received far too little publicity. This is without doubt because it, like the Malmstrom event (discussed later in this chapter), involved only military personnel who controlled all aspects of the incident. It is another of those cases that directly contradict the official Air Force position—and the position of the infamous Condon Report of 1969—that there have been no national security issues involving UFOs.

We know about this event because of the bravery of one man, Dr. Robert Jacobs, who headed up a team charged with photographing a side view of an Atlas missile launch from Vandenberg AFB, California, in 1964.[8] Dr. Jacobs decided to tell his story after concealing it for eighteen years as instructed by the Air Force. He has appeared on *Larry King Live*, where his fiery replies to idiotic rebuttal statements by Bill Nye are still on YouTube. He has also written of his event and videotaped an interview but other than that has remained rather low profile.

Dr. Jacobs is a professor at Bradley University, where he is shown on the faculty list as a professor of communication. He received his B.A. from the University of Southern California and his M.A. and Ph.D. from the University of California–Santa Barbara. In the 1960s, Jacobs was a lieutenant in the Air Force stationed at

Vandenberg Air Force Base, California. His specialty was in optics and the filming of ballistic missile tests at Vandenberg. When photographing the missile launches from Vandenberg, they were only able to get shots from below the launch, so it was desired to get a side view to see the stage separations. To do this Jacobs and his crew went north to the Big Sur area of California and set up their equipment.

I have several accounts of Bob Jacobs's story and have noted that his superior, Maj. Florence J. Mansmann, has backed Jacobs's story as accurate on several occasions. In researching his fascinating story I found Jacobs's story in his own words on the Web and contacted him to ask his permission to use the story. His story is included below.

> The background of this event is that we were testing ballistic missiles that were to deliver nuclear weapons on target. That's what they were there for. We weren't launching real nuclear weapons, we were launching dummy warheads. They were the exact size, shape, dimension, and weight of a nuclear warhead. I was the officer in charge of optical instrumentation at Vandenburg Air Force Base in the 1369th Photo Squadron and as such it was my duty to supervise the instrumentation photography of every missile that went down in that western test range.
>
> They counted down the missile and we heard engine ignition lift-off so we knew the missile was underway. We were looking down south, southwest, and the missile popped up through the fog. It was just beautiful and I hollered, there it is. Our guys on our M45 tracking mount with a 180-inch lens on it filmed the missile. And the big BU telescope swung over and got it and we followed the

thing. And sure enough we could see all three stages of powered flight boosters, they burned out and dropped away. And then of course, to our naked eye all we saw was a smoke trail going off into subspace as it headed off toward its target, which was an island in the Pacific. Well, that was our first filming of a launch and we got it.

We sent the film back down to the base and—I don't know exactly how long it was after the event, it might have been a day or two—I was called into Major Mansmann's office at the First Strategic Aerospace Division Headquarters. I walked into his office and they had a screen and a 16mm projector set up. There was a couch and Major Mansmann said sit down. And there were two guys in gray suits, civilian clothes, which was fairly unusual. Major Mansmann said "Watch this" and turned on the film projector. I watched the screen and there was the launch from the day or two before.

It was quite exciting. Because of the length of the telescope, as the Atlas missile entered the frame we could see the whole third stage. That was pretty exciting optics. We watched that stage burnout. We watched the second stage burnout. We watched the third stage burnout. And then on that telescope we could see the dummy warhead. It's flying along and into the frame came something else. It flew into the frame like and it shot a beam of light at the warhead.

Now remember, all this stuff is flying at several thousand miles an hour. So this thing [UFO] fires a beam of light at the warhead, hits it and then it [the UFO] moves to the other side and fires another beam of light, then moves again and fires another beam of light, then goes down and fires another beam of light, and then flies out the way it came in. And the warhead tumbles out of space. The object, the points of light that we saw, the warhead and so forth, were traveling through subspace about sixty miles straight up. And they were going some-where in the neighborhood of 11,000 to 14,000 miles an hour when this UFO caught up to them, flew in, flew around them, and flew back out.

Now when the lights came on, Major Mansmann turned around looked at me and said, "Were you guys screwing around up there?" And I said, "No sir." And he said, "What was that?" And I said, "It looks to me like we got a UFO." Now the thing that we saw, this object that flew in, was circular, was shaped like two saucers cupped together with a ping-pong ball on top. The beam of light came out of the ping-pong ball. That's what I saw on film.

Now Major Mansmann said to me after some dis-cussion about it, "You are never to speak of this again. As far as you are concerned, this never happened." And he said, "I don't need to emphasize the dire consequences of a security breach, do I?" I said, "No sir." And he said, "Fine. This never happened." As I started for the door, he said, "Wait a minute. Years from now, if you are ever forced by someone to talk about this, you are to tell them it was laser strikes, laser tracking strikes."

Well, in 1964 we didn't have any laser-tracking strikes. We didn't have any laser-tracking at all. Lasers were in their infancy in 1964. They were little playthings in laboratories. So I said, "Yes sir," and walked out and that was the last I talked about it for eighteen years.

After eighteen years it occurred to me that I could talk about this one incident because nobody ever told me it was classified top secret. If you parse what Major Mansmann said, he said, "You are to say this never happened." Well, that's not classifying it top secret, is it? That's why I felt free to talk about it. It's not a secondhand story. This happened to me. And I was a part of a United States Air Force cover-up for eighteen years.

The Air Force denied everything. Was I in the Air Force? The Air Force denied it. Was I ever at Vandenberg? Well of course I couldn't be because if I wasn't in the Air Force how could I have been at Vandenberg? Did I put a tracking site up along the California coast? No, there was no tracking site in California. Which is a crock! The tracking site is still there right where I put it. And they use it to show you every time the Space Shuttle lands in California—that's where you first see it from. And they are still photographing missiles from Vandenberg from that tracking site.

At any rate, to corroborate my story, Lee Graham tracked down Florence J. Mansmann Jr., the same major who had ordered me to shut up about it and he was now a Ph.D. at Stanford and a rancher in Fresno, California. And he wrote back to Lee saying everything Bob said in his story is absolutely true.

He corroborated my story and he continued to do that year after year, every time somebody brought it up, every time somebody would contact him he corroborated my story by saying, yes, that's exactly what happened. It takes a lot of guts to do that. I became a fan of Sonny's [Mansmann]; he is now deceased. He was my hero for a while.

This compelling story is but one of other indicators that we have extraterrestrial visitors who have great concern for our nuclear programs. Perhaps of equal importance is that it puts another stamp of authenticity on the fact that the Air Force, at high levels, has imposed censorship, covered up, and simply lied about their involvement in UFO-related issues to the public.

THE GREAT NORTHEAST BLACKOUT OF 1965

On November 9, 1965, at 5:16 P.M., the largest blackout in U.S. history occurred, shutting down power to the northeast from Pennsylvania north to Maine and west into Canada, including Toronto. In cities, including New York City, people were trapped in elevators of high-rise buildings, subways halted with people trapped in the pitch-black subway tunnels, and traffic was snarled to a halt as traffic lights went dark. The blackout lasted for up to thirteen hours in some areas and is considered one of the "good" blackouts because people for the most part remained calm and helped each other as best they could under extremely difficult circumstances.

It took six days for officials to report on the cause of the blackout. It is officially blamed on the tripping of a relay known as Q-29 on transmission lines in Ontario. Why the relay tripped was unknown but a number of sources claim that it was human error and that maintenance personnel incorrectly set the relay. However, research has not been able to verify this claim.

Of the event, President Lyndon Johnson wrote the chairman of the Federal Power Commission:

> Today's failure is a dramatic reminder of the importance of the flow of uninterrupted flow of power to the health, safety, and well-being of our citizens and the defense of the country.
>
> This failure should be immediately and carefully investigated in order to prevent a recurrence.
>
> You are therefore directed to launch a thorough study

of the cause of this failure. I am putting at your disposal
the full resources of the federal government and directing
the Federal Bureau of Investigation, the Department of
Defense, and other agencies to support you in any way
possible. You are to call upon the top experts in our na-
tion in conducting this investigation.

A report is expected at the earliest possible moment
as to the causes of this failure and the steps you recom-
mend to be taken to prevent a recurrence.[9]

What is of interest is that a number of well-reported UFO
sightings took place in the area of the blackout. Conspiracy theorists have taken this fact to blame the blackout on the UFO presence. This is to be expected and would not in itself be reason to
include the event. What brings the possible involvement of UFOs
into the area of relevance is that the issue caught the interest of Dr.
James E. McDonald, Dr. J. Allen Hynek, and Maj. Donald Keyhoe,
who all became involved in the investigation.

All three men knew that flying saucers or UFOs had been seen
near or above power plants and high-voltage power lines for years.
McDonald discussed the blackout subject with Maj. Hector Quintanilla, the intransigent head of Project Blue Book at the time, and
pressured him to admit that Blue Book needed to investigate the
possible UFO connection to the blackout. Quintanilla refused to
do so. When McDonald brought up the fact that Blue Book's own
astronomical consultant, Dr. J. Allen Hynek, had brought up the
possibility that UFOs were responsible for the blackout, Quintanilla had to reluctantly concede that an investigation was necessary.

Before confronting Quintanilla, McDonald had met with an
official of the Federal Power Commission in Washington to discuss a possible UFO connection. McDonald neither believed nor

disbelieved that UFOs were involved in the blackout, but the large number of reported UFO sightings in the blackout area needed scientific study. He was frustrated at the lack of knowledge displayed by the FPC official and learned few facts.

After months of research, a number of reasons why various outages occurred was uncovered but there was still no answer why the original Q-29 relay tripped, causing a chain of blackout events. Once again McDonald was stymied in his investigative efforts by unknowledgeable officials and peers who were unwilling to publically or even privately explore and research what McDonald viewed as factual data.

There is an interesting exchange between author Ann Druffel and Jacques Vallée in an interview with him for her book *Firestorm*.

Privately, Vallée had problems with McDonald's entire excursion into the UFO research field. He couldn't forget how McDonald had pounded on Hynek's desk during their first meeting, barely one month before.

"He told Allen, 'Look at this case!' and 'Look at that case!' And Hynek would say, 'Yes, I knew about those cases.' And Jim would say, 'How could you sit on this if you knew that witnesses were actually seeing these things?'"

Vallée knew why Hynek had not spoken out publicly; he knew why his good friend and mentor had remained silent for eighteen years: "At that time, Hynek said to me, 'It was very simple. If I had said so I would have lost my job, and I would have lost my credibility with the scientific community because these things are not proof! They are anecdotes. They are interesting anecdotes.' And Hynek kept asking McDonald, 'Where is the evidence, Jim? Where is the evidence? Where is the stuff you are going to take to the NAS to convince those guys?' And of course Jim felt—you could ascribe it to his scientific integrity and his intellectual integrity—that given the strength of the data, it should be presented no matter what. 'You should go public with it. It should be presented.'

"Or you could say he was a bull in a china shop, going off with preliminary data, with not enough evidence," continues Vallée. "Allen Hynek had his problems with Jim, which had to do with the fact that they were such different men, [with] different temperaments and philosophies. But I had my own problems with Jim . . . He didn't really understand how Hynek's position had changed, and why it had changed. And why, in fact, Hynek had been in a kind of impossible position with his job . . ."

Vallée pauses, remembering. "And I don't know who was right, you know? I was unhappy with both. What I would have liked to see was a real scientific panel. If Jim and Allen had gotten together, they could have created a team of scientists who could have gone public and really pushed the problem before their colleagues."

"Would it have taken both of them, though?" Vallée was asked.

"I think so," Vallee replied. (Druffel 2003, 147–148)

The presence of UFOs as the original cause of tripping the Q-29 relay is still being debated and there is no concrete proof to date. However McDonald learned that someone touring the plant where the Q-29 relay tripped asked his guide why the FPC had issued a statement that human error was behind the relay tripping and was told, "We had to tell the papers something" (Druffel 2003, 146).

THE MALMSTROM ICBM UFO INCIDENT

These important UFO events occurred during the Johnson administration. The events occurred on March 16, 1967, and involved Echo Flight, and then on March 24, 1967, Oscar Flight of Minuteman Intercontinental Ballistic Missile (ICBM) launch facilities.[10]

On the morning of March 16, 1967, maintenance crews and security personnel were at two of the launch facilities; they had performed maintenance work the previous day and stayed overnight at the launch sites. In the early morning hours reports came in from both groups that UFOs had been seen near or over the missile silos. It was reported that one security officer was so unnerved by his sighting that he never returned to work.

Around 8:45 A.M. in the belowground launch control center the deputy crew commander, Lt. Walt Figel, was on alert status when the alarm horn sounded indication that one of the missiles had gone offline. Lieutenant Figel, thinking that the crews had not informed him that maintenance work was being performed as required, called the site. He reached a security guard, who advised the commander that maintenance work had not yet started. However, he reported that UFOs had been seen hovering over the silos. Lieutenant Figel was perplexed, and as he pondered this information, more of his missiles started to go offline. In short order all ten of his missiles went offline and became inoperable. There had been no power failure and after a quick check it was discovered that all the missiles had suffered a guidance and control fault. This seemed to be impossible because each of the missiles was totally independent of each other.

The commander dispatched two security teams to the sites. They reported back that *all* the maintenance and security personnel present at both sites reported seeing UFOs hovering over the silos.

On March 24, 1967, the same event occurred at Oscar Flight, about twenty miles from Echo Flight. Robert Salas was the deputy missile combat crew director that morning. His recollection of the events is well documented in his excellent book, *Faded Giant* (Salas 2005), and on the Internet.

I met Bob and his wife at the International UFO Museum and Research Center in 2011 at the annual Roswell UFO festival where we were both speaking, and again at the 2012 event. I found Bob, a graduate of the Air Force Academy, to be personable, intelligent, and a gentleman but someone who has little time or favor for the fanatical fringe of UFOlogy as well as uninformed skeptics and debunkers.

In our discussions Bob told me that after the event he was debriefed and instructed to sign a nondisclosure agreement with Air Force security personnel that he would never speak or discuss the events of March 24, 1967, to anyone. For almost twenty years Bob honored that agreement until the 1990s. While thumbing through *Above Top Secret* by author and researcher Timothy Good, he saw a reference to the Malmstrom event. Through a Mutual UFO Network (MUFON) investigator, James Klotz, he contacted the Air Force to ask for information about the Echo Flight incident. There was no mention of UFOs in this request. The written reply from the Air Force said in essence that the event was still classified top secret but because of the time factor it would be declassified and they would send documents related to the incident.

In researching this incident I found a discrepancy in the dates of the two events. In *Faded Giant* it is stated that the events occurred on the same day. However, in my discussions with Bob he stated that they occurred a week apart. To clear up this discrepancy

I contacted him and he has allowed me to include his e-mail reply here:

> *The Oscar Flight shutdown (my incident) occurred on March 24, 1967. That date was confirmed by two sources. Robert Jamison was the maintenance officer who was sent to restart Oscar Flight in the late evening of the twenty-fourth, which he confirmed by noting that he was notified of the Belt sighting on the same night. The Belt, Montana, sighting was well documented in a Blue Book file and by newspaper accounts in the* Great Falls Tribune. *The other confirmation came from notes of Roy Craig who started to investigate the shutdowns for the Condon Investigation but was denied access to witnesses and info by A. F. Investigators. His notes indicate that a missile shutdown incident occurred on March 24 (info he received from Ray Fowler). He thought it was Echo Flight, but we have firm documentation that Echo Flight went down on March 16, 1967. At the time I wrote my book, I did not have this confirmation in hand and simply assumed both flights went down the same night because of a comment my commander, Fred Miewald, made to me. After reporting our incident to the command post, he turned to me and said, "The same thing happened at another flight." I had always thought he meant the same night, but what he had meant to say was that the same thing had happened a week earlier.*
>
> *I hope this clarifies the dates of the shutdowns. It will be interesting to learn whether or not LBJ was notified and you can find that information. Other witnesses have stated that when they were bringing the Echo Flight*

back online they stayed overnight at the Echo Launch Control Facility (E-1) and they recall seeing a lot of "high-level brass" there. Walter Figel, the deputy at Echo also told me that he was sent to Offutt AFB, Nebraska, to brief the chief of SAC, so it is likely the Pentagon and above knew about the incidents.

In March 2013 I spent two days researching at the Johnson library archives in Austin, Texas, but did not find any relevant information on the event. It is almost certain that Johnson would have been advised in his security briefings if ICBMs unexpectedly and without reason or logic go offline in a manner that Boeing, the contractor, said was impossible. This was certainly a matter of national security that would have been brought to the attention of the president. I have filed a declassification request with the Johnson library archives for Johnson's daily CIA briefing documents for that time period; also, the archivist at the Johnson Library stated that there would be eighty thousand additional documents released into the RAC Project files in early 2014.

In 1967, Dwynne Arneson was the officer in charge of the communications center for the Twentieth Air Division in Great Falls, Montana. In that position, he held the security classification of top secret/crypto/special compartment information/talent-keyhole. He remembers a message coming through in March of that year saying that a UFO had shut down ICBMs at a base in Montana. In 1975, while commanding a radar base near Loring AFB in Maine, he and his security people would meet with the SAC security at the base. On two occasions he was told by a security officer at Loring that UFOs had been seen hovering over the missile silos.

After leaving the Air Force he went to work for Boeing as a

computer systems analyst and his supervisor was Robert Kaminski. Kaminski was the engineer selected by Boeing to go to Montana and investigate what caused the shutdown. He told Arneson that all of those missiles were clean and did not shut themselves down, it had to have come from outside. More incredibly he stated that his office at Boeing called him and said they received a message from the Air Force telling them to stop their investigation and to not file a report!

I believe that these two events, chronicled by men of unquestionable character who, after careful screening held the keys to some of our nation's most awesome destructive power, prove that a nonearthly intelligence has great interest in our nuclear programs. This intelligence, whether they be extraterrestrials, interdimensional, or some other form of nonhuman intelligence, seems to be sending a message that needs to be taken seriously and given official scientific consideration and examination.

The Malmstrom event is not the only case where UFOs have shown great interest in nuclear programs; there are many more such as the RAF/USAF joint bases at Bentwaters in 1980 incident[11] or the lesser known Bentwaters/Lakenheath incident in 1956. But the shutting down of twenty of our ICBMs is documented to have happened, something that Boeing said was impossible, thus taking offline twenty missiles of critical importance to our national defense. For the Air Force to continue to take the public position that no UFO event has ever had any impact on our national security is absurd in the extreme.

Perhaps deep within the bowels of our intelligence community the keepers of the secrets, immune from political influence or pressure, are working on deciphering the meaning of the messages. That is my hope as the future of mankind may lie in the balance.

THE KECKSBURG, PENNSYLVANIA, UFO INCIDENT—
DECEMBER 9, 1965

This story has been compared to the Roswell incident by many people. However, when you study both events there are great differences between the two. With Roswell there is no question, and the Air Force admits, that there was a recovery of material on the Foster ranch. There are numbers of reports that nonhuman bodies and perhaps one living entity were recovered. With Kecksburg, the government has denied that anything was found at the alleged crash site and there has never been any mention of bodies, with the exception of unconfirmed rumor of a body or bodies found at the site. Kecksburg researcher Stan Gordon told me that recently accounts have surfaced suggesting that something was inside the object. But stories of the event do not discuss occupants or bodies.

Kecksburg is a small town about forty miles southeast of Pittsburgh just off the Pennsylvania Turnpike. This area of western Pennsylvania is rather mountainous with heavily wooded forests surrounding small towns.

On December 9, 1965, something resembling a large brilliant meteor streaked through the northeast skies over Canada and the U.S. It was seen in at least six states and caused sonic booms. The press reported it to be a meteor but a number of people in and around the small town of Kecksburg, Pennsylvania, said the fireball appeared to be a controlled craft that made corrections in its flight path as it flew overhead at a much slower speed than that of a meteor. Witnesses said that the fireball seemed to make a controlled crash landing in a remote ravine near the town. There are credible witnesses who were first to arrive at the scene of the "crash" after it was reported; these include locals and firemen who describe an acorn-shaped object in the ravine emitting various color flashes or arching of light. The news director of a local radio station was said to have arrived and photographed the object but his film was later confiscated when the military arrived. More recently, a documentary stated that only one witness, Bill Bulebush, actually viewed the object in the ravine and the others viewed a glowing blue light from a roadway above the ravine. Researcher Gordon told me that was not accurate. He has interviewed a number of people who went into the ravine and viewed the acorn-shaped object and noted the strange symbols around the base.

As in many UFO reports with a number of witnesses, stories vary, but in any case from one or more witnesses there appeared to be some sort of writing like hieroglyphics around a rim at the bottom of the bell-shaped craft. When the military arrived (as it has been reported), the area was cordoned off and taken over by them, allowing no one access to the site. Later, eyewitnesses in the town said a convoy escorting an Army flatbed truck carrying an object covered with a tarp came through town. Gordon told me one witness stated he briefly saw the object without the tarp.

The story has a number of interesting side notes. One of these is that John Murphy, news director from the local radio station, raced to the site after the station received calls from concerned witnesses about the object apparently crash landing near the town. Murphy arrived at the scene before any authorities, and it is reported that he saw the strange craft, took pictures of it, and interviewed locals who had seen the craft crash and had shown up on the scene. When military arrived and cordoned off the area his film was confiscated.

Murphy became engrossed with the event and wrote a radio documentary built around his sighting of the object, witness interviews, and the fact that his film had been confiscated by the military. Before the documentary was to air, two men in dark suits showed up at the station identifying themselves as government officials and asked to speak to Murphy in private. After about thirty minutes, the men left, leaving Murphy in a very agitated state. When Murphy finally aired the documentary it was heavily censored and nothing like the original, according to his wife, who had read the original. Stan Gordon told me that Murphy never publicly acknowledged he saw or took pictures of the object and that that information came from family members and those close to him.

After the airing of the documentary, Murphy, according to his wife, became depressed and refused to talk about the event to anyone. In 1969, while on vacation in California, Murphy was killed while crossing a road by a hit-and-run driver.

This is a very short synopsis of a very involved book-length story. The story has been told in various reports, books, and TV documentaries. This was a major and important UFO event during the Johnson presidency.

Stan Gordon has researched this event since it occurred. In the 1980s Gordon and researcher Ray Boeche sent out a number of FOIA requests and located the Project Blue Book file on the case. The Blue Book files were very limited and only stated that three men from Blue Book were sent to Kecksburg to investigate and found nothing. This goes against what a large number of credible local witnesses have reported. It does seem certain that something very unusual did land or crash in the forest near Kecksburg and that a large contingent of military and NASA personnel were on the site and removed an object on a flatbed truck. The witnesses have also stated that the military was very forceful in keeping citizens away from the site, even threatening some at gunpoint.

In 2001, investigative journalist Leslie Kean became interested in the event and Stan Gordon's research. She played a major role in a lawsuit against NASA to get documents on the case. In a paper she authored and published in the *International UFO Reporter*, Kean touches on a subject that I believe could play a significant role in the Kecksburg event. She poses the question: Could the Blue

Book personnel have been purposely sent to the wrong location as a diversion? As we have touched on and will see in greater detail in later chapters, Project Blue Book, except in the early Ed Ruppelt years, was nothing but a propaganda tool of the Air Force. In 1965, the abrasive Maj. Hector Quintanilla was heading up Blue Book. Quintanilla had no interest in investigation but only in finding a prosaic explanation for every UFO report and, in some cases, disregarding them completely. UFO reports of significance that had national security implications did not go to Blue Book but were handled under JANAP 146 (to be discussed in chapter 6). Under the circumstances it is reasonable to speculate that Quintanilla was directed to send three *investigators* to Kecksburg, where they were met by military personnel who directed them to a totally different area away from the crash site and they reported that they found nothing. The three men sent by Quintanilla were from the 662nd Radar Squadron near Pittsburgh and not from Blue Book.

The Air Force was under tremendous pressure regarding the UFO issue throughout the 1950s and 1960s as we shall see, and this theory is not as far-fetched as it may now seem. In the 1960s the brilliant atmospheric physicist, Dr. James E. McDonald, entered the UFO fray, butting heads with Quintanilla. After twenty years, Dr. J. Allen Hynek had become disgusted with Air Force lies and deception regarding UFOs and ended his consulting work with them. Combine this with Donald Keyhoe and NICAP, who were hammering away at an Air Force cover-up, and it's little wonder that the Air Force and military may have taken unusual steps toward disinformation, debunking, and witness threats to conceal something highly classified.

There is one other hypothesis that follows this line of thinking: the Army and the Air Force bungled badly the early UFO incidents from the 1940s, but as these incidents increased, so did the military's ability to act quickly to defuse the public's concern and knowledge of UFO events. We know that the military had trained and put in place highly classified rapid response recovery teams located not only around the country but around the world. These teams were trained in the recovery of foreign technology and how to deal with the public who may have been exposed to highly classified technology of terrestrial or extraterrestrial origin. One of these teams may well have been involved in the Kecksburg incident with Blue Book personnel playing an unwitting role. Of course, this is all speculation.

Kean and Gordon's extensive research has ruled out a number of possibilities, including a Soviet Cosmos satellite. They are left with two possibilities: a very secret government project or an extraterrestrial craft. Stan Gordon continues to research this event and new information continues to trickle in from people who have had various levels of involvement in the issue.

The five UFO events briefly touched on above form the nucleus of the major UFO events during the Johnson administration. Johnson's deep interest in space is unquestioned but little of consequence has been uncovered by my research, or the research of others in the Johnson Library in Austin. I have filed declassification requests with the Johnson Library archives for his daily CIA briefing documents that cover the weeks of the Malmstrom, Vandenberg, and Kecksburg event dates.[12]

As stated earlier Johnson, like FDR, was consumed with a war. However, the difference was that with World War II, FDR had the support of the majority to pull together and defeat the evils of the Axis powers. With Vietnam, the war was seen as a political war that should have never been waged. The hippie movement of the 60s took up the charge against the war and Johnson. He was continually pummeled by war protesters, which attracted the attention of his administration away from UFO-related issues.

Although Johnson was engulfed in a very unpopular war (as if any wars are popular), he most certainly would have been informed if twenty of the nation's nuclear deterrents went down, especially if it was related to UFOs. The importance of these events cannot be overstated; it was a time of war and great anxiety.

The research into these events continues.

5

PLAN FOR DISCLOSURE

THE NIXON ADMINISTRATION

Richard Nixon was a significant exception to the shift of power in UFO research from the executive branch to the military-industrial community seen previously in the Kennedy and Johnson administrations. Nixon came from the Eisenhower White House and was an insider to many of the UFO secrets revealed to the security-minded president. There are numerous reports of Nixon being present at White House meetings discussing the UFO issue. Nixon, unlike Kennedy and Johnson, was on the inside, and until Watergate, he wielded a big stick.

The Nixon administration's UFO involvement is compelling because of their collaboration with two principal figures in an attempt at disclosure: writer Robert Emenegger, and his partner, producer Allan Sandler, who produced the NBC documentary, *UFOs: Past, Present and Future,* that was covered in the introduction. This documentary gave a never seen before and never seen since view behind-the-scenes of the government's handling of the UFO issue. However, to understand their participation it is necessary to first understand the development of the Nixon administration, and its interest in the UFO issue and possible desire for disclosure.

In 1962, Richard Nixon was a broken man. He had narrowly lost the race for president to John F. Kennedy in 1960, and in 1962 he lost the race for governor of his home state of California to incumbent governor Pat Brown. It was after this last loss that Nixon declared he was retiring from politics, and famously said to the media: "You won't have Nixon to kick around anymore."

For a while Nixon stayed out of politics, joining a prestigious law firm and even arguing a case before the Supreme Court. In 1964 he edged back into politics when he introduced the GOP's presidential nominee, Sen. Barry Goldwater, at the 1964 convention. After Goldwater's defeat in 1964, the pieces of crushed conservatism in the U.S., a movement many thought was dead, were picked up by a new conservative star, Ronald Reagan. However, Reagan needed to hold public office before running for president and in 1966 he ran and won the race for governor of California. This put Nixon in the front-runner spot for the 1968 presidential race, a race he won by a narrow margin over Johnson's vice president, Hubert Humphrey. Although Nixon's first years as president were troubled by inflation and unemployment, in 1971, some drastic economic changes, including temporary wage and price controls, helped turn the economy around.

It was in foreign policy that Nixon excelled. His lists of accomplishments are impressive: opening up to China, détente with the Soviet Union, arms-limitation talks, withdrawal from Vietnam, and a host of other diplomatic matters.

What is hard for people today to remember or understand, especially younger people, is that Nixon was an extremely popular president prior to Watergate. His landslide reelection was almost historic in the size of the popular vote. Because of this, Nixon gained great power. Riding high in the polls Nixon was able to take on issues that would have been unheard of from other presidents. UFOs and possible limited extraterrestrial disclosure using the Emenegger-Sandler documentary is almost certainly one of these issues.

Nixon's interest in the UFO phenomenon had been rumored for years but really had little solid data to back it up. On the other hand his good friend and golfing buddy, comedian Jackie Gleason, had a well-known interest in UFOs and the paranormal. It was not an interest that Gleason denied nor did he expand on the extreme depth of his interest. His 1960s home in Peekskill, New York, was in the shape of a flying saucer that he called "the mothership" and he called the outbuildings "the scout ships." He also had a collection of some 1,700 books on UFOs and the paranormal, which were donated to the University of Miami Library after his death. It is clear that Gleason did have something far greater than just a passing interest in UFOs and extraterrestrial life. He could best be described as a serious armchair UFOlogist.

The most controversial of the Nixon-Gleason stories is told by his former wife, Beverly McKittrick Gleason. After their separation, she was interviewed by *Esquire* magazine to discuss a book she was writing about her time with Gleason. During the interview she spoke about the alleged late-night trip when Nixon took Gleason to see dead bodies of preserved aliens at Homestead AFB. The story has a number of variations but in general it goes as such:

McKittrick stated that during a round of golf at Gleason's Inverrary Golf Club, Nixon and Gleason discussed, among other things, UFOs and extraterrestrials. Later that night Nixon showed up at Gleason's home and whisked him away to Homestead AFB where they entered a hangar in a high-security area containing a crashed UFO and the remains of preserved extraterrestrials. Gleason returned home in a very disturbed state and eventually told his wife what he saw. Shortly thereafter the Gleasons separated and at some point in this time frame the *Esquire* article came out. In a 2003 telephone interview she stated that when the article was published Gleason called her and was very upset that she told *Esquire* the Nixon UFO story and what relationship they had still enjoyed was now over. However, he never denied her account of his late-night trip with the president.

This story has a number of variations, including that Nixon didn't go with Gleason but had him escorted to Homestead by a military officer to see the craft and entities. Another version has Gleason being escorted to MacDill AFB to see them without Nixon. What we do know as fact is that Gleason had an intense interest in the UFO issue, McKittrick related the Nixon-Gleason story to *Esquire*, and McKittrick was interviewed several times about the story.

The strange tale seems to have several problems. First, it is difficult to the point of being almost impossible for a president to go anywhere without Secret Service protection. Nixon complained about the level of protection he and his family had to endure and tried to reduce the size of his detail. There are stories that he did from time to time slip away from them while at San Clemente but they are anecdotal. Second, Homestead AFB seems an unlikely base to store alien artifacts because it is located in such a populated area. Bases in the secluded west seem better suited for something so highly classified. On the other hand, Homestead AFB is located near an area that for years has been a hot spot of UFO activity, the Bermuda Triangle. Finally, Richard Nixon may have been the president of the United States, but that didn't automatically give him need-to-know status on recovered extraterrestrial vehicles and entities. I think it's highly unlikely that the president had a few martinis, jumped into his car, picked up Gleason, and then drove past bewildered guards at what would be one of the most secure areas on the planet.

The story cannot be dismissed, no matter how unlikely, because it came directly from McKittrick, and the fact that Gleason never denied it carries additional weight. Considering what we know there most likely are some, perhaps many, factual elements within the story.

The real importance of the story is that McKittrick said Gleason told her he discussed the UFO issue while playing golf that day with Nixon. That is reasonable to accept as fact since we have established Gleason's deep interest in UFOs. Gleason publicist and biographer, James Bacon, stated in his book, *How Sweet It Is: The Jackie Gleason Story,* that Gleason always argued with columnist Bob Considine over UFOs. Bacon recalls that one day Gen. Emmett "Rosie" O'Donnell overheard one argument between the two, and he came up to Considine and said, "Jackie's right."

Gleason also, on a number of occasions, mentioned that Nixon shared his interest in the phenomenon. It is beyond the pale to believe that Gleason didn't discuss UFOs with the president. Gleason was in a position that would be the envy of any legitimate UFO researcher, direct access to a president who may have shared Gleason's interest and was privy to tightly held government UFO secrets.

McKittrick stated that for three weeks after the alleged late-night trip to Homestead, Gleason ate and slept little, but drank heavier than usual. He couldn't fathom, according to McKittrick, why the government continued to conceal an extraterrestrial presence. It seems reasonable that Gleason would press the president for some type of disclosure, and it's almost certain that is exactly what Gleason did. It is probable that Gleason was instrumental in convincing Nixon to at least take a hard look at some level of disclosure. Now being pressured by his good friend, Nixon could see that disclosure of an extraterrestrial presence combined with his other achievements in foreign affairs could make him a historic president.

When analyzing all the presidents from Roosevelt forward, I believe the presidency of Richard Nixon is the only administration that could possibly have benefited from ET disclosure. I think it is factual to say that Richard Nixon, although flawed, was a man of superior intellect, especially in the area of foreign affairs. This I'm sure could be argued by many, but I can think of three examples to support this statement.

First, some years ago I remember a CIA agent on a talk show telling of giving Nixon, as president-elect, a briefing on world events. Sitting in a schoolroom-type desk chair, Nixon was listening to this briefing on some obscure African nation. He listened for a while and then asked to inject a thought. He started explaining the history of the country, the background of which the CIA briefer was unaware. Soon Nixon was standing and the agent had taken a seat. Nixon went on to explain why the history of this country had brought them to this possible crisis and what the U.S. should expect. Nixon, because of his knowledge and grasp of foreign affairs, became the instructor and the CIA agent the student.

Second, former *Today* show host Bryant Gumbel, no Nixon supporter, appeared on *The Oprah Winfrey Show*. When asked by Winfrey whom he considered the most interesting person he had ever interviewed, Gumbel stated a couple of names but then added that by far it was former president Richard Nixon after his resignation from office. Gumbel said he had been invited to Nixon's New York City apartment for drinks and dinner. He said after a few drinks his tongue became a little loose and he said to Nixon and the other guests, "I can't believe that I'm having dinner with a man that at one time I thought was the epitome of evil." Gumbel went on to say that he was astounded by Nixon's intellect and grasp of world events.

Finally, it is now known that President Nixon was a confidante to President Clinton, especially in the area of foreign affairs. Clinton trusted Nixon's judgment, and speaking of Nixon's death he said, "I felt like I had lost my father."

I believe that Nixon was a statesman in the truest sense of the word. He certainly had flaws, flaws that brought down his presidency, but that's not the point of this discussion. My argument is that Nixon was the only president to be in a position, and have a reason and the knowledge, to disclose the existence of an extraterrestrial presence.

My logic is that in his first term he did some remarkable things and enjoyed great popularity. He had substantial public support, which resulted in power. Nixon wanted to go down in history as a great president who accomplished great things, and he did accomplish great things. If one thinks about it his accomplishments, including the opening to China, détente with Russia, and a nuclear arms treaty, had unquestionably made the world a safer place. If to that were added the disclosure of an alien presence, he would have gone down in history as one of the great American presidents. He was the only president with the knowledge, the power, and the desire who was, above all, positioned to benefit from disclosure. With the onset of Watergate, UFOlogists, the people of the U.S., and people of the world lost the chance for presidential disclosure for the foreseeable future.

When looking at the overall picture the pieces fit. Using hindsight, we can see that the making of a UFO documentary was the tool that would be used to add extraterrestrial disclosure to this list of impressive accomplishments. On the inside the holders of the UFO secrets were not happy with this course of action. However, Nixon at the peak of his power could and would not be challenged. Also, unlike Kennedy, Nixon did not have an adversarial relationship with the intelligence community. He and Gleason both held the FBI in high regard and Gleason actually did work for the FBI in Miami. The perfect storm for some form of UFO disclosure was brewing in the form of the documentary—only to be dashed by Watergate.

CONCLUSIONS

Starting in 1953, and supported by the Robertson Panel findings, the Air Force took a public stand that UFOs posed no threat to the security of the U.S. and in fact were just some form of naturally occurring phenomenon. This position was bolstered by the 1969 Condon Report that shut down all future *official* UFO investigations. The remarkable UFO documentary *UFOs: Past, Present, Future* is the only documentary or TV program before or after that supported UFOs as being extraterrestrial and having the support of the United States government. Even more remarkable there were no opposing or debunking views.

In contrast to *UFOs: Past, Present, and Future,* there are two other well-known major network documentaries. The first, *CBS Reports,* aired on May 10, 1966, was hosted by Walter Cronkite. In a private letter from Thornton Page of the Robertson Panel to Fred Durant, who had written the Durant Report on the Robertson Panel findings, Page stated that he was the technical consultant on the Cronkite special and structured the show around the Robertson Panel findings and recommendations closely following the Robertsonian profile. In the end, the documentary proclaimed that UFOs were the product of human error and foibles (Swords and Powell 2012, 195–196).

The second documentary of note was *Peter Jennings Reporting: UFOs—Seeing Is Believing.* This documentary aired February 24, 2005, on ABC. This two-hour prime-time special had possibilities and in the first hour there were some excellent interviews. The interview with the B-52 crew that encountered a UFO was exceptional, as were interviews with Dr. J. Allen Hynek, Dr. Michael Swords, and Jerome Clark. Of course they saw it necessary to include the obligatory skeptics and debunkers in the mix. It was the second hour where the program's credibility fell apart. The Roswell segment was perhaps the most biased and slanted report on the incident ever aired. As an example, Stanton T. Friedman told me he was interviewed for over an hour but only twenty seconds of the interview was used. He was referred to as a Roswell "promoter" rather than a nuclear physicist with fourteen years in top-secret government research. Maj. Jesse Marcel was called a TV repairman when in fact he was an amateur radio operator (ham) holding an FCC license for years. No mention was made that Marcel Jr. was an M.D., as well as a helicopter pilot and colonel in the Army National Guard. The list of biased reporting omissions goes on and on. The bottom line . . . the segment closed with Roswell being called a myth. The last segment on abductions was almost as biased as the Roswell segment. The only positive in the second hour was at the very end, as famed theoretical physicist Dr. Michio Kaku admonished the audience not to discount the possibility that some UFOs may be extraterrestrial craft.

It is important to remember that after the Robertson Panel of early 1953, the resulting Durant Report recommended that the Air Force start debunking UFO sightings and carefully watch private UFO organizations.[1] The goal was to quell public interest in the phenomena. Project Blue Book, which started as the official Air Force UFO investigation program, became a propaganda tool of the Air Force with little or no investigation. The fact is that important cases involving national security never did go to Blue Book. In a memo dated October 20, 1969, from USAF Gen. Carroll Bolender, "Reports of UFOs which could affect national security are made in accordance with JANAP 146 and Air Force Manual 55-11, and are not part of the Blue Book system" (Friedman 2008). When researcher Friedman passed this memo on to Blue Book consultant, J. Allen Hynek, Hynek was incensed to realize that he had been used by the Air Force as a propagandist while the important UFO events were concealed from him and the Blue Book staff.

The 1969 Condon Report is even more remarkable. A $500,000 contract to study the UFO phenomenon was signed by the Air Force with the University of Colorado. The director of the study was Edward U. Condon, a noted physicist, and a number of scientists would study the issue. Condon came to the so-called committee predisposed to believe UFOs were nothing but non-sense. At the end of two years of work, Condon prepared section one of the report, "Conclusions and Recommendations," and section two, "Summary of the Study," but took no part in the study sections; in fact from his conclusions it appears he never even looked at the four study sections. His reports, which were what the press and the Air Force looked at, said in essence that UFOs were a nonissue and the Air Force should discontinue any further study of the subject. This summary is 180 degrees in opposition to the other four studies of the Condon Report.[2]

In 1967, the board of directors of the American Institute of Aeronautics and Astronautics formed a technical committee to study the UFO issue. In their study they referred to Condon's "Summary of the Study" and stated: "We did not find a basis in the report for his prediction that nothing of value will come of further studies." On the contrary they found that "a phenomenon with such a high ratio of unexplained cases (about 30 percent) should arouse sufficient scientific curiosity to continue its study" (Sturrock 1999, 51).

It has been proven through the release of FOIA documents that the government has in fact remained deeply involved in the UFO issue. Ten years after the documentary was released, the Reagan White House Science Office questioned Emenegger about the film and showed interest in a remake. This documentary, when viewed in proper context, destroys the argument that the Air Force and the U.S. government have no interest in the UFO phenomenon. It also forms the thread that finally binds presidential involvement in all UFO issues since the 1940s.

Over the last two years I spoke and corresponded with Bob Emenegger via e-mail regularly. He never failed to answer my questions in detail and sent a host of data that supports his experience with the documentary.

On April 2, 2013, my wife, Alice, and I finally had the pleasure of meeting Bob Emenegger at his retirement home in Fayetteville, Arkansas. He and his wife, Margaret, live in an old Southern antebellum–style home right out of *Gone with the Wind*. The home is filled with antiques that Margaret loves to collect, including several full suits of armor. Unfortunately, Margaret had recently had a fall, breaking her hip and requiring surgery. She was staying in a nearby rehabilitation center to regain her ability to walk, so we didn't get to meet her. Emenegger had invited us to stay in the adjoining guesthouse, which we did, and had an enjoyable evening. We took him to dinner at a local restaurant where he regaled us with stories of his Hollywood days. The next morning I met him in his kitchen for coffee as Alice slept in. We discussed his many DoD contacts made during the making of the documentary that became lifelong friends. Bob lamented that with advancing age he was losing many every year. He still talks by phone with Bob Friend from Blue Book regularly.

Although in his eighties, I was amazed at the sharpness of his mind as we talked. He took me to his upstairs office where he still works to help UFOlogists unravel the UFO and extraterrestrial story. There is no question that he has had, and to some extent still has, access to some of the real insiders to the government-controlled UFO story. Emenegger chuckled and told me that the well-known UFO researcher and writer, Maj. Donald Keyhoe, called him when he and Sandler were working on the documentary and was furious that he was not given access by the DoD to the information that was given to them to make the documentary.

Stanton T. Friedman told me that he met with Emenegger and Sandler in Los Angeles and asked to be part of the documentary because of his background with flying saucers. Friedman, who to his credit has no ego problem, just laughed and told me they turned him down. I mentioned this to Emenegger and he replied that they knew Friedman had a solid background with UFOs but decided to stay with all DoD people in making the documentary.

At the time of the meeting, Friedman had in his possession a Russian document on UFOs that needed translating. Emenegger and Sandler said they could have it translated for him. Friedman turned it over to Sandler, who sent it off to the FTD at Wright-Patterson and within a day he had the translated document. Friedman said he was stunned, since that type of work usually took days. It indicated that the U.S. possessed some new and secret computer technology that could rapidly translate Russian documents. He told me that at that point he knew they truly had inside government sources.

There is an interesting side note to the documentary story. As touched on above, Emenegger had mentioned to me a couple of years ago that some people from the Reagan White House contacted him about the possibility of reprising the original documentary and bringing it up to date. It was my impression that this was just a feeler and it didn't go anywhere. Recently, he mentioned the event to me again and I realized there was more to the matter than just a passing contact. I asked him to e-mail me more details. Here are Emenegger's comments to me in his own words:

The work on UFO was not directed from White House (I asked if Reagan requested it and got no answer), the request was from two Reagan appointees (Bob Scott and

Ret. General Miller), heads of DAVA (Defense Audio/Visual agency) located at Norton AFB where the first project originated. While waiting for the "special UFO film material," I worked on a terrorist project with Rand Corp and participated in contact with the film studio to get a British film featuring the actual British SAS team in an daring rescue of an embassy to be shown at all U.S. military bases called the "Final Option" (I think). We also talked about interviewing captured terrorists red brigade in Italy. DAVA was soon moved and nothing move developed on UFO.

Why this is of interest is that it does have Reagan White House connections and Emenegger specifically asked if Reagan was involved and got no answer. I find that telling. Also, as we shall see in the Reagan chapter, the Reagan White House Science Office was involved in the FAA investigation of the Japan Airlines UFO event.

Bob Emenegger is a great fellow. We agree on some things and disagree on others. He has a sharp mind, and a twinkle in his eye when telling a funny story, but he tells the truth. He is a resource to all UFOlogists and he is my friend.

6

SWAMP GAS

THE FORD ADMINISTRATION

With the resignation of President Richard Nixon over the Watergate scandal, Vice President Gerald R. Ford became president of the United States on August 9, 1974. In the world of UFOlogy, Ford's administration is a true enigma. Ford served twenty-four years in the United States House of Representatives from Michigan's fifth congressional district. In 1966, southeastern Michigan, part of Ford's jurisdiction, had a major UFO flap and Ford became deeply involved in pushing a government investigation of the event. As we shall see, his involvement played a leading, but unintentional, role in the government commissioning the University of Colorado and Dr. Edward Condon to study the UFO issue (the Colorado Project) that resulted in the controversial 1967 Condon Report.

What makes President Ford's administration a UFO enigma, or at least odd, is that as vocal as he was over the Michigan flap while in the House of Representatives, once becoming vice president and then president he never again mentioned the subject of UFOs. After leaving office he was asked in a letter written by a UFO researcher and retired Air Force intelligence officer about his knowledge of UFO issues while in public office. Ford replied that while in public service he made many inquiries about UFO issues but said high-government officials always denied UFO knowledge. This is reminiscent of a later president, Bill Clinton, who stated in a public forum after leaving office that he had to admit that he did make inquiries about UFOs and Roswell in particular. He went on to say that "if they knew, they didn't tell me." One has to wonder who are these mysterious "they" and "high-government officials" and why do they apparently lie to presidents, or at least some presidents?

Over a period of six days in March 1966, UFOs were seen by hundreds of people in southern Michigan and Ohio, in an area between and around Toledo and Detroit. On March 14, in the early morning darkness a number of police officers from Washtenaw, Livingston, and Monroe counties viewed objects that darted about the sky moving very fast and making sharp turns. The objects would dive, hover, and shoot straight up while changing colors. Citizens were also seeing the objects and were calling the various police departments to report the sightings. Monroe County sheriff's office contacted Selfridge Air Force base and was told that the base had uncorrelated targets over Lake Erie.

On March 17 at 4:25 A.M. in Milan, Michigan, two police officers, Sgt. Neil Schneider and Dep. David Fitzpatrick, saw three or four toplike objects dart about the sky glowing red, white, and green. Willow Run Airport could not confirm the sighting on their radar.

On March 20, Dexter, Michigan, patrolman Robert Huniwell spotted an object in the sky around 9:30 P.M. He reported that the object, flashing red and green, hovered over a car, then was joined by another object and shot up into the night sky. The county sheriff ordered all deputies to the scene and they later chased an object but were unable to catch up to it.

A local, Frank Mannor, and his family saw the lights from their home and went to investigate. An object appeared to touch down in a nearby swamp. Mannor stated, "I got within five hundred yards of the thing and it looked pyramid-shaped. I've never seen anything like it." Mannor said the object appeared to be about the size of a car. It had a haze under it as it hovered then rose to treetop level and came back down while changing colors. The event was viewed by Mannor's wife and son. The object emitted a noise like a very high-pitched siren. Mannor's wife called the police.

Chief Robert Taylor and Patrolman N. G. Lee came to the scene and heard the sounds and saw the object in the sky around 10:30 P.M. Taylor watched the object through binoculars pulsating red with a light on each end. Washtenaw County Deputy Sheriff BuFord Bushroe also observed the object. "It looked like an arc. It was round. We turned around and starting following it through Dexter for five miles. It was headed west and we stopped. We lost it in the trees. Either the lights went off or it took off with a tremendous burst of speed. It was about fifteen hundred feet above the ground. It moved along at about one hundred miles per hour. We were doing seventy before losing it."[1]

There is no doubt that some very unusual sightings took place in southeastern Michigan and in Ohio in March 1966. What makes this group of sightings of special interest, besides being excellent sightings by hundreds of people, including many police officers, is that it brought into the investigation a member of the United States House of Representatives from Michigan Gerald R. Ford, and Dr. J. Allen Hynek, professor and chairman of the astronomy department at Northwestern University, and consultant to the Air Force's Project Blue Book.

As a consultant to the Air Force, Hynek was sent to Michigan by Blue Book head, Maj. Hector Quintanilla, to investigate the sightings. It was while in Michigan that Hynek made the biggest blunder of his professional career.

Quintanilla pushed Hynek to come up with a debunking press statement about what the sightings "really" were before the population got too excited (Swords and Powell 2012, 307). At a news conference after studying the sightings and going to the Mannor farm to view the site where the Mannors said the UFO landed, Hynek opined that swamp gas may be the cause of some of the sightings. He repeatedly stated that swamp gas was a possible explanation for only a few of the sightings. Hynek's admonishment that swamp gas was a possible explanation for only a *few* of the sightings was overlooked and his comments were ridiculed by citizens and scientists alike.

There are unconfirmed reports on the Internet that, while reviewing sightings in Michigan in the presence of others, he was told he had a call from Washington. He took the call in private and when he returned he seemed out of sorts. It thus has been speculated that he was directed by Washington to use the swamp gas theory in his later news conference. Whether that story is based on fact or hearsay is conjecture, but the swamp gas explanation at the news conference haunted Hynek the rest of his life.

The swamp gas fiasco caused worldwide outrage, and brought Rep. Gerald Ford of Michigan into the controversy. Hynek, for his part, was disgusted with the Air Force. He felt he had been used by the Air Force and from that point on his relationship with the Air Force and Quintanilla went into a rapid decline.

As stated above, Gerald Ford was the first of two high-government officials who expressed a deep interest in the UFO phenomenon, but after becoming president he avoided any discussion of the UFO issue. The other was Gov. Jimmy Carter of Georgia. Carter witnessed a UFO while governor and filed a UFO-sighting report. Carter's interest in UFOs and his desire for government information will be discussed in the next chapter.

In 1966, Ford made several passionate radio broadcasts to his constituents that he was pursuing a congressional investigation into the Michigan sightings. Ford wrote to Terry Mitchell, a UFO researcher sponsored by the University of Minnesota Program Service, thanking him for his endorsement of his proposal to have Congress investigate UFOs. He also wrote a lengthy letter to Rep. George Miller and Rep. Mendel Rivers, cochairman of the Science and Astronautics committee, to start a congressional investigation into the UFO issue.

It was these Michigan events and the "swamp gas" controversy that were the catalyst that forced Air Force Secretary Harold Brown to begin getting the ball rolling toward funding a university study into the UFO phenomenon. It also brought into the fray Dr. James E. McDonald, Maj. Donald Keyhoe, and President Lyndon Johnson, as discussed in chapter 4.

THE COLORADO PROJECT AND THE CONDON REPORT

The period starting just after the Robertson Panel in early 1953 and into the middle 1960s is a period that could charitably be called a time of discord between the Air Force and those trying to get answers from the Air Force on UFO issues. In fact there were times of almost a war between the Air Force and not only UFO-research groups, most notably Maj. Donald Keyhoe and NICAP, but members of the media and certain members of the U.S. Congress. It was truly a shameful time for the Air Force. There were hundreds, if not thousands, of legitimate unexplained UFO sightings of craft that performed well beyond the laws of known physics and seen and reported by respected civilian and military individuals. Within short order the Air Force debunkers would arrive to interview (perhaps interrogate is more suitable) the witness.

Their first approach was to attempt to convince the witness or witnesses that they didn't see what they thought they saw. If that was not successful, then the verbal rubber hoses would come out and discussions would become ugly, threats would be made, and people were told to keep their mouths shut. It happened hundreds of times all around the country. It was and remains a shameful and despicable part of Air Force history.

Project Blue Book originally was under the direction of Edward Ruppelt and was involved in studying UFO cases. After the arrival of Maj. Robert Friend, the focus of Blue Book changed from one of investigation toward a focus on the public's perception of the issue. The blame in this change is not to be directed to the affable Bob Friend but to his bosses at the Air Technical Intelligence Center (ATIC). During this time some in the media were taking the Air Force to task for censorship.

In 1958, an East Coast newspaper writer took on the project of polling over a thousand government radar operators and the results were astonishing. Eight out of ten reported tracking objects that traveled at thousands of miles per hour, could stop instantly, and make ninety-degree turns at speeds that would turn any human to mush. The writer followed with a poll of fifty commercial pilots. These men were almost unanimous in blasting the policy of Air Force censorship. They stated that they were treated like "incompetents" when interrogated by the Air Force and to keep their mouths shut, and this position was backed up by their employers. They were told that they would be liable for a $10,000 fine under the JANAP 146 regulation if they talked (Swords and Powell 2012, 284–285).

In 1963, Friend was replaced by the caustic and strong-willed Maj. Hector Quintanilla. Now all Blue Book efforts turned from any form of investigation toward public information or disinformation of legitimate UFO sightings. Major UFO sightings were

ignored whenever possible but when multiple extraordinary sightings made news, the Air Force issued prosaic explanations that
bordered on idiocy. People and the media who were being given
the idiot's treatment were becoming outraged. Powerful people
like Lyndon Johnson and Speaker of the House John McCormack were becoming involved in discussions of congressional
hearings. Time and again the Air Force's chestnuts were pulled
from the fire from on high before a congressional hearing was
formally organized. The Air Force was on the verge of bleeding,
and something had to be done. The Air Force cover-up of whatever information they possessed in their attempt to misinform the
public was saved by the Colorado Project and resulted in the closing of Blue Book.[2]

The Colorado Project, and the resulting Condon Report, are of
immense importance in understanding the state of UFOlogy today. Even more than the Robertson Panel and the Durant Report
of 1953, they established the massive U.S. denial, cover-up, and
the use of government disinformation relating to UFO incidents.
This still holds true even after governments around the world are
releasing formerly top-secret information and files on their respective countries' UFO events.

As stated earlier, in the 1960s the abrupt and caustic Maj.
Hector Quintanilla replaced the rather open-minded and soft-
spoken Maj. Robert Friend as the head of Project Blue Book. Quintanilla saw his job as being focused on simple data collection, then
with no research whatsoever, to find a conventional explanation
for all UFO sightings. He operated out of the Robertson Panel
playbook and tried to find quick conventional explanations for all
UFO events. His pushing of Hynek, as described above, caused a
worldwide public-relations nightmare with far-reaching consequences.

In 1965, the Air Force continued to face increasing pressure on UFO issues. It was decided to select a group of scientists to meet, discuss, and select a method to best address the UFO problem. The O'Brien Committee, as it became known, met and their recommendation was for the Air Force to contract with a major university for comprehensive research into the best UFO cases, which numbered in the hundreds.

This recommendation was left on the table until the Quintanilla-Hynek swamp gas fiasco. Within a few days of the Hynek press conference, the House Armed Services Committee called Secretary of the Air Force Harold Brown, Quintanilla, and Hynek to testify before the committee. The O'Brien Committee recommendation to contract with a university to scientifically study the UFO phenomenon was favored by Hynek and accepted. The job of finding a university to take on the research project went to the Air Force Directorate of Science. The problem was that the UFO issue was viewed in the academic community as an albatross. MIT, Harvard, UNC, USC, and Hynek's own Northwestern turned the project down even with dangling a $500,000 carrot.

Finally, after much inside political maneuvering, the University of Colorado and Dr. Edward U. Condon accepted the contract. The problem was that Condon didn't like the subject, didn't understand it, and didn't want to understand it.[3] The Air Force was secretly delighted as they had just the person they wanted, a director of the study who thought the issue absurd. From 1966 to 1968, when the report was finally issued, there was constant infighting between scientists who tried to do a respectable job and those, primarily Condon, who felt the work was "damn foolish." Scientists who disagreed with Condon were removed from the project. Condon seemed to become unstable and no longer acted like a scientist, becoming emotional and paranoid. He resorted to name-calling and referred to Hynek as a "kook" (Swords and Powell 2012, 329).

In the end, Condon's own summary of the report bore little resemblance to the conclusions of the actual report. The front end of the report, as written by Condon, should stand as one of the worst cases of bias documented in our recent history (Swords and Powell 2012, 331). The Air Force took off running with Condon's summary and promptly closed Project Blue Book for good. Since Blue Book had become nothing but an Air Force propaganda and disinformation outlet, not much was lost, except it did affect the public's perception of the issue. The media did the same, never bothering to review the report itself, and relied on Condon's summary.

Did this end the Air Force's involvement issue? Of course not. On the 20th of October 1969, Brigadier General C. H. Bolender developed a memo recommending closing Blue Book and stating that UFO reports that could affect national security would be made *as they always had* in accordance with JANAP 146 or Air Force Manual 55-11. The Bolender Memo, as it became known when finally released through the FOIA, authenticated what UFOlogists had suspected for years. Project Blue Book never got the important UFO reports, as those reports remained highly classified.

The memo was distributed to all Air Force commands. The Air Force was still very much involved in UFO investigations, but with the removal of the pesky Project Blue Book, they could now work in complete secrecy.

Before we end our consideration of the Colorado Project and the resulting Condon Report, there is another issue that puts even greater emphasis on the incredible level of incompetence within the Air Force on the UFO issue.

Just up the road from the University of Colorado sits the United States Air Force Academy at Colorado Springs, Colorado, the essence of "The United States Air Force Academy's Producing Lieutenants for Our Air Force and Leaders for Our Nation." In a period from the late 1960s to the early 1970s, a period during which the Air Force was paying the University of Colorado and Dr. Condon a half million dollars to turn out a biased fantasy (Condon's summary) that claimed the UFO phenomenon was rubbish, the Air Force Academy was offering a physics class (Physics 370) to its students called Introductory Space Science and using a textbook called *Introductory Space Science—Volume II*. Chapter thirty-three of this textbook had fourteen pages and was simply titled "Unidentified Flying Objects." The complete chapter is far too long to be included in this work, but below is the heading from chapter thirty-three and the short conclusion:

INTRODUCTORY SPACE SCIENCE—VOLUME II
DEPARTMENT OF PHYSICS—USAF
Edited by: Maj. Donald G. Carpenter
Coeditor: Lt. Colonel Edward R. Therkelson

CHAPTER XXXIII
UNIDENTIFIED FLYING OBJECTS

33.6 CONCLUSION
    From available information, the UFO phenomenon appears to have been global in nature for almost 50,000 years. The majority of known witnesses have been reliable people who have seen easily-explained natural phenomena, and there appears to be no overall positive correlation with population density. The entire phenomenon could be psychological in nature but that is quite

doubtful. However, psychological factors probably do enter the data picture as "noise." The phenomenon could also be entirely due to known and unknown phenomena (with some psychological "noise" added in) but that too is questionable in view of some of the available data.

This leaves us with the unpleasant possibility of alien visitors to our planet, or at least of alien-controlled UFOs. However, the data are not well correlated, and what questionable data there are suggest the existence of at least three and maybe four different groups of aliens (possibly at different stages of development). This too is difficult to accept. It implies the existence of intelligent life on a majority of the planets in our solar system, or a surprisingly strong interest in Earth by members of other solar systems.

A solution to the UFO problem may be obtained by the long and diligent effort of a large group of well financed and competent scientists, unfortunately there is no evidence suggesting that such an effort is going to be made. However, even if such an effort were made, there is no guarantee of success because of the isolated and sporadic nature of the sightings. Also, there may be nothing to find, and that would mean a long search with no proof at the end. The best thing to do is to keep an open and skeptical mind, and not take an extreme position on any side of the question.

So we have the half-million-dollar Condon Report coming out and stating that UFOs can be explained as something prosaic, or in Condon's words to the press, nothing but "damn foolishness." Of course the Pentagon embraced this report with great glee, while out in Colorado Springs their own academy was teaching their students that there may be as many as four extraterrestrial races visiting Earth.[4]

The *National Enquirer* was the first publication to break this story. The story was picked up by the *Lemoore Advance* in northern California, where interest was high over a number of recent UFO sightings in the area. Since the *Enquirer* has a somewhat spotty background, the *Lemoore Advance* wanted to verify the story and contacted the Public Affairs Office at the Air Force Academy. A Major Kilpatrick, the second in command in the office, verified the story as being accurate to the *Advance*.

The validity of this story caused quite a buzz, especially coming on the heels of the Condon Report. Once again the Air Force in the Pentagon was knocked back on its heels. Fortunately for them it was short-lived, as they now had the Condon distortion to fall back on. Using the Condon Report as the reason, they had the textbook reprinted and took out chapter thirty-three. When the facts don't fit your story, adjust them until they do—this but another example of the distortion of facts, concealment of facts, disinformation, and outright lies about a subject that an otherwise fine and distinguished branch of the military is powerless to deal with, and afraid to face.

1967 TO 1971—YEARS OF CONFLICT AND CHANGE

For a number of years before the arrival of Dr. James E. McDonald on the scene, UFO researchers pushed for congressional hearings before a scientific panel. Little progress was made, except that Speaker McCormack's House Subcommittee on Atmospheric Phenomena held closed hearings in 1958. There were also some aborted attempts at hearings, but nothing of great significance happened until the arrival of McDonald in 1966.

McDonald's casual interest in the UFO issue goes back to 1960 and early discussions with Richard Hall, the assistant director of the National Investigations Committee on Aerial Phenomena. However, it appears that his UFO work was very low key until he "came out" on the issue in 1966.

In 1968, McDonald was very concerned with what he was hearing concerning the Condon study going on in Boulder, Colorado. He had made contact with J. Edward Roush of Indiana, who sat on the House Committee on Science and Astronautics. He and Roush developed a relationship and McDonald discussed in detail the UFO issue and problems with the Condon investigation, and with Roush, McDonald had a sympathetic ear. Things heated up in early 1968 when *Look* magazine published an article about the conflicts in the Colorado Report research team, calling it "The Half Million Dollar Trick." McDonald wrote to Roush to impress upon him that congressional inquiry could no longer be put off. Three days later Roush was on the House floor asking for a hearing and taking the Air Force to task for commissioning what surely would be a faulty study. Roush said if the *Look* article was incorrect it needed correcting, but if it was correct it raised serious questions about the University of Colorado investigation and the federal contract process.

The ball was rolling for congressional hearings, but much work and politicking lay ahead. As a precursor to an actual hearing, a UFO seminar was proposed and set up. The seminar, or symposium as it was later called, required a great deal of work on McDonald's part. As someone who wanted to always move at rabbitlike speed, his efforts with the deliberate actions of Congress were very frustrating to McDonald and, at times, depressing.

It was during this time that McDonald called Dr. Bob Wood at McDonnell Douglas to ask him to participate in the conference. Wood was eager to participate but wanted approval from his superiors at McDonnell Douglas to do so.[5] In this conversation, Wood relayed a report to McDonald, a report he considered to be from a very reliable source at Vandenberg AFB. The report concerned Gene May, a Douglas test pilot who had been involved in X-15 test flights. As the story goes, May had taken the X-15 on a test flight some several years before with only fifteen minutes of fuel on board, yet May didn't land until three hours later. When he landed, May reported that he had been taken on board a UFO, X-15 and all! In checking this story, I found that Gene May was a Douglas test pilot from 1941 to 1952, but never was involved in or flew the X-15. I have no doubt that this story was told to Dr. Wood by his contact at Vandenberg, who Wood felt was very reliable. It appears then that the story is not true, but I have included it in the book on the chance that it is factual and the contact simply named the wrong test pilot and someone with knowledge of the event will read the account and come forward to set the record straight.

The Roush Hearings were held on July 29 under the auspices of the House Committee on Science and Astronautics with the speakers being, among others, McDonald, Dr. J. Allen Hynek, and Dr. Carl Sagan.

McDonald's address was rather lengthy but I believe brilliantly structured for a congressional symposium. A snippet from that address follows:

> *The type of UFO reports that are most intriguing are close-range sightings of machinelike objects of unconventional nature and unconventional performance characteristics, seen at low altitudes, and sometimes even on the ground. The general public is entirely unaware of the large number of such reports that are coming from credible witnesses . . . When one starts searching for such cases, their numbers are quite astonishing. Also, such sightings appear to be occurring all over the globe.*

His closing statement, which follows, is important to understand the thinking of this brilliant scientist who had only been
researching the UFO phenomenon, but in great detail, for two
years:

> *To conclude, then, my position is that UFOs are entirely*
> *real and we do not know what they are because we have*
> *laughed them out of court. The possibility that these are*
> *extraterrestrial devices, that we are dealing with surveil-*
> *lance from some advanced technology, is a possibility*
> *that I take very seriously.*
>
> *I reach that hypothesis, as my preferred hypothesis,*
> *not by hard fact, hardwire, tailfins, or reading license*
> *plates, but by having examined hundreds of cases and*
> *rejected the alternate hypothesis as capable of accounting*
> *for them.*
>
> *I am afraid that this possibility has sufficiently good*
> *backing for it, despite its low a priori ability, that we*
> *must examine it. I think your committee, with its many*
> *concerns for the entire aerospace program, as well as our*
> *whole national scientific program, has a very special rea-*
> *son for examining that possibility. Should that possibility*
> *be correct, if there is even a chance of its being correct,*
> *we ought to get our best people looking at it. Instead, we*
> *are laughing at this possibility.*

In general, McDonald was pleased with the outcome of the
hearing and looked forward to full congressional hearings. Unfortunately, this would prove to be the last official UFO symposium
or hearing held before Congress.

This short synopsis of the effort and the number of people
that McDonald talked with in Congress, people he prodded, ca-

joled, and lobbied over a two-year period does not give his efforts justice. It should also be noted that during this time McDonald was under attack from *Aviation Week* writer and UFO debunker, Philip Klass. He was attacking McDonald for what he saw as misuse of funds from an Office of Naval Research grant to study UFOs, a subject Klass found nonsensical. Since Klass was an outsider with the scientific community, he became an abrasive debunker to the number of scientists like McDonald who believed in the UFO phenomena. Unfortunately, McDonald underestimated the clout Klass possessed, and it would create many problems in times to come.

Was Klass on the government payroll as a paid debunker as some believe? To the best of my knowledge there is no hard evidence that this was the case. On the other hand it can't be ruled out. Klass was not a debater in the true sense; in fact no debunkers really are good debaters, as they simply don't know the subject they are debunking. There is a humorous saying that has been around for many years that seems to sum up the debunker well: If you can't dazzle them with brilliance, baffle them with BS. From what I've read, Klass operated in this area and employed what I would call a "smokescreen" approach to delay and derail legitimate discussion and debate.

To complicate the issue, there was a growing feud between McDonald and Edward Condon over Condon's lack of interest in any investigative efforts on Condon's part in the Colorado Project. Condon was limiting his own UFO investigations to wild stories of contactees and was giving lectures about their shenanigans, which kept receptive audiences highly amused (Druffel 2003, 229). The explosion finally occurred with the unauthorized release of the Low Memorandum from the Colorado Project files.[6]

With the release of the Condon Report in 1969, there was, needless to say, a dark cloud of despair over the entire UFO research community. The only hope to right the wrongs of the incompetent Condon Report was through a scientific symposium to be held by the American Association for the Advancement of Science (AAAS). The AAAS UFO Symposium came into being when Dr. Thornton Page of Wesleyan University, along with Dr. Carl Sagan as coorganizer, wrote to Dr. Dael Wolfle of the AAAS proposing the symposium at the 1968 meeting.

They listed six reasons for the symposium:

1. The subject was interdisciplinary.
2. It was of interest to the public.
3. Most scientists sneer at it but are not well informed.
4. Those scientists who have studied the problem disagree in their conclusions.
5. The Condon Report will deserve discussion.
6. The subject of UFOs would serve to inform the public on current knowledge in astronomy, atmospheric physics, and space biology.

In his letter, Page went on to say that Menzel and Condon refused to attend because of the kook factor. However he felt that McDonald, Hynek, Sagan, Klass, and some others would make for an interesting and lively discussion. As it happened, a 1968 symposium was not to be. In the background, Menzel and Klass fought to kill the idea. Finally, Sagan wrote to McDonald that the project would be put off until 1969.

There was fear now with McDonald, Hynek, and Keyhoe that the symposium would be abandoned, but in early 1969 indications were that Menzel and Condon had failed to derail the symposium and plans were again moving forward. Menzel is quoted as telling Page "that UFOs had nothing to do with outer space, and anyone who invoked the ETH to explain them was a crackpot or crank who should not be permitted on the panel." He went on to say, "If McDonald or any other of his ilk participated he would not and, in fact, would oppose the symposium."[7] Now the stage was set for a verbal scientific fistfight with Menzel, Condon, and Klass on one side and McDonald and Hynek on the other side.

What I found of great interest as I researched this segment was the participation of Carl Sagan, who I always considered anti-UFO in his views. Studying Sagan's participation and actions in organizing the 1969 AAAS UFO Symposium gives rise to the idea that he was pro-UFO, a feeling that was shared by Condon and Menzel, and a feeling that I began to embrace as I studied the events of this period. It was not until I read and reread the doctoral thesis of Paul E. McCarthy, *Politicking and Paradigm Shifting: James E. McDonald and the UFO Case Study,* that I began to realize that Sagan was playing a necessary role in bringing together two opposing factions for scientific discussion that he and Page felt were important. Sagan certainly had an interest in the UFO phenomenon and desired serious scientific study, but at no time did he then, or for the rest of his life, embrace or even consider the validity of the ETH.

The years of 1966 to 1971 were most certainly years of conflict and change. The internal conflict within the government and the scientific community are far too complicated and involved for many participants to be covered in any detail in this book. The doctoral thesis by Paul E. McCarthy, mentioned above, is an excellent source for those wishing greater detail on this period of UFO history.

What can be said with certainty is that the Colorado Project and the resulting Condon Report did derail scientific research into the UFO phenomenon, a situation that still stands today. It also played a major role in the loss of one of the greatest minds to research the UFO mystery, Dr. James E. McDonald.

One has to ponder where UFO research would be today if McDonald and Hynek had lived to continue their research. Combine their efforts with the work of up-and-coming UFO researcher and nuclear physicist Stanton T. Friedman, and there is little doubt that UFOlogy would be far advanced from its present state.

After becoming president after the resignation of Richard Nixon, Ford appointed Donald Rumsfeld his chief of staff, and later in 1975, secretary of defense. Rumsfeld had been a Ford confidante since Ford had been minority leader of the House and Rumsfeld was a U.S. congressman from Illinois. After his appointment as secretary of defense, Rumsfeld was instrumental in having Dick Cheney named chief of staff.

Two rather simple letters in the Ford library may indicate a far greater involvement by the Ford White House in UFO issues than research has indicated.[8] On March 3, 1975, Dr. J. Allen Hynek, then director of the Center for UFO Studies, sent the letter below to Donald Rumsfeld:

> Dear Don,
>
> In keeping with your kind request of being kept informed of developments within the Center, I am enclosing some material which may be of interest. The FBI Bulletin carried a long article about the Center for UFO Studies last month, and the Washington Post carried a follow-up article. Both are enclosed.
>
> If you are interested in how our toll-free number was used last year, enclosed is the annual operational report.
>
> Best Regards,
> Allen

On March 12, 1975, Rumsfeld replied:

Dear Allen,

Thanks for your thoughtful note and the materials concerning the UFO phenomena. I appreciate seeing the enclosures.

Sincerely,

Donald Rumsfeld

Although after becoming president, Ford no longer spoke publically about UFO issues this note indicates that at the highest levels of the Ford administration UFOs were a topic of great interest. These two documents indicate that interest but also raise other questions.[9]

First, it has long been felt by UFOlogists that both Rumsfeld and Cheney were (and still are) deeply involved in UFO issues going back many years.[10] From almost the beginning of the Ford administration these two men, close friends, held high positions of power. Now the question that must asked is what was behind Rumsfeld's interest in developments within the Center for UFO Studies? Was it at the direction of his boss, was it simple curiosity, or as an insider did he want to keep track of what was going on inside a much-respected UFO investigation operation?

One thing of importance is that in 1975 the president's chief of staff and soon-to-be secretary of defense stated in the letter to Hynek that UFOs were a *phenomenon,* which, according to Merriam-Webster, "is an observable fact or event." Words mean things and Rumsfeld's use of the word "phenomena" in writing to Hynek is telling. People will say that I'm reading too much into this simple statement, but I don't think so. I believe at the very least Rumsfeld knew that the official Air Force and government position that all UFOs could be explained as something prosaic and natural was absurd, thus his interest. At the most he was deeply involved on the inside of the government's cover-up of an extraterrestrial presence and wanted intelligence on what Hynek was doing and finding.

During the Ford administration and while Donald Rumsfeld was secretary of defense, a major UFO event occurred on the other side of the globe that was closely monitored by the U.S. In the late evening–early morning hours of September 18–19, 1976, citizens in the Iranian capital of Tehran were alarmed by a very large, bright object over the city. At that time Iran was a strong ally of the U.S. and had modern military equipment, including F-4 Phantom jets supplied by the United States.

Calls came in from citizens to the Imperial Iranian Air Force command, which in turn contacted the control tower at Mehrabad International Airport. The tower confirmed they had visual sighting. It was described by the tower operator, Hossain Pirouzi, who viewed the object from the tower's balcony with binoculars, as looking like a ceiling fan with four drooping blades.[11]

General Yousefi, assistant deputy director of operation for the Air Force, ordered an Iranian F-4 Phantom scrambled to investigate. (The F-4 is a Mach 2 aircraft.) As the pilot approached the object in excess of Mach 1, the object stayed ahead of the jet. With the jet now about 150 miles from Tehran, he lost the object. The object, in fact, had returned to Tehran and the pilot was instructed to return and try to get a visual on the target. When he got within twenty-five miles of the object, he lost all radio communication and instrumentation and, running low on fuel, he returned to base. As soon as he turned away from the object he regained the use of his electronics.

A second F-4 was scrambled, flown by Lt. Parviz Jafari. As Jafari approached the object he could see it was flashing intense red, green, orange, and blue lights much like strobe lights. The lights were so intense that Jafari could not make out a structure.

He got a radar lock on at a range of twenty-five miles and said the size appeared to be that of a 707 tanker. The pilot reported he was having trouble following the object because it was jumping around from one place to another. This was clearly well beyond the capabilities of any known aircraft.

Jafari was now flying at Mach 2 (close to fifteen hundred miles per hour) and still couldn't gain on the object. Since it was clear he couldn't catch it, he was ordered to return to base. When he turned the jet and started to return to base, the object also reversed and started to pursue the jet. In a short period of time it shot past the jet, nearly hitting it, and took up a position in front of the jet. As he approached, a smaller object seemed to break away from the main object and flew toward the jet. As it approached, Jafari lost radio communication and his weapons were jammed. The object seemed to make a straight line approach to Jafari, who thought a missile had been launched. He tried to launch a heat-seeking missile at the target but his missile system went out. He quickly turned his jet and descended quickly to return to base. As he did so, one of the objects followed him and appeared to be right on top of the jet.

As Jafari and the jet screamed past the airport, the tower operators could see a dark rectangular object almost sitting on top of the jet. When the jet made a diving turn the small object broke off the chase and rejoined the larger object. As the pilot and radar operator watched the object, another object came out of it and shot straight down toward the ground where the two men expected to see it crash, but instead it landed in the desert, lighting up the sandy area like daylight.

Upon returning to base, Jafari was debriefed and noted that a U.S. Air Force lieutenant colonel, Olin Moody, was present who took notes. Jafari was unable to find Moody after the debriefing.[12]

The next day the crew flew by helicopter to the spot in a dry lakebed, where the object landed the night before. Nothing unusual was found, but there was a nearby house, and the occupants were asked if they had seen anything unusual the preceding night. The couple replied that they heard a loud noise and a flash like lightning, but there were no storms in the area.

Lieutenant Colonel Moody had indeed taken shorthand notes of the debriefing and sent a Teletype message to the Defense Intelligence Agency, all of the military chiefs, the CIA, the NSA, the White House, and the deputy undersecretary of defense. This was a major UFO encounter that we know reached the highest levels within the Ford White House.

In looking at the Ford administration, we must also take into account that once becoming vice president and then president, Jerry Ford, a man who had seven years prior been a moving force in Congress to investigate what the government knew about UFOs, became a clam on UFO issues. Is there a pattern here with Ford, then Carter, and Clinton? The answer is probably both yes and no, and in all cases pure speculation. With Ford, after becoming vice president he was probably briefed on the basic background of the government's involvement in UFO research. As such Ford accepted the government's need to conceal knowledge of an extraterrestrial presence. With Carter and later Clinton, they were most likely considered risks by the keepers of the secret and kept out of the loop of UFO government intelligence. That is not to say that they weren't briefed to some extent, but were simply asked in a respectful but firm way to stay away from pursuing the issue.

7

PRESIDENTIAL SIGHTING AND NASA

THE CARTER ADMINISTRATION

President Jimmy Carter is unique in the history of modern presidents concerning the UFO issue. He campaigned that if elected president he would disclose to the citizens what the government knew about the UFO phenomenon. President Carter had seen a UFO while attending a Lions Club meeting in Leary, Georgia, before becoming governor. He witnessed the event with a number of other club members and filed a UFO-sighting report. Although the sighting made an impression on him, he did not file the report for almost five years, which happened when he was governor of Georgia.

A side note to his report is that he stated the sighting took place in October 1969. However, in checking the records of Lions Clubs International his Leary, Georgia, visit took place on January 6, 1969. Also, according to Lions Clubs' records, Carter's term as a Lions district governor ended in June 1969. This is important as we will see shortly.

District governors serve one-year terms, and during their terms are required to visit all clubs in their district and give a talk. While waiting for the dinner meeting to start, he was outside of a small restaurant in Leary with a group of ten or so men. The time was around 7:15 P.M. and one of the men noticed a strange light in the western sky and brought it to the attention of the others, including Carter. In a 2005 interview, Carter recounted:

And all of a sudden one of the men said, "Look over to the west!" And there was a bright light in the sky. We all saw it. And then the light got closer to us. And then it stopped, I don't know how far away, but it stopped beyond the pine trees. And all of a sudden it changed color to blue, and then it changed to red, and then back to white. We were all trying to figure out what in the world it could be, and then it receded into the distance. (Hylton 2005, 116)

To this day Carter still refers to his sighting as a UFO but he doesn't believe it was extraterrestrial because *he knows that the laws of physics don't allow for such things.* Many have since written that what the men saw that night was the planet Venus, but Carter insists that as an amateur astronomer, he was well aware of what the planet looked like in all its phases, and it definitely was not Venus. A further study reveals that the date confusion rules out Venus in the correct time period of January 6, 1969. Venus was in the southwestern sky on that date. Also, Carter stated that the object was the size of the moon and Venus is never the size of the moon. It appeared for only about ten minutes before departing and Venus would have remained visible for another two hours. Once again we have the grossly overused Venus explanation for what was most likely a legitimate UFO sighting.

Once in office Carter did not reveal any UFO information and was quiet on the subject. Many stories over the years say that he tried to obtain UFO information but was rebuffed as president-elect by then CIA director George H. W. Bush during an alleged briefing on November 19, 1976.

However, there is a long and convoluted story concerning Carter's attempts to get UFO information. Since the story is so complex and, I believe, quite questionable, I'll only present a very abridged version. There are probably some factual elements so it needs to be mentioned as part of the Carter administration.

As the story goes, Bush told the president-elect he didn't have the need to know but if he wanted information he should ask the Congressional Research Service (CRS) to prepare a briefing for the new administration.[1] After becoming president, he is said to have taken this advice and had his staff contact the CRS. An analyst in the Science and Technology Policy division of the CRS, Marcia Smith, was given the task to develop a report for the president on UFOs and extraterrestrials.

At some point Smith made the acquaintance of Daniel Sheehan, a graduate of the Harvard Law School and who was the 1977 general-counsel to the United States Jesuit National Headquarters. Sometime after this meeting Smith had Sheehan appointed as a special consultant to the CRS. It is said in some versions of the story that Sheehan, to prepare for a presentation to the Jet Propulsion Laboratory (JPL) in California, tried to get UFO files from the Vatican but was denied access. He asked to see the secret Project Blue Book files, which he was told were now in the possession of the Library of Congress and stored in a basement vault. He was granted access and went through a number of security checks, including having his briefcase taken from him before entering the vault. For some reason the guards didn't see a legal pad he was carrying under his arm. There is no explanation why the legal pad wasn't in the briefcase, but in any case he claims to have slipped it into the vault or research room. (Having done research in presidential library archives I can say that this would be very difficult.)

Once in the room, he discovered many boxes of microfilm. In looking through the microfilm, he came across photos of a disc-shaped craft that seemed to have plowed into the side of a hill and was tilted up at an angle. There was snow on the ground and men in uniform who he assumed were Air Force taking measurements of the craft.[2] Sheehan states that he sketched or traced, using the microfilm projector, some of the images on the cardboard backing of his legal pad and left the viewing room.

Sheehan reported all the information he discovered back to Smith and his boss at the Jesuit National Headquarters. Smith is said to have developed two reports from the information given her by Sheehan, one that said there were at least two to six very advanced civilizations within our own galaxy. The second report stated the Air Force felt it certain that a significant number of UFOs were craft from these civilizations visiting Earth. The reports are said to have been put together and sent to Carter.

That is a very abridged version of the story, a story that has many variables depending on what version you read. There is no question that Daniel Sheehan has a distinguished academic background as a social activist and Marcia Smith held the government position outlined in the background story. With that said their involvement in the Carter UFO issue brings forth a number of questions. The first of these questions concerns the rumor of DCI Bush's refusal to give president-elect, or after he was in office, President Carter, classified UFO data. I have a problem with this for a couple of reasons.

Many in UFOlogy have opined that DCI George H. W. Bush was on the inside of UFO information, even a member of MJ-12. I have found nothing to substantiate this belief, although Bush's record as a public servant over many years spans a number of high-level government positions and dedicated government service. Bush only served one year as director of the CIA but was a strong supporter of the CIA and the intelligence community in general. The new CIA headquarters is named the George Bush Center for Intelligence. However, as the DCI he was really a short-timer compared to other directors of the Central Intelligence Agency.

I spent two days at the Bush Library in College Station, Texas, and with the help of an archivist, could not find a hint that President Bush was on the inside of UFO-related issues. Of course this could be because President Bush was so attuned to security that any documents of his possible involvement would be carefully concealed. It is possible, even probable, that after Bush became vice president and then president his background and knowledge of UFO issues increased substantially, and will be discussed in chapter 9.

I have trouble with the Bush briefing story for one simple reason: It's illogical. Director Bush could have simply brushed off the request in any number of ways. He knew Carter's feelings toward the CIA, and Carter's feelings toward him. He knew Carter was going to replace him as DCI, and in fact Bush was replaced by Adm. Stansfield Turner in March 1977, who served until January 20, 1981, when he was replaced by William Casey after Ronald Reagan became president.

There is no question that Bush briefed Carter as president-elect and as the new president on any number of subjects. But it is illogical to believe that he incited the ire of the incoming president by telling him that as president he didn't have the need to know on UFO issues. If Bush did in fact want to retain his position as DCI, which I doubt, this slap in the face was a sure kiss of death to retain that position. If he knew he was on the way out, as I believe, why incite the new president and make it more likely he would order his new DCI to dig into the subject if he in fact was an insider to UFO data as many believe, and he was committed to total security? None of this really adds up when the simple out would have been to lie to Carter. There is another possibility, and that is that Bush was not on the inside of UFO knowledge, didn't like Carter and knew that Carter didn't like him, and this was his chance to give Carter the verbal middle finger.

One other thing to consider in the Bush-Carter briefing matter: DCIs are administrators appointed at the will of the president. If presidents are to be briefed, most certainly the DCI will be present, but the briefing will be carried out by the experts in the agency in a particular field, not the DCI.

My second issue with this story is that of Sheehan's request to see classified Project Blue Book files. I do not dispute Sheehan's story as he related it to the Disclosure Project news conference at the National Press Club in 2001. My concern is that according to the National Archives all Project Blue Book files have been declassified. In 1970, Blue Book files were transferred to Maxwell AFB (Air University) where they were available for public viewing until 1975, when they were microfilmed by the Air Force for internal use and transferred to the National Archives. Now, according to the National Archives Web site, all Blue Book records have been declassified and are available for public viewing on ninety-four rolls of 35 mm microfilm. It seems most likely that this is what Sheehan viewed and it's almost certain that a number of UFOlogists have also viewed these files.

I don't know what Mr. Sheehan saw on the microfilm but it sounds very similar to film reported to be Russian footage of a UFO crash in Siberia and very likely a hoax. It can be found on YouTube by searching "Russian Siberia UFO crash." Also, in his address before the press conference Sheehan never mentioned that a report was written by Marcia Smith and sent to President Carter, which of course is the core of the story.

Third, anyone remotely involved in UFO research knows that Project Blue Book, except during the Ruppelt years, was simply a public relations and disinformation program, as has been covered earlier in this book. Serious UFO reports were then, and still are, covered in accordance with JANAP 146 or Air Force Manual 55-11. UFO incidents of a truly serious nature or having national defense significance were never sent to Blue Book but handled elsewhere in the Air Force and intelligence community.

Finally, one would have to wonder why the new president wouldn't rely on his handpicked friend, Adm. Stansfield Turner—the newly appointed DCI—to spearhead Carter's desire to secure the government's knowledge of the UFO phenomenon. It seems the logical thing to do instead of having people he didn't know and probably didn't trust gather this information for him. Again, we have a logic issue with this story.

Where logic does come into play is that once in office Carter, who had campaigned to open up government records on UFOs, became silent. From this there is only one logical conclusion: Carter was briefed to some extent on the government's background and knowledge of an extraterrestrial presence and was impressed with the possible dire consequences if this knowledge was released to the public. However, Carter was still no favorite with the intelligence community, especially military intelligence. Prior to the 1980 election Carter had stated in a news conference that the U.S. had developed "an invisible plane" which at the time was the highly classified stealth program. Many publications, including *The Washington Post*, took Carter to task for divulging a highly classified government secret for political gain.

THE CASH-LANDRUM INCIDENT

Around 9:00 P.M. on December 29, 1980, Betty Cash, Vickie Landrum, and Landrum's seven-year-old grandson, Colby, were driving on a deserted two-lane road in the Piney Woods area of Texas. They were returning to their home in Dayton, Texas, just northeast of Houston, after having dinner out of town. Although within forty miles or so from Houston, this is still a very lonely and desolate area not far from the Sam Houston National Forrest. The road they took was Farm to Market Road 1485 that was lightly traveled, especially at night.

In this densely wooded area they noticed a light ahead just above the treetops. Their first thought was a plane on approach to Houston International Airport, but as they rounded a bend they saw a strange diamond-shaped object hovering over the road. The object was huge and described as about the same size as the town's water tower. The diamond-shaped object was flat on top and bottom and orange flame was being emitted from the bottom of the object in rapid bursts. Cash stopped the car in the roadway, and although it was a cool evening and they had been running the heater, the car became extremely hot. Both Cash and Landrum got out of the car but Colby became very agitated and hid under the dashboard. The object appeared very bright with blue lights ringing the center and they seemed to be a dull silver metallic color. As flame erupted from the craft, it would rise and when the flame subsided, it would float down toward the roadway.

Landrum returned to the car to comfort her grandson but Cash stayed outside the car, apparently mesmerized by what she was seeing. When she finally returned to the car the door handle was so hot it burned her hand. Once in the car they saw the craft move upward and at the same time a group of helicopters arrived (twenty-four by Cash and Landrum's count), both small single-rotor birds and large twin-rotor CH-47 Chinooks, and surrounded the object. The craft seemed to pull itself together and moved off surrounded by the helicopters, and a shaken Cash and Landrum drove on to Dayton.

The event lasted about twenty minutes and the craft and choppers were reported by others in the area, including an off-duty police officer and his wife. Later that evening Cash and Landrum started to have health issues, with Cash's the most serious. She was hospitalized a few days later and diagnosed with what appeared to be radiation poisoning. Cash's daughter stated that her mother was placed in a room with a radiation warning symbol on the door. Cash died at seventy-one, exactly eighteen years after the encounter, and Landrum died in 2007 at eighty-four. Colby is still alive with no apparent health issues. Cash and Landrum suffered from illnesses for the rest of their lives after the encounter.

The military was contacted but denied knowledge of any such event, or of having helicopters in the air in that area. Eventually a lawsuit was filed against the government for their health issues but was thrown out of court for lack of evidence.

I have read numerous accounts of this case and feel certain that this was not an extraterrestrial encounter but a test gone wrong of some classified military craft with experimental nuclear power. My logic in making that statement is as follows: Experimental aircraft always have chase aircraft in the air monitoring the craft, in this case the helicopters. The number of helicopters seems to indicate something beyond the norm, especially the Chinooks, which are troop carriers. Perhaps the craft was in distress and the military was positioning itself to secure an emergency-landing area. Reports are that the helicopters had no markings, and since it is widely believed that there exists within the military a very secret quick-response team for just such events, both terrestrial and extraterrestrial, this fits.[3] Finally, an extraterrestrial craft would not be chased by helicopters but rather by jet aircraft. Since none were seen, this is another indicator that this was a military project. There have been unconfirmed reports that this could have been an experimental nuclear-powered troop carrier called a WASP II, but I can find no official or unofficial information that such a craft existed.

This event occurred in the closing days of the Carter administration and it is most probable that Carter was not informed. This, I believe, is but another example of the military's sophisticated development of their ability to quickly take charge of highly classified incidents after the bungling of the Roswell incident.

VICTOR MARCHETTI

Victor Marchetti is a former CIA official who is not considered a UFOlogist but who has spoken out on the UFO cover-up in books and articles. His books and comments tie not only into the Cash-Landrum incident but his whistle-blowing efforts go back as far as the Nixon administration.

Marchetti first became involved in intelligence work in the military in 1952. He joined the CIA in 1955 and became an expert on Soviet Third World aid, especially to Cuba. In 1966, Marchetti was promoted to special assistant to CIA director Richard Helms. By 1969 he had become disillusioned with the CIA and resigned. That started a series of books critical of the CIA. His book *The CIA and the Cult of Intelligence* is important because it is the first book the federal government ever went to court to censor before publication. The CIA demanded that 366 passages be cut from the book, but Marchetti fought back and the censored passages were reduced to 168. The UFO issue plays a small role in his efforts, but his thoughts are important because of the legitimacy he was given by the legal actions of the government and the CIA against his work. Below is an excerpt from a magazine article published in 1979:

> *We have, indeed, been contacted—perhaps even visited— by extraterrestrial beings, and the U.S. government, in collusion with the other national powers of the earth [sic],*

is determined to keep this information from the general public.

The purpose of the international conspiracy is to maintain a workable stability among the nations of the world and for them, in turn, to retain institutional control over their respective populations. Thus, for these governments to admit that there are beings from outer space . . . with mentalities and technological capabilities obviously far superior to ours, could, once fully perceived by the average person, erode the foundations of the earth's [sic] traditional power structure. Political and legal systems, religions, economic and social institutions could all soon become meaningless in the mind of the public. The national oligarchical establishments, even civilization as we now know it, could collapse into anarchy.

Such extreme conclusions are not necessarily valid, but they probably accurately reflect the fears of the "ruling classes" of the major nations, whose leaders (particularly those in the intelligence business) have always advocated excessive governmental secrecy as being necessary to preserve "national security." (Marchetti 1979)

Although Marchetti's writings cover a wide range of CIA issues, including the JFK assassination, and are not focused on the UFO issue, he does give UFOlogists a rare look inside the agency. His comments are in accord with the Brookings Institute findings from the 1950s that warned of contact with a vastly superior extraterrestrial race or races and possible devastating consequences of such contact.

Marchetti admits he has no firsthand knowledge of a cover-up but says the debunking efforts have a pure CIA flavor in their operation, and because of the very sensitive nature of the issue it was never openly discussed within the agency. He did say that he knew firsthand that the CIA had UFO collection facilities located around the world, something he found extremely intriguing.[4] Also, he heard rumors from high places that the CIA possessed extraterrestrial artifacts. Of course rumors come in all shapes and sizes. However, with the legitimacy afforded Marchetti by government legal action the odds of his reported rumors being true are very high indeed.

8

JAL FLIGHT 1628—THE HUDSON VALLEY SIGHTINGS

THE REAGAN ADMINISTRATION

Ronald Wilson Reagan took office on January 20, 1981, by a landslide victory over one-term president Jimmy Carter. The charismatic, conservative Reagan would serve eight years and become one of the most popular presidents in American history. Reagan would also be known by UFOlogists and those on the inside of UFO research as the most open proponent of the existence of UFOs and an extraterrestrial presence as any president in history. It seems clear that Reagan was at the very least enamored by the UFO phenomenon, as has been reported by a number of friends and family members. This was due in part to two sightings the former president had before becoming president.

The most important of these sightings occurred in 1974 while governor of California. Reagan and two of his security personnel were aboard a Cessna Citation on a flight to Bakersfield, California. Reagan's attention was called to a bright light that appeared to be following the plane. He went to the cockpit and pointed it out to the pilot, Bill Paynter, who was somewhat unnerved by what he saw. Paynter said it appeared to be several hundred yards away and a fairly steady light. It then appeared to become elongated and shot up at a forty-five-degree angle at a high rate of speed. Paynter said he knew of nothing that could accelerate with such a burst of speed.

The governor had asked the pilot to follow the strange light, which he did until it shot up and out of sight. Reagan is said to have discussed this sighting with the Washington bureau chief for *The Wall Street Journal*, Norman C. Miller, but never publically spoke of it again.[1] Some years later Paynter was asked if he thought Reagan believed in UFOs and he replied, "How could he not believe after what we saw that night in the plane."

The Internet is full of Reagan UFO stories as an actor, governor, president-elect, and after becoming president. Most are fabrications or perhaps snippets of truth in fabricated stories. One of the more bizarre stories is told by actress Shirley MacLaine. MacLaine claims that actress Lucille Ball told her that Reagan had confided in Ball some years before and told her that on the way to a party in Los Angeles with wife, Nancy, they encountered a UFO on the ground blocking their car. An alien exited the craft and addressed Reagan telepathically with one message, "Leave acting and go into politics." This of course would have most people laughing at such a seemingly foolish story, except that Ball in her biography, as did entertainer Steve Allen, confirmed that when the Reagans appeared at the party late, they appeared shaken and Reagan said they had seen a UFO. However, there was no mention of a close encounter with an alien. That came later when Ball disclosed her private conversation with Reagan to MacLaine.

Another dubious story but nevertheless of interest is the transcript of a supposed recording made in March 1981 of a briefing by CIA director William Casey to President Reagan at Camp David. Along with Casey, the president was allegedly briefed by a CIA black projects insider known as the Caretaker on the UFO issue.

The Caretaker is said to have been in charge of all UFO issues since 1960 for the CIA.

The Caretaker briefed the president on the crash of two ET spacecraft in the Roswell area of New Mexico in 1947: Several dead aliens (or EBEs—extraterrestrial biological entities) were recovered, all dead except one with only minor injuries. All were taken to Roswell Army Air Base, the wreckage sent to Wright-Patterson AFB, and the living EBE was sent to Sandia Labs, where special housing was set up for him. He lived there until his death in 1952 and supplied the government with a great amount of technical information.

The Caretaker went on to discuss four other races of extraterrestrials that visit Earth, one of which is considered hostile and behind the alien abductions. There were a number of other issues discussed, one of which was said to be so highly classified that they were not prepared to go into it with the president at that time.

The reason that this very skeptical story is of some interest and is mentioned here is that the Caretaker is said to have briefed both presidents Nixon and Ford but not Carter; Carter was "out of the loop." Considering how involved Congressman Ford was in the UFO issue because of the Michigan incident, and then he never again publically discussed UFOs after becoming president, seems to make this a remote but possible fit. Also, the briefing, when read in total, does have a Reagan tone to it. However, one must ask, where is the recording that the transcript was made from? Who transcribed it? Who released it? Perhaps there are bits of fact mixed in with a fabricated story, especially the MacLaine-Ball story, but there are simply too many unanswered questions for this story to reside anywhere but in the dubious file.

There is one very reliable story that occurred during the Reagan administration that deserves serious study and does involve members of the President's Science Office.

JAPAN AIR LINES FLIGHT 1628

Just after 5:00 P.M. on November 17, 1986, Japan Air Lines Flight 1628, a cargo flight of wine from France to Japan, had just crossed the Canadian–Alaska border and was heading for a refueling stop in Anchorage. The plane, a Boeing 747, had a crew of three, the pilot, copilot, and flight engineer. The plane was flying at thirty-five thousand feet in the dark with just the glow of the setting sun on the horizon to the west.

Capt. Kenju Terauchi first noticed some lights of what he thought was another plane to his left and below his plane. He assumed they were the lights of patrol aircraft that constantly patrolled this area close to the Russian border. However, when making a navigation adjustment as ordered by Anchorage flight control, the captain noticed the light stayed with him and seemed to be tracking his craft.

Now he saw what appeared to be three lights, one large and two small lights that seemed to "jump around" the large light in a manner unlike any normal aircraft. Suddenly the two small lights shot instantly right in front of the 747's cockpit. Terauchi said the cockpit filled with brilliant light and he felt warmth on his face. As the lights around the two craft (Terauchi referred to them later in his interviews as "spaceships") dimmed, he could see the craft were somewhat square and each about the size of a DC-8 jet. He said the objects flew about 150 to 300 meters in front and slightly above his craft. He tried to photograph the objects but his camera was on autofocus and would not focus on the objects. Radio transmission was out during the time the two objects flew in front of the plane so they could not report to Anchorage.

Finally the objects moved away from the plane and radio contact was made with Anchorage. From that point on there was a running of radio communication between 1628 and Anchorage, who then brought in Elmendorf AFB air-traffic control. At first ground radar only saw the 747 but then started to pick up intermittent returns in an area about eight miles off the 747's port side. The smaller objects had apparently merged with the larger object and lighting conditions allowed Terauchi to see a huge walnut-shaped object the size of two aircraft carriers. The drawing he made of the object after landing is remarkable.

The crew now became quite unnerved seeing a strange flying object that dwarfed the 747 in size. Terauchi felt they had to get away from it and requested permission to do a 360-degree turn. With permission granted they began the turn but the object continued to track the plane. A number of controllers and supervisors had gathered in the Anchorage ARTCC, listening and observing the unfolding events when Elmendorf advised they had solid contact with an uncorrelated target.

Shortly thereafter, the crew advised that they had lost visual sighting of the objects. A few moments later Elmendorf advised that they had picked up an object now in trail (behind) the 747. Within a few moments the UFO(s) disappeared and within twenty-five minutes Flight 1628 landed in Anchorage where the crew was met by FAA, U.S. government, and JAL officials. The fun began when Kyoda News in Japan got the story and released it on December 29, 1986, and UPI reporter Jeff Berliner broke the story in the U.S. on the same day.

The story got legs and pressure began to build on the FAA, whose position had always been that they don't investigate UFO incidents involving commercial or civilian aircraft (an odd position from an agency who investigates even the most minor of incidents involving civilian or commercial aircraft).[2] With the pressure mounting the FAA tried to dismiss the story by just staying away from it, but the debunkers jumped in saying the pilots were seeing planets, making the pilots look like idiots and enraging an interested public who wanted a logical explanation. The story began to grow and the FAA was forced into action. John Callahan, the

FAA's manager of the Accidents, Evaluation, and Investigation division in Washington, was brought into the issue. In January 1987, he received a package of data from Alaska containing all the reports, transcripts, and radar data from the 1628 event. He reviewed the data and then reported his findings to his boss, Harvey Safeer, and then the next day in FAA headquarters in Washington to administrator Adm. Donald Engen, and representatives from the White House science office and the CIA.

The audiotapes of the ground-to-air discussions and the radar tapes were played and replayed several times. Callahan said the White House and CIA people were very excited so he asked what they thought the object was and one of the CIA people said, "It's a UFO and this is the longest recorded tracking of a UFO that we have." The CIA said they were taking all the data and admonished them that the meeting they had all attended and the event itself had never happened.

Callahan did not tell them that he had made copies of the records and recordings and they were back in his Atlantic City office, assuming they would know that he did have copies. He put them on his office credenza, expecting someone from the CIA to pick them up. That never happened, and they sat on the credenza until he retired several years later, when they were packed up with all his office belongings and sent to his home. They resided in a box in his garage until in 2001 when he agreed to tell his story at a National Press Club event organized by Steven Greer. All of this material is now in the public domain.[3]

It is a known fact that President Reagan's aides worked hard to keep the lid on the president's interest in the UFO issue. He made a number of references to UFOs and extraterrestrial life in various speeches and talks, which caused his aides no small amount of grief. Since this story made news around the world it's hard to believe that President Reagan wasn't aware of it since people from his own science office were present at the FAA briefing. Most likely he was briefed on the story or demanded to be briefed on it. If we reflect back on Bob Emenegger's story in chapter 6 about being contacted by Reagan appointees with an interest in an updated version of Emenegger's documentary, *UFOs: Past, Present, and Future*, it certainly is not a big jump to think that Reagan may have been behind the effort and it was aborted by his aides.

There is another fascinating glimpse into the Reagan White House. A longtime time UFO investigator, Colman S. von Keviczky, a former major in the Hungarian army and founder and director of the Intercontinental UFO Galactic Spacecraft Research and Analytic Network, was invited to a special White House briefing apparently on the Strategic Defense Initiative (SDI). It's not clear exactly why a UFO investigator was invited to such a meeting, but it is known that von Keviczky held some definite and controversial opinions on SDI.

The name of his organization sounds more like a caricature of a UFO investigative group than a real project. However, although he was not well known in the U.S., he and his group were familiar in European and Asian countries, most notably Japan.

Von Keviczky held the belief, and was very vocal in his belief, that SDI was really a double-edged sword designed as a defense system against an alien invasion and ICBMs. This is a view that was shared by some others in the UFO community.

Von Keviczky was a bit of a thorn in the side of George Keyworth, science and technical adviser to President Reagan. Keyworth was recommended to Reagan by Dr. Edward Teller, sometimes called "the Father of the H Bomb," and was a prime mover for pushing the SDI concept in the Reagan administration. Keyworth then was also a major proponent of SDI within the White House. Of course Reagan's many public comments about a threat from another world fueled the speculation by some that SDI was really intended to repel an alien invasion.

The White House briefing with Keyworth and von Keviczky became confrontational with von Keviczky standing and stating in loud voice that SDI should be called UDI, or UFO Defense Initiative, not SDI. After the briefing, von Keviczky went to Keyworth's office and presented him with a document called "Heed Memorandum for Actions to the 99th Congress," concerning SDI and the UFO problem. Two months later he followed up with a letter to Keyworth requesting that the document be sent to President Reagan.

All of this is fascinating, but SDI as envisioned by Reagan was probably impractical with existing technology. Certainly research was undertaken and advancements were made, but SDI in its original form changed its focus under subsequent administrations.

The views of von Keviczky are interesting and perhaps a little amusing but his view simply does not stand up to logical thinking. SDI was an extremely complicated scientific project to protect the U.S. from missile attack, or that's its stated purpose. It is illogical for two primary reasons: Many scientists felt the technology was still well beyond our capabilities to produce a workable system as proposed to protect against a large-scale ICBM attack, much less to defend against the abilities of an invading force of extraterrestrials thousands, if not millions, of years more advanced than the inhabitants of this planet. Second, few findings by respected UFOlogists have indicated any real hostile intention of alien visitation.[4]

Certainly over the years there have been stories of aircraft being lost while attempting to intercept UFOs with orders to force them down or shoot them down if necessary. Planes and pilots were lost in the early years because of this order. It can be debated if the loss of pilots was due to actions taken by the UFOs or pilot error because of the great pressure of a frightening situation. In any case, the futility and idiocy of the order was soon rescinded. We also have cases of the pursuit aircraft having its arms becoming inoperative as the pilot tried to fire or the UFO simply taking off at incredible speeds before being fired upon. This seems to indicate benign intentions of whomever or whatever is operating these objects.

THE HUDSON VALLEY SIGHTINGS

The Hudson Valley sightings are similar in many ways to the Belgium Wave of sightings discussed in the next chapter. The sightings began on December 31, 1981, and continued until 1986. During that four-plus-year span, over five thousand reports of the same triangular objects were filed.

The first known sighting took place on New Year's Eve 1981 when a retired police officer was in his backyard in Kent, New York, just before midnight when he noticed a group of red, green, and white lights. His first impression was that he was seeing an airplane that was having some difficulty, as it was too slow and too low. As the craft approached him he quickly realized it was no plane. It was a V shape of lights connected by a huge solid body. There was no sound until the object was very close and then he heard a humming sound.

This was the beginning of four years of sightings that were remarkably similar. On the night of March 24, 1983, residents of the city of Yorktown flooded police switchboards with reports of huge flying objects. People pulled over on the Taconic Parkway to watch a huge object float across the sky. Of particular interest is the report of an object of similar appearance by guards at the Indian Point nuclear power facility. At one point it is reported that it moved as close as thirty feet from the reactor, causing the security supervisor to consider calling in the Air Force. Guards at the plant estimated the object to be about a thousand feet long. Once again we have UFOs interested in nuclear facilities. Another witness saw the same object over the Croton Falls Reservoir appearing to scan the surface of the water with a red laserlike beam. The account of this witness takes on even more importance when the Belgium Wave is discussed in the next chapter.

Dr. J. Allen Hynek did a thorough investigation of the Hudson Valley events and wrote a book on his findings, *Night Siege: The Hudson Valley UFO Sightings*. But Dr. Hynek was virtually alone in his study of the events. Government officials from local to the federal level all but ignored the events. No matter that the sightings took place within close proximity to some of the country's busiest airports; on the surface at least, no interest was shown by even the FAA which is charged with airline safety.

The fact that the FAA keeps UFOs at arm's length is legendary with UFOlogists. A classic example is the UFO O'Hare Airport incident. In that case, to be covered in detail in chapter 11, a circular disc hovered over the United Airlines gate at O'Hare for some fifteen minutes before shooting straight up at incredible speed, cutting a hole in the heavy overcast sky allowing those on the ground to look into the hole and see blue sky. The FAA wanted to deny the event occurred until tapes of conversations between airport personnel were made public.

In this case we have a craft without a transponder hovering over one of the busiest airports in the world, seen by hundreds of people including pilots and maintenance personnel, and the FAA wanted to bury it. The case was investigated by Dr. Richard Haines's National Aviation Reporting Center on Anomalous Phenomena (NARCAP) which resulted in a 154-page report.[5] One investigator stated, "The FAA treats the smallest safety issue as very important. It will investigate a coffee pot getting loose in the galley and falling as the plane is landing" (Kean 2011, 69). Yet the FAA wanted to bury its head about an unknown object in the restricted airspace over one of the world's busiest airports.

This is yet another example that fuels the conspiracy theorists' belief that somewhere deep within the government, out of reach of even the president of the United States, there exists a powerful group that has an iron grip on the disclosure of UFO events.

9

THE BELGIAN WAVE AND STS-48

THE GEORGE H. W. BUSH ADMINISTRATION

The history of UFOs and George H. W. Bush as we know it goes back to his alleged refusal to brief President-elect or President Jimmy Carter on UFOs as discussed in chapter 7. That part of his UFO involvement was covered in that chapter so we will move ahead to his years as vice president and then president in 1989. All told Bush served twelve years in positions where he would have possible access to inside UFO information. As touched on in chapter 7, many UFOlogists feel his time as DCI put him on the inside of UFO intelligence, but as I stated earlier I don't necessarily share this belief. Since he was highly regarded and trusted within the agency he may have had greater access to UFO information from those deep within the CIA who were involved with UFO issues even though he was only DCI for one year, and with the complexity of the UFO story that is not time to scratch the surface of the phenomenon.

With that said, his CIA background would put him in a position as vice president in an administration very tuned to the UFO issue to have greater access to UFO intelligence than any other vice president with the possible exception of Richard Nixon. It is not unreasonable to think that he would have been party to UFO briefings by Reagan's DCI, William Casey, and the experts the DCI brought in to brief the president and vice president. As Reagan's vice president and a former DCI this is a logical assumption.

Following Reagan as president, Bush then could be the best informed president of UFO issues since Truman and Eisenhower. Of course Truman and Eisenhower's knowledge of the issue was in the infancy of the UFO phenomenon, so Bush's knowledge would have far greater depth because of the accumulation of many more years of intelligence. This may sound as if I'm contradicting my position in chapter 7, but that's not the case. I simply find problems with the Bush-Carter briefing story at that point in history because with one year as DCI he simply didn't have the background to be well-versed with the UFO phenomenon. However, as a trusted member of the intelligence community, a vice president for eight years in an administration that was very tuned in to UFO issues, and then as president with his background in intelligence, he was (and is) conceivably one of the most knowledgeable men alive as to what the government really knows about UFOs.

During the Bush 41 administration two major UFO events occurred that the president most certainly would have been briefed on. The first was the remarkable Belgium Wave of sightings, and the other occurred in space, the Space Shuttle STS-48 event.

THE BELGIAN UFO WAVE

The Belgian Wave, as it has become known, is of great importance in UFOlogy because of the length of time it covered (from November 1989 and going well into 1991), the thousands of witnesses to numerous sightings, the Belgian air force F-16 attempts to intercept, radar confirmation, and the openness of the Belgian government and air force in dealing with and asking for support from the population.

The events started in November 1989. On November 29, thirty or more groups of people, including many police officers, scattered across Belgium witnessed a large, triangular, flat object move soundlessly across the Belgian countryside. This huge craft, with lights underneath that some described as being like spotlights sweeping the ground, moved silently from town to town as the population tracked the object.

This sighting would become a wave of sightings that occurred well into 1991. One of the stranger aspects of the sightings was the inability to clearly photograph the objects. Because of the duration and number of the sightings, many people kept cameras close at hand and took a number of photographs of the strange craft. Many photographers claimed the objects were clearly viewed and expected clear sharp photographs. However, when developed the images were blurred and seemingly out of focus. There seemed to be no reason for this anomaly until Auguste Meessen, professor of physics at Catholic University in Louvin, made a study of the pictures and theorized that infrared light could be the cause for the exposure problems. He tested his theory by exposing film to infrared light and then photographing objects. The results were the same as photographs taken of the UFOs.

There was one fair photograph of the craft taken by a man known only as Patrick, which shows a triangular craft with lights on each corner. The photo was studied worldwide and declared authentic by a number of experts. In 2011, Patrick came forward to admit he faked the photograph. Some believe the man was pressured or otherwise bought off to claim responsibility for the hoax. Overall it's not really of any great importance because in any major UFO event there will always be the possibility of hoaxers who attract the attention of skeptics and debunkers. But if this event was a hoax, one would have to believe that Belgium has a population of thousands of hoaxers, including the military and many police working in concert to perpetuate such an involved, yearlong hoax.

Maj. Gen. Wilfried de Brouwer of the Belgian air force has commented in detail on many events of the Belgian Wave of UFO sightings.[1] At the time of the Belgian Wave General de Brouwer was the head of operations of the Belgian air staff and went on to have a distinguished career retiring as a major general and chief of staff.

On November 29, 1989, there were 143 reported sightings in an area around Eupen, Belgium. One of the more astounding reports came from two policemen who saw an object around 5:15 P.M. while on patrol. The object, hovering above a field, lit the area with such intensity that the patrolmen could read a newspaper in their patrol car. The craft was triangular with what was referred to as three spotlights shining to the ground and with a flashing red light in the center. The craft was totally silent as it moved about at a slow speed. It moved over the town of Eupen, where it remained for thirty minutes and was seen by a number of witnesses. The object then moved to a lake where the two policemen observed it hovering and emitting two red beams of light with a red ball at the end of each. The beams and the red balls returned to the craft, then another cycle started. At 6:45 P.M. the officers saw a second craft appear that made a forward tilting movement, exposing a dome on top and what appeared to be lit rectangular windows. That craft departed about forty minutes after the first. Other craft were reported in different areas around the town. By the time the event was over eighteen police officers reported similar sightings as well as seventy civilians (Kean 2011, 26).

The reports continued to come in over the ensuing weeks and months and the air force had no option but to get involved. It was decided that two F-16s would be kept at the ready and if there were reports from credible ground witnesses and radar contact the jets would be scrambled. This arrangement resulted in a truly remarkable incident.

On March 30, 1990, a police captain called the Belgian military to report a large triangular object passing overhead. After checking, it was confirmed that two ground radars, one at a NATO installation, were picking up an uncorrelated target in the area the police captain indicated. The object was moving slowly. F-16s were scrambled and ordered to intercept and identify the object. One of the jets locked on to the object with its onboard radar and saw the object pick up speed. For an hour the fighters tried to make visual contact as the object made maneuvers impossible for any known craft to make. The objects seemed to be playing a game of cat-and-mouse with the fighters. At one point, one object dropped from ten thousand feet to five hundred feet in less than five seconds. The rapid change in speeds and abrupt maneuvers were far beyond the capability of any known aircraft and would be fatal to any human on board. Finally, after about an hour of the F-16s dogging the mystery craft, they disappeared. A press conference was held and cockpit footage from one of the jets' radars clearly showed the abrupt speed and altitude changes.

General de Brouwer describes another important event in Kean's book that I have included as written.

A few day before, [de Brouwer had described another sighting of an object by an engineer several nights earlier that floated at low altitude over his house, was rectangular in shape, and looked like an upside down aircraft carrier] *on March 12, 1991, a total of twenty-seven reports were filed from a small area southwest of Liege. On two occasions a craft was seen over the nuclear power plant of Thiange. One witness said it was directly above the*

*red lights on top of one of the enormous chimneys.[2] It
hovered there for approximately one minute, beaming its
lights on the outside of the structure while another light
pointed directly into one of the chimneys. After it finished
its "inspection," the UAP started moving slowly and flew
straight through the enormous white plume of the chimney
before disappearing in the dark.* (Kean 2011, 32)

The importance of this incident once again indicates that UFOs
(or UAP as they are called in some areas) have a definite interest in
nuclear programs worldwide regardless of whether they are weapons systems or for peaceful usage. It is also reminiscent of the
Hudson Valley Sightings, in particular the sighting discussed in the
previous chapter that took place at the Indian River nuclear plant.

There are many similarities between the Hudson Valley events
and the Belgian Wave events. There is also one huge difference.
The Belgian Wave was thoroughly investigated by the Belgian government and air force and the citizens were asked to help with information about their sightings. The Hudson Valley Sightings were
all but ignored by U.S. officials including the Air Force, the FAA,
and the intelligence community, as well as local authorities.

STS-48

STS-48 refers to a particular Space Shuttle mission that was
launched on September 12, 1991, carrying the Space Shuttle *Discovery* with a payload designed for upper atmosphere research.
On September 15, video from the shuttle showed a number of objects that appeared to be controlled and an unusual flash of light
that seemed to cause one of the objects to race off at incredible
speed. NASA theorized that the objects were ice particles and the
flash was from the firing of a jet thruster. However, some experts
dispute this explanation for a number of reasons. Since it remains

a controversial subject, a short version of events is included here for the reader's consideration and additional research if so desired.

From the shuttle's onboard camera, with part of the Earth in the background, what appears to be a distant object moves from left to right just inside the edge of the Earth. Two quick flashes are seen and the object hesitates for a split second, then reverses course and races back toward space just as a streak of light passes through the original location of the object. This video has been in constant controversy since it was first released. One academic, Dr. Jack Kasher, professor of physics at the University of Nebraska, worked for ten years in research and development of the so-called Star Wars defense system and has studied the video for the last two years. His findings state that it is definitely not a normal occurrence, such as the shuttle thruster firing and ice crystals being pushed around, but that it is a true spacecraft.

Astronaut Buzz Aldrin takes an opposing view, stating that there is always a lot of debris floating around in space. Ice crystals are common around the shuttle and Aldrin is not impressed with the video. Dr. Edgar Mitchell, the sixth man to walk on the moon, takes a different view from Aldrin. He thinks we should keep an open mind to what we see in space and should continue to study the video.

Another opposing view is Dr. Mark Carlotto, a digital imaging specialist, who reminds that these are actual NASA videos and the integrity is without question. Dr. Carlotto goes on to explain that if a thruster did indeed fire, it would have slightly changed the altitude of the shuttle, but it is obvious there is no change in the shuttle's altitude. It is also determined that at the time of the incident the shuttle was above Australia and Alice Springs where the United States maintains the largest satellite intelligence gathering facility in the world. If we have developed Star Wars operational systems, the Alice Springs facility would be the logical place to implement that technology and equipment. One final bit of intrigue: After this video was released, NASA stopped all live feeds from shuttle cameras.

The STS-48 event is controversial and included here because it brings together opposing views and discussions in the scientific community so sorely needed to advance the understanding of the UFO phenomenon. We must have increasing participation within the scientific community and reasonable scientific discussion, putting aside the stigma that UFOs are voodoo science before any real advances can be made in understanding the real nature of the UFO phenomenon.

10

THE ROCKEFELLER INITIATIVE
THE CLINTON ADMINISTRATION

When William Jefferson Clinton took office as president, we know he had a very deep interest in the UFO phenomenon. We also have reason to believe that he was an incoming president, like Jimmy Carter, who was on the outside of the loop of government knowledge of UFO issues.

In his book, *Friends in High Places,* Assistant Attorney General Webster Hubble states that early in his administration Clinton asked him to look into two things: who killed John F. Kennedy and what the government really knows about UFOs. Hubble's efforts were unsuccessful and, in 1995, President Clinton signed Executive Order 12958 that released over eight hundred million pages of previously classified and historically important information. It is believed that Clinton's chief of staff, John Podesta, played an important role in the promotion of this executive order.

In November 1995, while giving a speech in Belfast, Northern Ireland, Clinton replied to a letter he received from a thirteen-year-old youngster inquiring about the alleged Roswell UFO crash in 1947. Clinton's reply, made with a humorous tilt was, "Now, Ryan, if you are out in the crowd tonight, here's the answer to your question. No, as far as I know, an alien spacecraft did not crash in Roswell, New Mexico, in 1947. And Ryan, if the United States Air Force did recover alien bodies, they didn't tell me about it, either, and I want to know."[1]

Clinton's comments were said in a lighthearted tone but raise some interesting points. If President Clinton did have at least some information on Roswell as an extraterrestrial event, he would not have been lying to young Ryan because when Roswell occurred in July 1947, there was no "United States Air Force," it was still the U.S. Army Air Forces. The United States Air Force did not come into existence until September 18, 1947. That may seem a silly technical point but presidential speeches are carefully prepared and reviewed by a number of staff members and everything in them is carefully considered. The second point is the inclusion of "they didn't tell me about it, either, and I want to know." This is of greater importance since the president is implying that there are government secrets that are kept from presidents.

On September 14, 2005, former President Clinton, in an interview in Hong Kong, talked about Roswell and UFOs. In the question-and-answer session he stated that he thought Roswell "an illusion, I don't think it happened." He admitted that he attempted to find if there were any secret government, documents that revealed things, and if there were such documents they were concealed from him. He went on to say that he wouldn't be the first president who underlings had lied to, or who bureaucrats had waited out. He also acknowledged that there may be career persons hiding these secrets from presidents; if so they eluded him.

President Clinton, in his candor, admitted the very real possibility or even probability that there are people within our government who have control of very dark secrets, secrets that presidents are not in the loop of need to know. This has been suspected and supports one basic thesis of this book that discusses a paradigm shift with control of extraterrestrial secrets from presidents to a select small group of government bureaucrats and certain leaders within the military-industrial complex.

President Clinton and his wife, former secretary of state Hillary Clinton, have been associated with the well-known Rockefeller Initiative, the attempt by the late Laurance Rockefeller to have the government, or in particular the Clinton administration, to disclose closely held UFO secrets. Although called the Rockefeller Initiative, much of the funding came from former real estate developer and billionaire Robert Bigelow, now of Bigelow Aerospace, in Las Vegas, Nevada. Although there is much information in the Clinton Library in the form of documents and letters between Rockefeller and his staff and the Clinton White House, there is little of substance to substantiate either of the Clintons' support of the Rockefeller Initiative. It is a fact that Hillary Clinton did meet with Rockefeller at his JY Ranch near Jackson Hole, and Rockefeller hosted President Clinton at the ranch while Clinton was vacationing at Jackson Hole. It's also reasonable to think that Rockefeller bent Clinton's ear on disclosing UFO information and giving amnesty to both military and civilian personnel involved in UFO-related issues and who remain covered by a confidentiality agreement.

There are numbers of letters from Rockefeller and his lawyer, Henry Diamond, to Dr. John Gibbons, Clinton's science and technology adviser, and a number of other people in Rockefeller's disclosure initiative. Rockefeller brought into the initiative a number of people involved in UFO research who were passionate about UFO issues, and Rockefeller (or Bigelow) funded research by many well-known and respected UFOlogists, including Dr. John Mack of Harvard. However, after reviewing many of these documents, I have formed the opinion that Bill Clinton's relationship with Laurance Rockefeller was a patronizing relationship with a very wealthy elderly man from a very powerful and influential family. Clinton had absolutely no intention of trying to open the government's UFO files. In fact, it appears Clinton could not have done so even if he wanted it done, as there are clear indicators that he attempted to secure this information for his own knowledge and his efforts were rebuffed as discussed earlier in the chapter. Clinton did sign Executive Order 12958 and that was helpful in declassifying hundreds of thousands of UFO documents but it was not UFO specific, and whatever teeth the order originally had, it has since been greatly reduced by subsequent presidential orders.

It is reasonable to believe that any president who is set on uncovering government-held UFO information would at least attempt to work through the intelligence community and in particular the CIA. (Remember, in chapter 3, the head-butting between JFK and Allen Dulles for UFO data.) However, when we look at Clinton's first CIA director, James Woolsey, he is noted for having almost no contact with Clinton; in fact, it is reported that during Woolsey's two years as CIA director he never had a private meeting with the president, and only twice were there semiprivate meetings. Woolsey is quoted as saying, "It's not that I had a bad relationship with the president, the relationship didn't exist."

We must return once again to the world of presidential realism and say that if a president knows or has been briefed on even a small part of UFO issues, there is nothing to be gained from a political standpoint, and the possibility of much to be lost, for a president to disclose the existence of an extraterrestrial presence. The only possible exception would be the Nixon administration, as discussed in chapter 5.

There is another aspect to some level of official disclosure that is of immense importance: The door to disclosure cannot just be cracked open a bit; it will be thrown wide open by the demands of the public. This will expose a history of abuses of the public trust, the breaking of laws, criminal acts that may include murder, and corruption in the amassing of great wealth and the resulting power for that wealth. Disclosure would not be a pretty picture to a number of powerful people and a reason, I believe, that presidents are gently, or if necessary, forcibly told to stay away from the issue.[2]

THE PHOENIX LIGHTS

On the evening of March 13, 1997, around 8:00 P.M., hundreds—if not thousands—of persons in and around Phoenix, Arizona, witnessed a V formation of lights or orbs that moved slowly over the city from west to east. Hundreds of witnesses said the lights were part of a huge V-shaped structure that many estimated to be over a mile wide. The object was first seen in Nevada around 7:00 P.M. and then moved southwest to Phoenix where some say it hovered briefly before moving on slowly to the southeast and Tucson. At times the object or craft was extremely low and completely silent.

Two years earlier, Dr. Lynne Kitei and her husband, both physicians, had several encounters with large orange orbs seen from their house in suburban Phoenix. The first night, just after dusk, she noticed three orange lights that formed a pyramid near their backyard. Both she and her husband took photos and videos of the strange lights. Kitei and her husband had seen the lights on other occasions and their photographs have given photo experts some of the best photographic proof that the lights are not any of the conventional explanations offered by the military or debunkers.

Two years later, on March 13, 1997, Dr. Kitei did not see the huge V craft but did photograph three orbs over the city, one of the few videos of this mass sighting. From that time, and for the next seven years, Dr. Kitei dedicated herself to investigating and trying to find an answer to the mystery of the Phoenix Lights. I wrote to Dr. Kitei sometime ago after viewing her excellent documentary to ask if there were any new developments that could be included in this book. She returned a detailed reply that was most helpful. The first paragraph of her note to me shows her dedication toward getting answers to this phenomenon and is reproduced here.

> *Hello Larry,*
> *Thank you for your kind interest in the Phoenix Lights. There is MUCH MORE to the story than I could ever squeeze into an eighty-minute film. The documentary is merely an overview of the topic. On the other hand, I hope you have the opportunity to read the latest edition of my book, as it was a 750-page journal that I condensed to the most credible information I discovered after pushing my accomplished medical career aside for seven years (while remaining anonymous) trying to find a logical explication for what I witnessed and documented on film up close and personal two years before thousands saw the same phenomena statewide.*

For seven years she stepped away from a very important and lucrative medical practice to devote her energies full time to research the mystery of the Phoenix Lights. Originally she supplied the local press with her pictures as "Dr. X" over fear that her research could hurt her practice, but in 2004 she went public with her book, *The Phoenix Lights: A Skeptic's Discovery That We Are Not Alone.* The book was then made into a documentary that won a number of national and international awards; it is highly recommended.

As Dr. Kitie said in her note to me, there is far too much to this story to squeeze into a documentary or into this book to do it justice. The number of quality witnesses is staggering and the response of the military has been typically disjointed and contradictory. The explanation that the event was flares has been disproven by time line and photographic study. This is a major modern UFO event that is unique because of the number of witnesses, many from the scientific community.

Typically I have little interest in reports of lights in the sky at night. There are a lot of lights in the night sky, a lot of lights that move. However, the Phoenix Lights, like the Tehran incident or Bentwaters, are some of the exceptions. Also, there is another issue to the Phoenix Lights that needs discussion and involves the Clinton administration.

On the night of March 13, 1997, a U.S. reconnaissance satellite, a satellite that could have seen the lights over Phoenix, went offline for unknown reasons. Not only did it go dark—it was lost and has never been found. About that same time it is reported (unofficially) that the military went to DEFCON 3. At the time President Clinton was staying at the home of golfer Greg Norman. It is reported that late that evening the president is said to have tripped on a step causing a serious knee injury. That was widely reported, but there is also a different take on the story. According to reporter Steve Wilson of the *Arizona Republic,* Clinton was notified of UFO activity in Arizona and was hustled off to a secure location to oversee U.S. defense activities. This information was passed to Wilson by an unnamed source he said was highly credible in the field of UFO research. Wilson is said to have held this story for a time because he had no backup, only this one informant. He finally released it because he said the Clinton-Lewinsky scandal reporting was so irresponsible that his lack of backup seemed insignificant.

Digging deeper into the story of the night of March 13, 1997, more unusual facts and unconfirmed anecdotes have surfaced. Clinton, for instance, is said to have hurt his knee while the Secret Service was hustling him to a helicopter to get to a secure location. He ended up secured belowground at Bethesda Naval Hospital as a result of his knee injury. For a couple of days news reports described the type of surgery Clinton would need and how long the recovery would be. Some reports state that he showed up a couple of days later appearing completely healthy. That report is not true; Clinton was on crutches for about two months, so there is little doubt that he did suffer an injury.

In the July issue of *Scientific American* it was reported that on the evening of March 13, 1997, the Hubble telescope detected bursts of gamma radiation coming from space, something apparently very unusual. There is also a story written by staff writer Jack Dorsey of the *Norfolk Virginian-Pilot*, dated December 6, 1997. At the same time strange craft and objects were being seen over Phoenix (allowing for time zone differences). Troubleshooter 615, a Navy HH-60H helicopter, while hovering over the landing area on the frigate *Jesse L. Taylor* cruising eighty miles off Cape Hatteras, suddenly and without explanation, shot forward, clearing the frigate's hangar, then clearing the deck, slamming nose-first into the Atlantic fifty yards off the starboard bow. The helicopter and crew vanished in an instant. Both were retrieved from three hundred feet of ocean by a salvage vessel and no indication of any problem with machine or crew was found. The Navy has stated the cause of the accident may never be determined. Eleven minutes after this event, President Clinton was rushed from the home of Greg Norman and, in the rush, damaged his knee.

In his article, Dorsey sees a possible connection to all these events. I don't necessarily share that belief but there is no question that March 13, 1997, was a strange time indeed. First, the question of why would the president be alerted because of a UFO sighting two thousand miles away? The answer could be that this was no ordinary UFO sighting. According to Dr. Kitei and her research, as well as a review of her photographs by Dr. Bruce Maccabee, there was not a single craft sighted on March 13, but a number of objects sighted starting in the afternoon and continuing until almost dawn the next day. These included orbs of light that were photographed by Dr. Kitei at various times, the huge triangle-shaped craft seen by many, and the huge V-shaped craft seen by others.

The Air Force denies any knowledge of the event or that any aircraft were launched. Unnamed sources within the Air Force have stated that two fighters were launched and one got close enough to an object to photograph it. It was also stated by this informant that the pilots were badly shaken by what they saw. The next day Dr. Kitei contacted Sky Harbor Airport tower personnel who verified to her that they watched objects at about a thousand feet in restricted airspace through binoculars, but the objects did not appear on their radar and were uncorrelated.

What we know as fact is that thousands of Phoenix and surrounding area residents saw a remarkable object (or objects) a mile or larger in size float silently over the city, sometimes at rooftop level, without any obvious concern for being seen. In fact, it almost appeared that the object or objects wanted to be seen. This sighting was so out of the ordinary that the military, who most certainly was aware of the events, could reasonably expect to consider invasion as a possibility. With that in mind, the president most certainly would have been rushed away from the Norman compound and returned to Washington.

It has been discussed by those familiar with radar that radars are tuned to detect objects that fall into certain areas that would conform to aircraft traffic and filter out very fast or slow moving targets. For instance, airport radars may not be tuned to detect a stationary object in the air or objects traveling beyond the speed of aircraft such as meteors. It is also possible that NORAD could have been aware of the Phoenix objects and the military was alerted. This, of course, is all speculation. What is not speculation is that the people of central Arizona on March 13, 1997, viewed a phenomenon that remains unique in UFOlogy.

THE 1994 OHIO SIGHTINGS—THE JANUARY 2000 SOUTHERN ILLINOIS SIGHTINGS

There are three additional sighting of special interest that occurred during the Clinton administration. These events, like the 1966 southern Michigan sightings, are significant because of the number of police involved and that they actually followed the objects for a number of hours while being in contact with their dispatcher by radio.

Around midnight on December 14, 1994, in Trumbull County, Ohio, 911 operators began getting calls from people who were witnessing a very strange bright light moving in an erratic manner. Police from a number of townships were alerted and all reported pursuing a brilliant object of immense size and close to the ground. One police sergeant actually got his cruiser close to the object and at that instant his car cut off and his radio stopped working. He stated that the object was so bright that the surrounding area was bathed in a blinding light. He got out of his cruiser and watched the object while both frightened and totally mystified. When the object, which was completely silent, moved away the police cruiser restarted on its own, and his radio once again began to operate. This is a phenomenon that has been reported about close encounters with automobiles for years. The fact that for years vehicles with internal combustion engines stall when involved in a close UFO encounter, then restart on their own without the operator trying to engage the starter adds great depth to the mystery.

The quality and integrity of the officers who reported sighting this object are without question. There is also no question as to the number of solid citizens who placed 911 calls to local police. What adds to the intrigue of this sighting is that on April 17, 1966, a number of police officers chased a similar object from Portage County, Ohio, over eighty miles well into Pennsylvania. In March 1966 the Michigan UFO chase took place that resulted in the "swamp gas" fiasco.[3]

Several months prior to that sighting, there was a remarkable Holland, Michigan, sighting. On March 8, 1994, well over three hundred people, including police officers, reported mysterious lights over Lake Michigan. There were a number of lights reported at high altitude and brightly lit craft seen just above treetop level. There were so many 911 calls that the 911 operator called the National Weather Service radar operator at Muskegon, who advised he was monitoring the objects on his radar. The operator advised that he had never seen returns perform in the manner these objects, huge in size, performed. One object moved twenty miles in seconds. He said they would hover, accelerate rapidly, and make right angle turns at incredible speeds. The radar operator was adamant that these were solid returns from very large objects, much larger than airplanes. He said they would form up in a triangular pattern, then "jump all over the place." The sighting has never been explained.

On January 5, 2000, southern Illinois was rocked by another major UFO event. In the early morning hours, witnesses around Highland, Illinois, started reporting unusual brightly lit objects in the sky. In all, five police departments became involved in the sighting. Sightings of the object or objects took place from sunset to sunrise the following morning and one witness videotaped the objects.

The significance of these sightings seems to indicate that, for whatever reason, this area of the country seemed to be a hot spot of UFO activity at the time. Could the Great Lakes, with their vastness and great depth, be the draw? One can only speculate.

11

STEPHENVILLE UFO AND THE CRAWFORD WHITE HOUSE

THE GEORGE W. BUSH ADMINISTRATION

The administration of George W. Bush is much like the administration of his father, George Herbert Walker Bush, from an intelligence standpoint. After spending two days in the George H. W. Bush library in College Station, Texas, I was not able to locate any documents relating to the UFO or the extraterrestrial issue. Bush senior is believed by many UFOlogists to be one of the keepers of the secrets because of his service as CIA director. The fact is that Bush served just less than one year as director. His successor, Adm. Stansfield Turner, served almost four years, followed by William Casey who served six years. During the Eisenhower administration, Allen Dulles served eight years.

It is true that Bush senior has a varied and distinguished record of government service, but I see no reason to believe that he was on the inside of the UFO issue during his short term as CIA director. The case could be made that Allen Dulles under Eisenhower, and William Casey under Reagan, could be expected to have far more in-depth UFO knowledge than did Bush 41 in his short term as director. There is every reason to believe that whatever knowledge Bush 41 had from his time as DCI, vice president, and president was passed on to his son, Bush 43.

September 11, 2001, turned Bush 43 into a wartime president with tightened security that is still very much felt today. Any hope of a UFO breakthrough was dashed by the terrorist attacks that brought down the Twin Towers of the World Trade Center, the attack on the Pentagon, and the crash of United Airlines Flight 93 in Pennsylvania. From that date, and for the next seven years, the Bush presidency was consumed with punishing those responsible for the attack and fighting worldwide terrorism.

There were three UFO events during the Bush administration that directly affected the president. The Stephenville, Texas, sighting is one of the most remarkable sightings in modern UFO history. The other two are of little importance.

On November 20, 2003, the FAA and NORAD both detected an uncorrelated target within the restricted airspace around the White House. Jet fighters were scrambled and an evacuation of the White House was started. However, nothing was seen and the evacuation was canceled.

On April 27, 2005, an uncorrelated target made a slow approach heading north from northern Virginia toward D.C. The object moved in a direction that would take it to the White House; both President Bush and Vice President Cheney were taken to the White House bunker. Helicopters were sent aloft but the object disappeared from radar.

On January 8, 2008, in and around Stephenville and Dublin, Texas, in Erath County, a town that is bisected by the well-known Route 281, known as the Hill Country Highway, one of the country's most remarkable UFO events occurred. To make it even more remarkable, it brought into play the president's home in nearby Crawford, Texas.

The first sightings occurred between 6:00 and 6:30 P.M. near

Stephenville. There were a total of eight witnesses located in four different areas who described a very large, very bright, and completely silent object. Two of the witnesses stated that the object moved at a high rate of speed and then became motionless. One other witness only saw the object motionless and the other only saw it moving rapidly. Four other witnesses saw the object between 6:40 and 7:15 P.M. in the Dublin, Texas, area and one final sighting around 9:30 P.M. near Comanche, Texas, which is in Comanche County southwest of Stephenville on Route 67/377.

There have been numerous newspaper articles about the sightings with witness interviews. Reporter Angelia Joiner interviewed the officers and they saw not just lights but a craft of immense size. One officer on duty in Stephenville stated to Joiner that when he saw the craft, which he estimated to be about a half mile away, his first impression was that it was a huge aircraft but then realized it was hovering and he knew that no aircraft that large could hover. He estimated the size to be in the area of five hundred to six hundred feet. The craft was at first level but then turned to a thirty- to forty-degree angle and started to rise. It then went vertical and moved off to the northwest. The craft had a number of flashing lights, similar to strobe lights, of red and white and some red outer lights that were constant. There were two very large constant whitish-blue lights that were about the size of a nickel held at arm's length.

The officer went on to say that when the object went vertical, a third light came on as it started to move away. He did get a lock on it with his radar gun; it was moving at twenty-seven miles per hour and accelerating. He then lost sight of it in the trees. He remained quiet about the encounter because of concerns about his credibility and his position on the force. When the story broke in the papers, he found that two other officers had witnessed the same object and he contacted them. He made a sketch of what he had seen and took it to the two other officers who verified that it represented what they had seen.

Other reports have included military F-16s in the area; some accounts have them chasing the object. Carswell AFB has F-16s that operate in a military operating area (MOA) that takes in a small part of Erath County but not Stephenville. They were contacted but said they had no jets in the air the night of January 8. That statement was retracted a few days later and they advised that there were ten F-16s training that night in the MOA.

This is far from a complete overview of the events in the early evening of January 8, 2008. There were many more witnesses who viewed the events and whose names and stories have been reported in the media. I have chosen not to include their names or their detailed stories as they have been well documented and are available for those wishing to do additional research into this intriguing story. However, there is one aspect of this story that does need additional discussion.[1]

On January 19, 2008, the Mutual UFO Network (MUFON) started their investigation into the Stephenville incident. The result was a detailed report written by a group of distinguished scientists and researchers, some with Ph.D.s, and authored primarily by Glen Schulze, who has an extensive and detailed background in radar with many government agencies, including the CIA and NSA, and Robert Powell whose background is in device physics, primarily in the field of semiconductor chips.

Their seventy-seven-page report was published July 4, 2008, and is a detailed study using interviews and available radar data obtained through FOIA requests to ten different government agencies. Their report states that they received almost three million radar returns from the FAA but were unsuccessful with the military commands they contacted. Simply stated, they were stonewalled by the military, my words not theirs. In any case the radar returns from the FAA corroborated the sightings reported by the witnesses. In addition, the radar study revealed some intriguing, even astonishing facts.

1. There was a real and physical object that was observed by the witnesses.
2. The object(s) was not any known aircraft.
3. The object was huge, perhaps a thousand feet in size.
4. It could hover, fly slowly, and accelerate to over two thousand mph.[2]
5. At one point the object flew toward the Crawford Ranch, which is restricted airspace.
6. The military had F-16s in the air but no attempt was made to intercept the object.
7. The object was violating FAA and MARSA rules with no transponder.
8. Military air traffic was heavy in the area and strayed into civilian airspace.
9. A military AWACS was aloft at 41,000 feet crisscrossing the area for four hours.[3]

The importance of this story cannot be underestimated. It is a clear indication of the military's involvement in concealing evidence of a very real phenomenon for whatever reasons. It clearly shows the involvement of the military cover-up of an event that is now backed by scientific research. The questions are many: Was it ours? If so, why fly it in an area where it could be seen? Was it extraterrestrial? Why didn't the military respond to this incursion? Were they blind to this object that was clearly seen on FAA radars? Were they blind to the fact that the object was heading to restricted airspace around the Bush ranch?

There are of course the debunkers who come on like overzealous referees in a football game, blowing their proverbial whistles and yelling "foul." In this case debunker James McGaha in a Committee for Skeptical Inquiry (CSI) article has opined that MUFON "cherry picked only 187 points of noise and scatter" out of almost three million in their analysis. Is McGaha an expert in radar with the credentials of Schulze? I think not. If they did "cherry pick," I say so what? When I review documents in an archive, I may go through thousands of documents, but I "cherry pick" documents that are relevant to my research. McGaha goes on to say that what the witnesses saw were flares being deployed by the F-16s. Flares, like the planet Venus, are an overused excuse for legitimate UFO sightings. With that said, flares can be disconcerting to the untrained eye. They are bright, and in this case McGaha says they were LUU-2B/B illumination flares, which are very bright, float on a parachute, and last a minimum of four minutes. However, the question must be asked: Would flares ever be deployed in this area? The Brownwood MOA is authorized for air operations at a minimum of seven thousand feet so the deployment of dangerous flares over this well-known dairy country is very questionable.[4] Also flares have certain characteristics: they float down on a parachute, they leave a very noticeable smoke trail, and they burn out in a few minutes. If flares were part of air exercises in the Brownwood MOA, then those in residence would know what they were. If it was a first-time event the Air Force would certainly have advised Erath residents that they had seen a flare drop. It goes beyond the pale to believe that flares had anything to do with what was seen by some residents of Erath and surrounding counties. It seems McGaha stands alone with his flare theory.

In summarizing the MUFON report, the authors conclude what the residents of Erath County saw was a very real and physical object. It is also highly unlikely that so many witnesses at different locations in a close geographic area over a period of three and a half hours would misidentify known objects. What they saw was huge in size and could hover, travel slowly, and accelerate quickly in a manner beyond the capabilities of known aircraft.

One other intriguing question: Why, with the object headed straight for the president's home, did the jet fighters not attempt an intercept, or why did several F-16s deviate from required airspace? Perhaps the answer is they did attempt an intercept but were flying below radar coverage. There are witness reports that interceptors chased the object at low altitude. Since the FAA radar coverage sent to MUFON stopped at 8:00 P.M., that question cannot be answered.

This is a fascinating story that continues to unfold. The people of Erath County know what they saw and have rightfully become incensed by the foolish and absurd treatment they have received from debunkers. They are also incensed with how the Air Force and the military have ignored simple requests for a reasonable explanation from the military of their involvement in the events of January 8, 2008.

Having children and grandchildren in New Braunfels, my wife and I have spent much time in south Texas for the last thirteen years. I know Texas and Texans well. I know them to be hardworking patriots who support and take pride in the military. They don't deserve the treatment they have received from the military in the Stephenville incident.

There is one other UFO event that occurred during the Bush presidency that did not involve the president but deserves some discussion.

In November 2006, a number of United Airlines personnel reported seeing a disc-shaped object hovering over a United Airlines gate at Chicago's O'Hare Airport. Personnel included both ground employees and pilots. The sky was overcast at 1,500 feet and the object hovered just below the overcast. As the object was being observed, it suddenly shot straight up at tremendous speed, cutting a perfectly round hole in the overcast and allowing blue sky to be seen through the hole.

There was much buzz amongst the United employees until United officials told their employees not to discuss the incident. However, a *Chicago Tribune* reporter got wind of the story and started to investigate. He was told by both United officials and the FAA that no such event occurred but he continued to get credible off-the-record accounts from numbers of witnesses. Finally a FOIA request was made by the newspaper uncovering that both United Airlines and the FAA were well informed of the event.

The *Chicago Tribune* then broke the story and it made news around the world. The FAA, for their part, started backfilling by saying that an unusual weather phenomenon was the cause. Investigative journalist, Leslie Kean, checked this explanation with atmospheric physicists and found the FAA explanation to be impossible under the conditions that existed at O'Hare that day.

The story of how an unknown craft could be in the restricted airspace of one of the world's busiest airports, and why officials have shown no interest in investigating the event, and in fact tried to cover it up, remains unanswered.

12

THE PODESTA FACTOR

THE OBAMA ADMINISTRATION

In October 2002, former chief of staff to President Bill Clinton, John Podesta, stood before the podium at the National Press Club and addressed a conference sponsored by the Syfy Channel. He made the following statement in his address:

> *I think it's time to open the books on things that have remained in the dark; on the questions of government investigations of UFOs. It's time to find out what the truth really is that's out there. We ought to do it because it's right; we ought to do it because the American people quite frankly can handle the truth; and we ought to do it because it's the law.*

Podesta was making those remarks in the context of the implementation of Executive Order 12958, which declassified millions of pages of previously classified documents. He reaffirmed his UFO and disclosure interest in a foreword for journalist Leslie Kean's book *UFOs: Generals, Pilots, and Government Officials Go on the Record* (2011).

The arrival of the Obama administration in 2009 made many in UFOlogy rejoice at the possibility of real disclosure. This was mostly based on the fact that John Podesta, as codirector of Obama's transition team, seemed to be an inside track to disclosure. That has proven to be a fantasy.

There is no doubt that when Obama took office he had an agenda, perhaps a burning agenda, but it was in the area of health care reform and not disclosure of an extraterrestrial presence. It is laughable to believe that Obama would take on disclosure of an extraterrestrial presence; he or his advisers saw that this would not benefit him or his administration. There is also another consideration and that is, unlike Carter, Reagan, and Clinton, Obama has shown no interest in the UFO issue. He has made a couple lighthearted comments about UFOs and extraterrestrial issues, but beyond that he seems to have little interest in the subject. If Bill Clinton, who has a very great interest in the subject, was unable to get solid UFO information, it's unlikely that Obama would have received any serious briefing from those that keep the secrets. There is no indication that the disclosure of the existence of an extraterrestrial presence is included in any way in his agenda.

However, in politics things change, and in December 2013 John Podesta was brought back into the White House as a presidential adviser. The administration was facing second-term problems that have plagued previous administrations. New blood with fresh ideas seemed necessary and Podesta, along with his pro-disclosure opinions, was their choice. Will Podesta have any impact to move this administration toward any level of disclosure? That remains to be seen.

So far during the Obama administration, with a few exceptions, the UFO phenomenon has been relatively quiet. There have been two stories that have caused a stir but there is no indication that Obama knew about, or had any interest in, either.

In April 2011, the FBI launched The Vault on the Web to let the public see and research released FBI FOIA documents and the press noted the Hottel Memo, which actually had been in the public domain since the 1970s. The memo, dated March 22, 1950, was from Guy Hottel, head of the Washington, D.C., field office to Director J. Edgar Hoover. The subject of the memo was a story passed on to a field agent by a third party who told the agent that an Air Force investigator told him that three flying saucers were recovered in New Mexico. The memo went on to say: "They [the saucers] were described as being circular in shape with raised centers, approximately fifty feet in diameter. Each one was occupied by three bodies of human shape but only three feet tall, and dressed in metallic cloth of a very fine texture. Each body was bandaged in a manner similar to the blackout suits by speed fliers and test pilots."[1]

This memo is dismissed by UFO debunkers and some skeptics because it comes from a third party and, according to the FBI, they didn't investigate the story. That may or may not be the case, but the head of the D.C. field office thought it important enough to send a memo to the director. I have written the FBI office of public information for documentation that this memo was not investigated by the FBI.

The second story involves a thirty-five-year CIA veteran, Chase Brandon, who served in the CIA Clandestine Service for twenty-five years. In relating his story on Coast to Coast AM in June 2012, he stated that he was in the historical collection vault at the CIA Langley headquarters where he said he saw a box simply labeled "Roswell." He took the box down and thumbed through its contents, which contained written documents and photographs that proved to him that the Roswell incident was without question an extraterrestrial event. He will not elaborate on what he saw since he says it would violate his security agreement with the CIA.

He went on to say: "Some written material and some photographs, and that's all I will ever say about the contents of the box. But it absolutely, for me, was the single validating moment that everything that I had believed, and knew that so many other people had happened, was truly was what occurred."

This story has many critics who question why a now ten-year contract operator for the CIA on the director's staff as the agency's first liaison officer to the publication and entertainment industries was able to amble around in a top-secret vault. It's a good question and one that I've written to the CIA's public information office for their explanation.

Until proven otherwise I'll stand by my belief that the Obama administration is the least likely administration in recent history to become involved in disclosure. In fact, at least at the present time, I don't see disclosure from any administration as a reasonable occurrence. My research continues to support the opinion that the Nixon administration was the only administration that gave any serious consideration to any form of formal government UFO disclosure, and the advent of Watergate put a quick end to any efforts in that direction.

ROBERT T. BIGELOW

There is an important player in the current UFO issues who needs to be mentioned. Billionaire Robert T. Bigelow of Las Vegas, Nevada, and owner of Bigelow Aerospace, has become an important financial backer of UFO research. Bigelow also operates Bigelow Aerospace Advanced Space Studies (BAASS) that the Federal Aviation Administration now refers people to who want to report UFO encounters.

Bigelow is an extremely interesting person who grew up in Las Vegas at the time when nuclear aboveground tests were being conducted in the nearby desert. Present also were UFOs which were seen by many residents of the area, including his family members. In this environment he developed a deep interest in space and space exploration. He has stated that he knew early on that to realize his dream of space exploration, he would need substantial financial resources and he chose to focus on real estate development as a means to build a solid financial base. In that effort he was immensely successful and was able to use his substantial wealth toward the realization of his dream. That dream included the founding of Bigelow Aerospace in 1999 and has launched two experimental space modules, Genesis I and Genesis II, with plans for near-future space habitats. He is working under contract with NASA to develop his BEAM module for resupply work to the International Space Station. This fits nicely with the Obama administration's 2011 budget of investing $6 billion over five years for companies to develop spacecraft to carry people into space. NASA would then contract with these companies to transport astronauts into space rather than developing and using their own hardware. It is a program that appears to be moving ahead rapidly.

In addition to his space interests, with Bigelow Aerospace he also has a deep interest in the UFO phenomenon and other paranormal issues. His interest in these areas is handled through his BAASS organization. Bigelow is reported to have supported, or continues to support, a number of well-known UFO researchers and research organizations such as MUFON and CUFOS. As reported in the Clinton chapter, he was a major backer of the Rockefeller Initiative.

In September 1996, Bigelow purchased the 480-acre Sherman Ranch, also known as the Skinwalker Ranch, which lies southeast of Ballard, Utah. The ranch was known as a hot spot for UFO and paranormal activity. The last owner, the Gorman family, was forced to leave the ranch after only twenty months because of the number of frightening paranormal events that occurred almost daily.

After purchasing the ranch from the Gormans, Bigelow assembled a group of senior scientists along with scientific equipment to investigate the ranch. For several years the ranch was manned by scientists 24-7 and a number of UFOs were seen. Paranormal events occurred, but nothing of a repetitive nature that could produce true scientific evidence.

With such a background of interests and his wealth, Bigelow and his work are controversial. He has his supporters and his critics. He certainly seems to be leading the field in privatized space exploration. His most criticized work seems to be in UFO research and his relationship and financial interest in such organizations as MUFON. This book takes no sides in the issue and has given this brief overview of Mr. Bigelow because of his work with current space-related projects and his support of UFO research.

THE CITIZEN HEARING ON DISCLOSURE

I will close the presidential chapters with a brief discussion of the Citizen Hearing on Disclosure. This, I believe, is the most important event to date of the Obama administration relating to the UFO issue. Today, it is an ongoing event that can be viewed at www .citizenhearing.org.

From April 29 to May 3, 2013, a mock congressional hearing was conducted at the National Press Club in Washington, D.C. There were thirty hours of testimony from forty witnesses to a panel of six former congressional members. The basis of the event organized by UFO activist, Stephen Bassett, was to bring before the press and the population the accumulated evidence of an extraterrestrial presence visiting Earth, and to press Congress for hearings aimed toward disclosure of the government's knowledge and involvement in an extraterrestrial cover-up.

Giving testimony at the event were some of the best-known

UFOlogists from around the world, as well as pilots and government officials. A number who testified have also contributed in some way to this book and include Stephen Bassett, Stanton T. Friedman, Nick Pope, Antonio Heneeus, Jesse Marcel Jr., Robert Salas, Donald Schmitt, and Dr. Robert Wood.

Although criticized by some because of the rather large twenty-thousand-dollar stipend paid to the former congressional members, they all seemed truly impressed by the depth and quality of the testimony. That was made clear in their statements after the event and it should be understood that a negative assessment of the hearings would not have required the return of the stipend.

This was a watershed event because of the number and quality of many of the witnesses. I have stated a number of times in this book about "the mountain of evidence" that flying saucers or UFOs exist. This event was an example of that mountain of evidence. That's not to say that all forty of the witnesses don't carry some controversial baggage, and some have questioned the credentials of a couple of witnesses. In an event this large that's to be expected, especially when it is such a controversial subject. However, and this is especially true of many of the researchers, their depth of knowledge and the thousands of hours of tedious research, I think, were truly astounding to many. The people I'm speaking of are not armchair researchers but boots-on-the-ground people who have paid their dues with hundreds of thousands of air miles, extended time away from home and family, and contrary to what some may believe, none is getting rich.

In November 2011, the White House Office of Science and Technology on the White House Web site posted that there is no evidence that life exists outside our planet, and that the government is not hiding any evidence of an extraterrestrial presence. This official position was not unexpected and is in concert with the views expressed in this book that there is nothing to be gained by this administration, or any past administration with the exception of the Nixon administration, from any form of disclosure.

At the start of writing this book, I wrote to all of the living presidents asking them for an interview to discuss their thoughts on the UFO phenomenon. I made it clear that I was not looking for classified information, but rather their personal thoughts on the issue. I received a respectful reply from the spokesman for each, declining my request for various reasons but wishing me well with my book. I also wrote or e-mailed several high-ranking presidential assistants rumored to be on the inside of UFO issues, but received no replies. While doing research in the Johnson Library in Austin, Texas, I e-mailed a request to retired admiral Bobby Ray Inman for an interview. Admiral Inman is believed to have a long history in his intelligence work with UFO issues. Although his office was located on campus near the Johnson Library, the interview was refused.

A good friend, a retired Air Force colonel and now a D.C. lobbyist, contacted on my behalf several of his friends, all retired Air Force general officers of two-, three-, and four-star rank. He told them of my book and asked if they would be willing to talk with me about UFO issues. Of the group, all but one said they didn't mind discussing the subject with me but really didn't have any inside knowledge of the issue. One, a three-star general, even said he had been fascinated with the subject for years. However, one of the group, a two-star general who had held a very sensitive position in an Air Force command that would be knowledgeable of UFO intrusions into U.S. airspace, made it very clear that he wished to have no contact with me.

What we can take from this is that those in the know will not talk. The fact is that there is nothing to be gained from those in the know discussing UFO issues and perhaps much to lose.

Dr. Jesse Marcel, Jr., with the author at the 2013 Roswell UFO Festival. We lost Jesse two months later to a heart attack.

(Photo from author's private collection)

The brilliant atmospheric physicist Dr. James E. McDonald

(Courtesy of the University of Arizona–Tucson)

Dr. J. Allen Hynek, consultant to the Air Force for twenty years before founding the Center for UFO Studies in 1973

(Courtesy of the Center for UFO Studies)

Robert Emenegger in his home office.

(Photo from author's private collection)

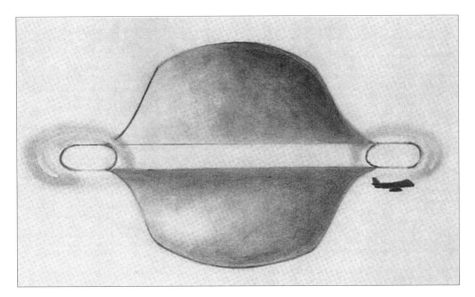

Sketch of object seen by crew of Japan Airlines Flight 1628 over Alaska. Note the size comparison with the 747 aircraft in the foreground.

(Courtesy of Donald Schmitt)

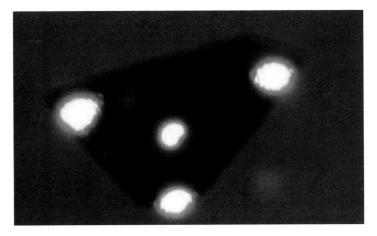

Photo taken of object during the Belgian Wave of UFO sightings.

(This photo was released into the public domain by J.S. Henrardi)

Left to right, Stanton T. Friedman, Kathleen Marden, the author

(From author's private collection)

The famous McMinnville, Oregon, UFO photo taken by Mr. Paul Trent in 1950

(Courtesy of the McMinnville Telephone-Register)

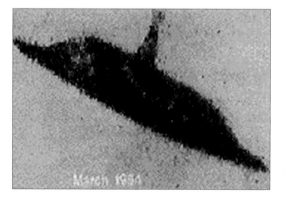

UFO photograph taken in 1957 at Rouen, France, by the gun camera of a French fighter aircraft before it flew away. Notice the similarity between the McMinnville and Rouen objects.

(Courtesy of NICAP)

James Jesus Angleton, chief of CIA counter-intelligence from 1954 to 1975

(Courtesy of the CIA)

Arthur C. Lundahl founded the National Photographic Interpretation Center, was a confidante to President Kennedy, and played a major role in the Cuban Missile Crisis. He was a strong believer in UFOs and the ETH.

(Courtesy of the National Photographic Interpretation Center)

Edward U. Condon, author of the flawed Condon Report on the Colorado Project

(Courtesy of Washington University Libraries)

Robert Salas with wife, Marilyn, on right, with author and wife, Alice

(From author's private collection)

Spectacular sighting of three orbs over Phoenix taken by Dr Kitei in 2002.

(Courtesy of Dr. Lynne Kitei, M.D., and www.thephoenixlights.net.)

Some have been burned by irresponsible UFO researchers who have quoted them out of context or have disclosed privileged information. A taped telephone conversation between Admiral Inman and a questionable UFO researcher that the admiral believed to be confidential was released to the public by the researcher. This embarrassed Admiral Inman and burned him toward discussing the issue with outsiders. I feel sure this played a role in his refusal to meet with me, although I was in walking distance of his office for two days.

This may be somewhat in variance to the view held by Steve Bassett, but that's reasonable in any discussion and something that I believe Steve would acknowledge as totally acceptable. Differing views are always good when investigating an unknown. What is important is that if the government continues to push back on disclosure, even in the simplest form. With his efforts, Bassett is building public support for congressional hearings to force the issue. For his continuing and tireless efforts toward disclosure, my hat is off to him. It is also one of the purposes of my work with this book.

13

THE ABDUCTION PHENOMENON

In UFO research there are, as said at the beginning of this book, so many different aspects to this very complicated story that it is necessary for the writer and/or researcher to focus on one specific part of the story. To do otherwise would dilute the importance of their work because of the immense scope of the subject. Since my interest from an early age was the sighting of what were then called flying saucers and is where my interest has always been focused, this is what the book has focused on. It is what I believe is the core of the UFO phenomenon and it is from this core that come the many related issues.

As researchers and students alike know, the different issues within the UFO phenomenon are many and varied. Biblical and prebiblical writings indicate to many an off-planet presence commonly called ancient astronauts, and explain the mysteries of the pyramids, Easter Island, and the greatest of all, Puma Punku, just to name a few. The subject of alien contact, or in the words of Dr. J. Allen Hynek, "close encounters of the third kind," is in itself an issue of tremendous importance. Of course the government involvement and cover-up is another story of huge importance, as is the media's reluctance to properly cover a true scientific issue. The issue of crop circles is yet but another clue in the search for understanding the UFO phenomenon.

These and many more are issues that make up the fabric of the complete and very complicated UFO story. As I look at the overall UFO issue, it is my belief that the most important of these related issues is that of alien abductions.

I have focused my attention in this book on UFO sightings and the retrieval of the remains and possible living extraterrestrial entities. Other issues, such as the government involvement and cover-up of research into the phenomena, have been discussed. However, I think it is important to include a chapter on the abduction issue as it is of great importance to the overall UFO story and resulting research. Dr. John Mack of Harvard and Bud Hopkins have been the leading researchers in this area of study. Since their passing, the baton of research has been turned over to Kathleen Marden, the MUFON director of abduction research. Kathleen is the niece of Betty Hill, who along with her husband, Barney Hill, were the first UFO abductees to gain national and international attention after their 1961 abduction. Marden is considered the leading expert on the Betty and Barney Hill UFO abduction case and authored a book on the incident with noted nuclear physicist Stanton T. Friedman, *Captured! The Betty and Barney Hill UFO Experience* (2007). Kathy's interest and work ranges far beyond the story of her aunt and uncle. She has coauthored with Stan Friedman, *Science Was Wrong* (2010), and with Denise Stoner, *The Alien Abduction Files* (2013). Kathy has a B.A. from the University of New Hampshire and participated in graduate studies there and at the University of Cincinnati. She was a social worker and educator before starting a twenty-three-year career in UFO abduction research. She has lectured around the U.S., appeared on many radio and televisions programs in the U.S., Canada, and the U.K., and authored many articles on the abduction subject. In 2012, she was honored by MUFON with the MUFON UFOlogist of the Year award.

I first met Kathy in July 2012 and again in 2013 at the International UFO Museum and Research Center, where we were both speaking during the annual Roswell UFO Festival. I immediately liked this charming lady who was attending with Stanton T. Friedman, her coauthor on the books mentioned above. When we had a free moment or two we chatted about a couple of subjects of mutual interest. Not being an expert in the abduction area of UFO research, I later wrote Kathy and asked if she would consider writing a general overview of the abduction issue as it exists today for my book. She replied that she was traveling to promote their new book but she had written a paper for author Bret Oldham for his book *Children of the Greys,* and she would be glad to send the paper for my use.[1]

I gladly accepted her offer. Kathy's comments and paper follows:

THE ALIEN AGENDA
BY KATHLEEN MARDEN

When Larry invited me to contribute a statement for his book regarding the perceived alien agenda, my first thought was that "experiencers" have described to me several agendas by a number of prominent ET groups. I had recently completed a yearlong research project designed to identify commonalities among abduction experiencers, which gave me additional insight into the perceived alien agenda. (See "Commonalities Study Final Report" at www.kathleen-marden.com.)

Participants in the study mentioned contact with several ET types, including 3½- to 4-foot tall Greys, 4½- to 5-foot taller Greys, insectoid praying mantis types, Reptilians, and human types (such as Nordics, Annunaki, and late-stage hybrids). A tiny percentage of the respondents mentioned less prevalent groups, such as tall whites, goldens, and browns, short, pudgy blues, and Yeti types. The most prevalent group in this study is Grey nonhuman entities. Anecdotal reports suggest that the Grey and Insectoid groups are working cooperatively with one another on medical experiments and education involving humans. Space limitations make it impossible for me to discuss all the different perceived agendas, so I will state simply that the most positive experience reports were with Nordic types (highly spiritual, benevolent, compassionate), and the most negative accounts came from individuals that claimed abductions by Reptilians (cruel, insensitive).

For the purpose of this paper, I will focus primarily upon what I have learned from abduction experiencers about the Greys' perceived agenda. Certainly it is impossible to voice an unequivocal opinion pertaining to this subject matter, as it comes primarily from the subjective experiences of individuals, but a quantitative analysis of experiencers' responses increases one's chance of finding valid information. It is fortuitous, in my opinion, that some experiencers retain conscious, continuous recall of at least part of their abduction experience and have eyewitnesses, plus circumstantial evidence. Eighty-eight percent of the respondents in "The Marden-Stoner Study on Commonalities Among Abduction Experiencers" had conscious recall of at least one abduction experience and were not alone when it occurred. More than two-thirds observed a craft at less than a thousand feet and 56 percent saw nonhuman entities prior to at least one abduction experience. In addition to this, more than 60 percent had witnesses with conscious recall for at least part of the experience.

It becomes increasingly difficult when information is retrieved exclusively through hypnosis, unless there are additional witnesses whose independent testimony, under hypnosis, confirms *the detailed memories of the first witness. This is because hypnotic subjects have a propensity to confabulate fantasy material when no real memories exist, especially when they are asked to recall details. Only 38 percent of the study's participants had undergone hypnosis to facilitate recall. The fact that the vast majority of participants had conscious recall of some of their experiences strengthens the validity of their testimony about the alien agenda.*

Taken together with a March 2012 article that appeared in Life Science magazine, I have gained additional insight into what I and others perceive to be the Greys' agenda. The article spoke of a U.S. military plan developed during the 1950s that outlined the seven steps to contact we would take if we discovered intelligent life elsewhere.* By all accounts, it appears that our alien visitors are following similar protocols. Step one would begin with remote surveillance and data gathering and eventually move toward close approaches, to determine whether or not the planet's inhabitants are hostile. Frank C. Feschino Jr.'s book Shoot Them Down: The Flying Saucer Air Wars of 1952, *lists case after case of aerial encounters during the summer of 1952 where U.S. fighter planes were on twenty-four-hour nationwide alert to "shoot them down" if they refused to land. This documented evidence indicates that our alien visitors have every reason to perceive us as hostile.*

Steps four and five include securing plant and animal specimens and the abduction of intelligent beings. It brings to mind the many historical reports of landed UFOs with their occupants collecting "soil samples." The abduction of intelligent beings by nonhumans is well documented in several compelling evidence reports dating back to 1957. (Villa Boas, Betty and Barney Hill, Buff Ledge, Hickson/Parker, Travis Walton, Smith/Stafford/Thomas,

---

* Natalie Wolchover, "If We Discover Aliens, What's Our Protocol for Making Contact?" March 29, 2012. LifeScience.com.

Allagash, Romanek, etc.) Thousands of humans have reported being taken into an alien environment where they were subjected to intrusive physical examinations, mind scans, images of cataclysmic events, the acquisition of advanced knowledge, and sometimes healings. It occurs around the world across racial, cultural, religious, educational, and economic lines.

Unexplained marks, such as patterned bruises, scoop marks, puncture wounds, sunburnlike redness, and rashes, are commonly reported by abduction experiencers. A highly significant 83 percent of the abduction experiencer participants in the commonalities study stated that they had awoken with unexplained marks on their bodies, whereas only 20 percent of the control group replied in the affirmative. Long, thin bruises (like finger marks) were most often found on women's calves or thighs, suggesting that a reproductive procedure had transpired. Often the women remembered at least part of the procedure. Scoop marks (tissue samples) were most commonly reported near elbows, ankles, and behind knees. Puncture wounds were often found on hands and rib cages. Several men believed that tissue had been extracted from their thymus gland (a specialized organ of the immune system). A few experiencers were released with patterned burn marks on their shoulders or necks and sunburnlike rashes. Over 50 percent of the experiencer group stated that they experienced nosebleeds immediately after an abduction experience. Several stated that their physicians had been concerned about significant scarring in their nasal cavities. One mentioned that his physician found a strange metal object (presumably a tracking device) high in his nasal passage and another told of expelling a suspected implant from her nose the day after an abduction experience.

A significant 69 percent of the female experiencers reported gynecological abnormalities, whereas only a third of the control group made the same report. This statistic offers compelling evidence of an increased percentage of gynecological problems among abduction experiencers, purportedly as the direct result of reproductive procedures performed on them by nonhumans. Two respondents from the experiencer group mentioned that they had tested positive for pregnancy, but following an abduction found that they were no longer pregnant, and there had been no cramping or bleeding. Both recalled observing fetuses purportedly being gestated in tubes on craft and hybrid-baby presentations. Some believe that they have carried genetically altered fetuses to full term.

Illnesses that might be generated by the stress, related to alien abduction, were reported by a significant percentage of the experiencers. Forty percent stated that they suffer from migraine headaches, although only 8 percent of the control group does. Thirty-eight percent reported chronic fatigue and immune dysfunction syndrome or reactivating mononucleosis diagnosis, whereas less than one percent of the general population has CFIDS. This is a highly significant finding.

When we combine this with our discovery that nearly three-quarters of the experiencer group had difficulty falling asleep and staying asleep, we have to question whether or not this is the result of post-traumatic stress disorder stemming from the abduction experience. It is interesting to note that sleep quality improved when experiencers overcame their fear of alien abduction.

One can raise a speculative argument that illnesses among experiencers are caused by the procurement process, when abductees are moved through solid surfaces, by the alien environment, or by the Greys' experiments. It has been reported by some experiencers that the Greys have attempted to raise their vibrational frequencies either as a healing process or for transport.

Despite the constellation of medical symptoms common among abduction experiencers, there have been some positive outcomes reported. Half of the participants in the Marden-Stoner

Commonalities Study stated that they were able to heal others for at least a short period following an abduction experience. This gift persisted for an extended period of time for some of the participants, but not for others. I have received numerous anecdotal reports from individuals that claim to have been healed during an abduction experience.

It is interesting that nearly three-quarters stated that they are more sensitive or intuitive than they were prior to contact and nearly 8 percent stated that they had developed new psychic abilities after a contact experience. Additionally, 88 percent reported that they had witnessed paranormal activity in their homes, such as light orbs that dart or float through the air and poltergeist activity.

Sixth in our military's seven steps to contact are low-level approaches to make our presence known. This brings to mind the gigantic carpenter's square–shaped craft sited over Arizona, Nevada, and Sonora, Mexico, that was observed by thousands of witnesses on March 13, 1997. Its "otherworldly" appearance and flight pattern was initially covered up by Arizona's governor, Fife Symington, but later revealed by him. On November 7, 2006, a dozen employees, including pilots and supervisors at Chicago's O'Hare Airport and several witnesses outside the airport, observed a low-level approach by a disc-shaped object that hovered over gate C-17. Close approaches by unconventional aerial craft are being reported to the Mutual UFO Network on a fairly consistent basis. One has to pause and consider the possibility that our ET visitors are weighing the pros and cons of implementing the eighth step: Overt contact.

One must ask, "Are we a species that can accept overt contact without suffering too many negative consequences?" Or would people from around the world experience fear and a sense of complete powerlessness? Would the world experience ontological *shock so great that governments, public institutions, and economic endeavors would collapse, at least temporarily? Would media outlets engage in fear mongering to increase their ratings without easing the public's fears? Given the many human concerns that arise when we consider the consequences of overt contact, one has to hope that our Grey visitors (and others) are sensitive enough to protect our primitive, warlike species until we move ahead on an evolutionary scale.*

Consider the idea that the Greys are significantly different than humans. Their communication style is telepathic. Their physical structure is reportedly different than ours, suggesting that they are a nonmammalian species. We are told that they have the ability to pass through solid surfaces and can enter locked buildings at will. By all appearances they are an ancient, highly developed species. Perhaps they are so different than humans that overt interaction would be impossible. Or perhaps they don't want to be held accountable for their behavior toward us. They know that we might possibly attempt to defend our planet from a perceived invasion by them. It follows that their only options would be to engage in warfare against us, possibly resulting in our destruction, or leave our planet and the human experimental subjects that have been a part of their grand longitudinal study. Given the possible negative consequences of overt contact, it seems that their current policy of covert interaction has served them well.

It is clear from Kathleen Marden's paper that the abduction phenomenon is a very controversial and uncomfortable, yet a very real subject. It is a subject that was embraced by Harvard Medical School tenured professor, and Pulitzer prize–winning author Dr. John E. Mack. His book *Abduction: Human Encounters with Aliens* in 1994 resulted in a Harvard committee to consider censuring him for his alien-abduction views and work. After fourteen months the committee "reaffirmed Dr. Mack's academic freedom to study what he wishes and state his opinion without impediment."

I think one of the most impressive and dramatic videos on UFOs I've seen and one that moved me like no other was taken from the Stéphane Allix documentary *Experiencers* showing Dr. John Mack and his associates going to the Ariel School in Ruwa, Zimbabwe, and interviewing sixty-two very bright children who'd had a UFO experience in their schoolyard. This was not abduction as such but it seems certain that it is an authentic "close encounter of the third kind," as per Dr. J. Allen Hynek's category of UFO sightings, and abduction was conceivably the intention of the visitors. Since it is believed that many experiencers are abducted at an early age, then periodically abducted as they reach puberty, and then through adulthood and childbearing years, there seems to be a sexual basis to the abductors' motives. I cannot recall any abduction of the elderly. It is for this reason that I believe the Ruwa incident was a planned abduction that for some reason didn't materialize.

I highly recommend viewing the video of this event by typing in Stéphane Allix documentary *Experiencers* on YouTube. I in no way mean to reduce the importance of what other adult abductees have experienced, but children are special in their innocence and their story is moving and compelling. On September 27, 2004, Dr. Mack was struck and killed by a drunk driver while in London to give a lecture on T. E. Lawrence. Dr. John Mack was as special as the children.

I again want to thank Kathleen Marden for allowing me to include her paper on the abduction phenomenon in my work. Kathy possesses a keen intellect and is a hardworking UFOlogist in the so very important field of alien abductions. She also is special.

14

FINAL THOUGHTS

The original book idea was to document Robert Emenegger's fascinating background story in making the documentary *UFOs: Past, Present, and Future*, and the later revised version titled *It Has Begun*. That idea soon expanded to include all of the modern presidents' involvement in UFO events starting with Franklin Roosevelt to present. After getting well into manuscript development, I started to see that using presidential history as a thread to tie modern UFO history into one ever-evolving story could also serve as a sort of textbook for the great majority of people who have a very real interest in UFOs but yet a limited knowledge of this very complicated subject. It is also my hope that my efforts in this endeavor will present the more knowledgeable student or researcher a bit of a different perspective from which to view the phenomenon, especially the military's, and, in particular, the Air Force's handling of the issue.

Although I have studied and researched the UFO phenomenon for over fifty years, in researching this book the most surprising revelation that I encountered was that from 1948 to 1953 there reigned total confusion and discord within the Air Force, as well as a policy (or nonpolicy) that was chaotic, rudderless, and contradictory. The release of the *Estimate of the Situation* destroyed Project Sign, the only group that actually officially researched the UFO issue (Ruppelt and his work at Blue Book being the exception). The death of Sign came from its belief, after much research, that the extraterrestrial hypothesis was the only logical answer to the UFO question. This was the conclusion in their *Estimate of the Situation* that was passed up the chain of command until it finally ended up on Gen. Hoyt Vandenberg's desk. The inflamed Vandenberg smacked the *Estimate* back to the Sign group with orders to rewrite. This is not surprising, as Vandenberg was a member of MJ-12 and he was not about to let this document stand. MJ-12 was willing to let the Air Force do the footwork on UFO sightings but as Sign started to get too close to some answers it was time to show them the errors of their ways. Sign had been given a death notice. The ending came on November 12, 1948, when Sign personnel were ordered to appear before members of the intelligence community at the National Bureau of Standards in Washington. We don't know who attended, since the records of the meeting remain sealed. Perhaps Vandenberg himself was there, but if not the meeting was still run as he directed. Project Sign was through, it was humiliated and crushed, its personnel sent to other duties and replaced with the housekeeping Project Grudge (Swords and Powell 2012, 67).

From that point until the Robertson Panel in 1953, the Air Force stumbled and bumbled along while facing an increasing number of remarkable UFO events they never investigated but rather tried to explain away. Grudge was not investigative; it was a propaganda tool and was finally disbanded and replaced in 1952 by Project Blue Book and the very capable Edward J. Ruppelt.

Let me be perfectly clear that I have the highest regard for the Air Force and their personnel. Prior to World War II the Army Air Corps was all but nonexistent. At the start of the war young men, some who had never driven a car, were taken away from their families, taught to fly fighters and bombers, and sent on missions where one in four would not return. These young men (and young women) performed brilliantly and with great courage. After the war, test pilots put their lives on the line every day (and in many cases, losing them) at Wright-Patterson, Muroc, later Edwards AFB, testing new aircraft designs while setting speed and altitude records. And, of course, the pilots and crews who flew in combat in so many conflicts over the last sixty years. My hat is off to all of them: Air Force, Army, Navy, Marines, and the Coast Guard.

My complaint is with the Air Force and military in general who bungled the UFO issue so badly and continue to do so. Countries around the world (the U.K., France, Belgium, Russia, Spain, South American countries . . . the list goes on) have opened their files, yet the United States stands alone like the stupid ostrich with its head buried in the sand, ignoring the obvious.

It is clear to this writer, and supported by the work of Swords and Powell in their excellent book, *UFOs and Government: A Historical Inquiry,* that from 1947 to the 1969 Condon Report the Air Force was in a state of constant bewilderment relative to the UFO issue, bombarded by NICAP and Donald Keyhoe on UFO issues, and trying to dismiss creditable sightings with ridiculous explanations (the planet Venus was used ad nauseam) and total lies. The Air Force and other elements within the government continue today with a debunking rhetoric, believing that it will eventually become reality. The book mentioned above makes this situation a well-documented fact.

The Condon Report took the monkey off the back of the Air Force and allowed them to finally close Blue Book, and from then on they could publicly state that they no longer had an investigative interest in the UFO issue. It's an absolute lie and a disgrace to a fine branch of our loyal military. What a pathetic situation.

THE LAMENTABLE FACT OF UNREPORTED SIGHTINGS

One of the greatest hindrances to the advancement of UFOlogy and the push for disclosure is the large percentage of sightings that go unreported. Those who report a UFO can suffer consequences that take many different forms. They may be faced with the simple giggle factor or in more extreme cases suffer discredit or even disgrace. In a few cases some have reported threats of bodily harm from officials. Commercial pilots are warned by their companies not to report UFO sightings, and sightings by military pilots are closely controlled. The FAA that investigates even the smallest issue with commercial aircraft says they have no interest in UFOs. When a disc-shaped UFO, discussed in chapter 11, was seen by a number of workers and pilots hovering over a United Airlines gate at O'Hare Airport, the FAA denied they had any information on the event. United Airlines for their part told their employees to keep their mouths shut. It was not until a tape recording of conversations between United Employees and FAA personnel became public was the event acknowledged by the FAA. It's for this reason that only a small percentage of UFO sightings are reported.

The government—using propaganda, disinformation, and outright lies combined with witness intimidation, the roots of which go back to the Robertson Panel and later Condon Report—has succeeded in defusing the public's UFO interest. Reports that are spotty and few are reflected in the public's interest. An increase in reliable reports will also increase the public's interest. Therein is the reason to encourage the reporting of all sightings regardless of how significant they may seem. Disclosure will only happen because of public pressure, and public pressure will only come from a greater awareness of the issue. It's all in the numbers.

While working on the book, I have had a number of people who had a UFO story to tell . . . usually off the record for one reason or another. One of those stories was told to me by a young

woman I'll call Sandy. Sandy is an executive with a well-known
West Coast business involved in the entertainment-and-publishing
industry. She had an interest in this book, and we discussed consulting possibilities by phone through my agent. In the conversation she mentioned that she'd had a UFO encounter that had made
her a believer rather than the staunch skeptic she had been prior to
the encounter. I was intrigued and sent her an e-mail and asked if
she would consider telling me her story at some future time. We set
a date but with her busy schedule it had to be rescheduled several
times. Finally we got together by phone and talked for about thirty
minutes. Her story is fascinating and believable.

A couple of years or so ago she and friends would camp out
occasionally on weekends at a lake in central California. The lake
was in an agricultural area and was a source of irrigation for the
surrounding fields. She and a friend left after business hours on a
Friday evening with plans to meet more friends at the lake several
hours away. By the time they got into the rural agricultural area of
central California it was dark.

The landscape was open rolling farmland with almost no traffic on the road. Sandy's friend was driving and as they chatted
Sandy noticed lights off their left that seemed to be moving along
with them a couple of hundred feet away and about twenty feet off
the ground. Sandy called her friend's attention to the lights and
their first thoughts were that the lights were a crop duster. After a
few moments they realized that whatever it was it appeared to be
round with white and blue lights that seemed to rotate around the
perimeter. After some discussion with Sandy about size it was determined that it was probably about twenty-five feet in diameter.
After much back and forth discussion about general shape, Sandy
admonished me that it was dark and the rotating lights made it
difficult to determine the exact shape. Finally, I brought up the
much used description of two dinner plates placed together top to

bottom. She thought for a few moments and said that would be close except more rounded. She went on to say that whatever this was, it matched the speed of the car and followed the contour of the ground.

Finally becoming more and more concerned, they slowed and stopped the car, hoping the object would move away. However, the object also slowed and stopped to match the car. The object hovered motionless about twenty feet above the ground, just wobbling slightly.[1] They started off and increased their speed to much above the speed limit. The object again paced them, matching their speed. Sandy said the object approached a stand of trees that separated two farms and the object abruptly jumped up to just above the trees and then back down again to just above the field after clearing the trees.

Their anxiety was building as was their speed when the object suddenly shot ahead and in front of the car directly over the road. It was at that point that Sandy said she really "freaked." Then all of a sudden the object was gone, leaving two badly shaken young women alone on a deserted road in central California. The rest of their trip was uneventful. However, the next night the object or one similar to it made a brief appearance over the lake. It was only viewed for a few moments before disappearing. Sandy said that they all noticed that during the brief appearance over the lake all the animals in the area, especially dogs, became very agitated.

In many ways this sighting is like so many reported over the last half century with perhaps one major difference: the length of the sighting. Sandy said the total time the object paced the car was at least thirty minutes and probably a little longer. The length of this sighting may not be unique among UFO sightings but it is most certainly rare. I asked Sandy if she or her companion noted any loss of time when reaching the campsite, or if she or her companion had experienced any sightings prior to or after this sighting. She replied in the negative to both, except for the brief sighting the following night. In both cases the object was in view, then it was gone. Both women couldn't say for sure if it flew away or just vanished.

Another aspect to this story is that it is yet another example of how many quality UFO sightings go unreported. There are no statistics, it could be one in a hundred or one in ten thousand, but it is a fact that most do go unreported because of the stigma attached to the UFO issue. We have seen over and over that credible people who have witnessed major sightings that are totally unexplainable come forward only to be ridiculed by armchair debunkers with ridiculous explanations of what these people saw. In many cases these sightings have been life changing for the witness, and to be ridiculed by debunkers who have no conception of what the person actually saw can be crushing. To compound the problem, even the friends of the witness may apply the snicker factor to what was a major event in that person's life. This is a situation that must end if disclosure is to move forward.

In writing the final chapter for this book I have struggled over the disclosure of my own UFO sighting. I realize that in telling my story it could hurt my credibility as an unbiased UFO researcher. After much thought and personal debate I have decided to include it as it may in some small way benefit others and encourage them to tell their own stories. Also, it's time for me to practice what I've been preaching.

In the overall picture it was rather insignificant as far as UFO sightings go but it made a big impression on me and I think of it often. Invariably when I have told others about my experience I get attempts at making silly eerie sounds or jokes and other rather stupid comments. It's frustrating because my simple sighting made a lasting impression and the idiocy of comments I received made me . . . well, angry. On a small scale it served to give me the insight to understand those who have had major sightings and choose to remain silent, as Sandy did.

My sighting occurred sometime midwinter, probably February or March 1995. My home at the time was in a remote wooded area overlooking a tidal creek off the Great Wicomico River between the Potomac River to the north and the Rappahannock River to the south, and about five miles from the Chesapeake Bay in Virginia. My house was located on a creek that was remote and sparsely populated with only a few homes located along its high banks that wound around points of land for about three miles. The southern shoreline was totally unpopulated and heavily wooded with high banks.

On the day in question I was in my lower-level home office, sitting at my desk behind a picture window that looked out over the creek. It was around 3:00 P.M. in the afternoon and I was alone. Across the creek on the southern shore was a cove where the high banks dropped down to form the cove. At the low point in the shoreline was a very large tree, probably an oak that was surrounded by smaller pines and poplars.

Looking across the creek, my attention was drawn to two large birds, probably ospreys, circling in a tight circle above the tree mentioned above and almost like they were in a thermal. Then I noticed that in the top of the tree there was what I would call a frantic rustling deep within the branches. Since this was winter there were no leaves on the tree, but still a thick growth of limbs. The mind is a very fast computer, and when you visually notice something unusual, your mind tries to reason what you are seeing. My first thought was the two birds were circling over the tree because there was another osprey caught in the top of the tree, possibly tangled with fishing line, a common occurrence with birds, primarily with gulls, on the bay that is so popular with sport fishermen.

The frantic rustling lasted for perhaps five seconds or so before an object rose out of the top of the tree. My instant thought then was of a mylar party balloon, and at first glance it appeared silver in color. I soon realized, as it floated up out of the tree, that it was much larger than a party balloon and it now appeared to be gunmetal gray in color (I have no explanation for the change in color or when it occurred). My vantage point was about a third of a mile from the tree and the object was sort of teardrop shaped. If you visualize a miniature hot-air balloon about five feet across and six feet high without a gondola below, that would be a good representation of the object. Its size would be about that of your thumbnail held at arm's length.

As it floated upward in a sort of wobbly motion, it appeared to be rotating on a vertical axis. My thoughts now turned to a weather balloon. Again, the computer in my head was trying to figure out what I was looking at as it rose to just above the tree level on the high banks on either side of the cove.

Reaching just above the top of the tree line it started to move laterally to the west, or to my right. I assumed that it was being pushed latterly by wind currents as it cleared the tree line. As I continued to watch, something happened that unnerved me. A brilliant beam of light came from the object that seemed directed at me. The light lasted only a second or so and went out. This occurred two more times as I watched the object float over the treetops on the far side of the creek. My reasoning then was that as the object rotated, it had some sort of highly reflective panel that was reflecting the sun that was low on the western horizon in the late-winter afternoon.

I jumped from my desk and ran upstairs to our great room where I had a pair of binoculars that I kept on our wet bar. I grabbed the binoculars and went out onto a large deck that ran the length of the house and overlooked the creek. However, once out-side, the object was no longer in view.

It should have still been in view but it wasn't. I can speculate why it disappeared, but I won't. I was disappointed, but I must admit I was also relieved.

I returned to my office and tried to sort out just what I had seen. As strange as it may seem, after following the UFO phenom-enon at that time for some thirty-five years, the strange aerial object didn't register in my mind as a UFO, or in terms of an extraterrestrial sighting. Let me say here that at no time did it op-erate in any manner that one would say defied the laws of known physics, as has been the case in so many UFO sightings, at least not that I saw.

Since my house was located in an area close to many military installations, most of which were involved in experimental re-search, this became my focus. NAS Patuxent River and Naval Flight Test Center was only about twenty-five air miles from my house as the crow flies. Pax River flew drones over the area fre-quently as well as experimental Navy aircraft.

The sighting didn't fit the flying saucer mold as I had known it. In recent years, as I became more involved in UFO research, I have read about somewhat similar sightings of small orbs or craft de-scribed by many people that could fit the type of object that I saw.

As I reflected on my sighting, a number of things became clear. First, weather balloons don't descend into a treetop and then with a furious rustling rise out again, and they don't rotate on a vertical axis. Being pushed by wind after rising above the tree line made sense except for two things: it would not stop rising as this object did and start a flat drift to the west, it would continue to rise as it moved laterally. Also, this was a crystal-clear, cloudless day. The prevailing winds would have been from the north or northwest.

What about the beam of light? It very well could have been a highly reflective panel on the object that reflected the setting sun as it rotated, but that in itself indicates some sort of special craft. Also the light was instant on and instant off and that didn't seem to fit the sun-reflecting theory.

I have no idea what I saw that winter afternoon but I think of it often. I now believe the two birds were in a thermal caused by the object powering to rise out of the treetop, and I feel certain the object was controlled. I know what I saw on that crystal-clear winter day and it was a very real solid object. In all probability it was military, perhaps a secret military vehicle being tested out of Pax River, but I can't rule out the extraterrestrial explanation of a probe looking at our very secure military interests in the area. My great regret is that I didn't pick up the phone and call the NAS Patuxent River public-information office and report the sighting.

My reason for telling the story of my encounter is to give credibility to my ability to understand the feelings of witnesses to sightings far more incredible than mine. It is very difficult to articulate the feeling of utter frustration and disgust a witness feels when they tell their story about something they witnessed that was extraordinary, something they know beyond any question was real, as real as their own automobile in their driveway, and then have an armchair debunker try to tell them that what they really saw was swamp gas or a lighthouse or a cloud formation. These people are crushed. They know what they saw and to be ridiculed by imbecilic debunking clowns, or puppets of those on the inside, is reprehensible in my opinion.

I have related the story for the reasons given above. I consider the many people, pilots, military personnel, police officers, and solid citizens who have had far more remarkable sightings, close encounters, even abductions than I have, who have come forward only to be ridiculed. They don't deserve that treatment, a treatment given birth years before by actions from within our own government.

If what I've written offers any small support to these folks, then any risk I run of credibility loss is worth the telling of my story.

THE IDIOCY OF DEBUNKING

Another aspect of the UFO phenomenon is the UFO debunkers that I have touched on throughout this book. Unlike skeptics, most of whom are genuine in their skepticism but are also open-minded, the debunkers are bent on discrediting even the most reliable of UFO witnesses and often espousing explanations that border on pure idiocy. How seemingly intelligent people can make so many unintelligent statements without doing any research is beyond comprehension unless some are working for those on the inside of UFO knowledge.

An example of this is UFO debunker James McGaha, a retired Air Force pilot and now an amateur astronomer who is the director of the Grasslands Observatory in Arizona. McGaha's theme centers on his belief that UFO witnesses are not "trained observers." He seems to feel that only astronomers are trained to view things that appear in the sky. He especially likes to take aim at pilots, both military and commercial, who he says "are trained to fly planes, not identify objects in the sky." To say that military pilots, who have to identify other aircraft as friend or foe in times of war, or commercial pilots, some of whom have had frightening UFO encounters and who have their lives and the lives of their passengers at stake, are not trained observers of objects in the sky is laughable.

McGaha, on *Larry King Live*, also stated that what a number of officers and enlisted MPs at the Bentwaters AFB UFO event in England saw on two nights was the light of a lighthouse. No matter that these men had been on that base for months or years, and only on those two nights were they fooled by the light from a lighthouse. No matter two or more of the MPs saw an object on the ground. No matter that one of the men walked to the object, made notes of symbols on the object, and touched the surface, which appeared like molten glass. No matter that these two men saw the object lift off the ground and fly away silently; McGaha still says these men saw the beacon from a lighthouse.

One of the men was the deputy base commander, who was charged with the protection of a base that secretly housed nuclear weapons. As the late Lord Hill-Norton, chief of defense staff, U.K., said, "The men saw exactly what they said they saw, or you have to believe the entire group was hallucinating."[2]

I have no idea of McGaha's record of Air Force service or if he flew in combat. But it's beyond my comprehension to understand how he can say with a straight face that pilots are not trained to observe what they see in the sky or are not good observers of what they may see in the sky. I would venture to say that if he made that statement to the great general Chuck Yeager, or Yeager's close friends and pilots of exceptional ability, Clarance "Bud" Anderson or aviation legend "Bob" Hoover, he would receive vulcanized eardrums.

Another UFO debunker is Bill Nye, known as "the Science Guy," who hosted a PBS show of the same name on PBS Kids, directed at a preteen audience. The show was created by comedian Ross Shafer and produced by Disney Educational Productions. For whatever reason, Nye has been used by various television shows, most notably *Larry King Live* and some news programs to offer counter (debunking) views to UFO sightings or events seen by a number of witnesses. One of the most memorable of the Nye debunking attempts came on *Larry King Live*. Dr. Robert Jacobs recounted a UFO event where he photographed a missile launch at Vandenberg

AFB that was covered in chapter 4. In that event, Jacobs's crew photographed an Atlas missile warhead that was apparently attacked by a UFO as it was traveling at over eight thousand miles per hour. Nye, when asked for his opinion, opined that perhaps the missile was attacked by another of our government's secret projects to test that particular weapon's platform. This occurred in 1964 when our government was having trouble getting missiles off the launch-pad without blowing up. To think that some other government agency had a system that could fly circles around a missile warhead at that speed and fire some sort of plasma beam at the warhead and knock it down is laughable idiocy. Jacobs's response to Nye was a classic response to the stupidity of many UFO debunkers.

Another classic Nye appearance on *Larry King Live* involved the 1967 event when launch control officer Robert Salas described the UFO event that appeared to shut down their entire ICBMs (a story covered in an chapter 4). In Nye's attempt at debunking, he stated he had heard rumors that some of the men were drinking. The idiocy of this statement is a reflection of Nye's ignorance of the subject, his ignorance concerning the effects the depressant alcohol has on the human body, or his debunking bias. As someone who has consumed adult beverages in his life, and on occasion perhaps a few too many, the old fable of "pink elephants" is pure fiction. Discussing the Roswell incident on *Larry King Live*, Nye talked about Project Mogul using Skyhook balloons when in fact Mogul used conventional weather balloons. It's another example of debunkers having little depth of knowledge of the UFO issue or the particular event they are attempting to debunk.

Three of the better known UFO debunkers are now deceased: Dr. Donald Menzel, Phillip J. Klass, and Dr. Carl Sagan. Menzel was covered in chapter 3 and will not be discussed here. Klass and Sagan were important in UFO research and need a brief discussion.

Klass was an electrical engineer and editor of *Aviation Week*

& Space Technology. He was also a rabid and somewhat abrasive UFO debunker. Klass became involved in UFOs in 1966, and his initial theory was that UFO reports were an unknown type of plasma or ball lightning. He butted heads with Dr. James E. McDonald and even campaigned to have McDonald's government research funding cut off. Finally, after his ball-lightning hypothesis was widely criticized by those on both sides of the UFO issue as unscientific, he abandoned it and directed his debunking to other theories. He was known to make monetary challenges for solid UFO artifacts, including ten thousand dollars to anyone who produced any part of a crashed spacecraft. He challenged UFOlogist Stanton T. Friedman over what he thought were inconsistencies in the typeface on the Cutler-Twining memo. He publically offered Friedman a hundred dollars for every official document Friedman could produce (up to a maximum of ten) in pica typeface from the same government office and same time frame that produced the Cutler-Twining memo. Friedman sent fourteen official documents along with a bill for a thousand dollars. Klass sent a check, which Friedman photocopied, cashed, and then made public. Klass, incensed, threatened to sue. Friedman laughed at him and the issue ended. Klass died August 9, 2005, at age eighty-five.

Carl Sagan could probably be labeled more of an extreme skeptic than a debunker. Sagan was a very bright man with a scientific and inquisitive mind. He was simply too bright not to look at the accumulated evidence of the UFO phenomenon without having some desire for scientific study. In 1969, as stated in chapter 7, Sagan played a major role in the American Association for the Advancement of Science (AAAS) UFO Symposium. He and Thornton Page fought for the symposium and were felt by Menzel and Condon to be pro ETH. The truth was that Menzel and Condon were the radicals and Page and Sagan approached the subject with real scientific curiosity. The statement by Sagan below is quite telling and also puzzling because it seems to contradict Sagan's later statements on extraterrestrials visiting Earth.

> *It now seems quite clear that Earth is not the only inhabited planet. There is evidence that the bulk of the stars in the sky have planetary systems. Recent research concerning the origin of life on Earth suggests that the physical and chemical processes leading to the origin of life occur rapidly in the early history of the majority of planets. The selective value of intelligence and technical civilization is obvious, and it seems likely that a large number of planets within our Milky Way galaxy—perhaps as many as a million—are inhabited by technical civilizations in advance of our own. Interstellar space flight is far beyond our present technical capabilities, but there seems to be no fundamental physical objections to preclude, from our own vantage point, the possibility of its development by other civilizations. (Sagan 1963)*

It could be that Sagan, like Menzel, was on the inside of the group but I think that is unlikely. Also, Sagan unlike the others really had more of an open mind on the subject of UFOs and treated it fairly, although he publicly, especially in later years, wrote off the extraterrestrial hypothesis. At this point I can't document my belief that Sagan knew far more about UFOs and an extraterrestrial presence than he admitted, but the last sentence in his statement is a clue. As stated above, I don't think he was an insider who used his gentle and compelling manner to promote debunking the ETH. On the other hand, the feeling continues to nag me that Sagan may have also led a Menzel-type double life.

McGaha and Nye are not the only debunkers active today; there are many more including *Skeptic* magazine's Michael Shermer, or to a lesser degree SETI Institute's affable Seth Shostak. There is one characteristic shared with each debunker: the call for hard evidence in the form of a craft, an alien, alive or dead I suppose, a piece of a craft, or as Seth Shostak has said, even an ashtray from a craft to prove they exist. These requests or demands bring two things to mind. First, there are scientific theories of things that scientists embrace as existing but have never touched or seen. Black holes come to mind. None of these debunkers has ever touched a black hole or seen one but they believe they exist. Astrophysicists who search for black holes use indirect observations but they know they exist. However, thousands, probably hundreds of thousands, of reliable witnesses, including almost all the world-renowned scientists working in New Mexico in the late 40s and 50s, have seen flying saucers and UFOs and a few have even touched them. This, then, is obviously imposing a double set of standards to reject a scientific issue on which they won't even take the time to do the most basic of research.

My second thought is that the debunker who wants solid evidence, evidence that they can touch, only needs to get the proper security clearance, then have the need to know and they'll have all the hard evidence they could possibly want. It exists. It's locked away and guarded somewhere—S-4 (a highly classified part of Area 51), Dugway, Wright-Patterson, who knows, but it does exist.

How refreshing it would be for a debunker to take the time, make the effort, to become truly knowledgeable of the UFO issue and then debate from a position of strength and knowledge. On the other hand if they did, as Allen Hynek did, they most likely would no longer be debunkers.

DISCUSSION

At the beginning of this book I stated that UFOs do exist and went on to describe what I considered a true UFO or flying saucer. It is my hope that the casual observer, the agnostic, and the skeptic will at least have a better understanding of this fascinating phenomenon, and will view the subject with an open mind.

This book has not solved the UFO riddle but hopefully it has put a very complicated issue into a better perspective by viewing UFOs using presidential administrations as a connecting thread from World War II to the present. In taking this approach I focused on the core issue, which is the unquestionable fact that UFOs, that is, aerial objects that perform beyond known laws of physics, exist.

In my attempt to establish this as fact we have touched on a number of issues.

First, I have tried to include what I feel are some of the best sightings and UFO events of the World War II and postwar eras. Since the better events also seem to involve better-quality witnesses, we have the dual advantage of studying remarkable UFO events that are well reported.

There is little question that at the top of the list is Roswell, and the list of quality witnesses is impressive. Unfortunately, the passage of time is rapidly reducing the number of those witnesses still with us.

Roswell is unique in a number of ways and one of the most notable is that with the large number of witnesses that have come forward, and documented evidence that has been uncovered, the burden of proof to establish whether it was an extraterrestrial event or something prosaic is no longer on the researcher, but rather it's on the government. They have had sixty-seven years to disprove the mountain of evidence accumulated by researchers and have succeeded in only making their position worse with each attempt. When you consider that the Air Force has had at least three different stories of what took place at Corona, New Mexico, in 1947, and over the years have presented thousands of pages of documents, their story only becomes weaker. The fact is they only need to provide one document, one official document stating or authorizing troops to clean up Project Mogul debris on the Foster ranch, a document that would now be declassified. Make no mistake, there was a cleanup by troops, that's a given, and make no mistake, there was paperwork generated to authorize that cleanup. I was in the precomputer military and I know that nothing happened without paperwork. It could be a simple hand receipt or something more involved, be it nonclassified, classified confidential, secret, top-secret, or a top-secret code word. As far as Roswell, the ball is in the court of the Air Force to produce that one simple document.

Second, we have discussed the skeptics and their legitimate question: Where is the evidence? To the skeptics I say you only need to have an open mind and look around, look at the facts. With that thought in mind let us take a look at the Fermi Paradox.

In 1950, the great physicist, Enrico Fermi, was working at Los Alamos National Laboratory in New Mexico. One day, while walking to lunch, he was discussing with Edward Teller, Herbert York, and Emil Konopinski the rash of recent UFO sightings in the area that most of the scientists had seen. The discussion turned to the probability of faster-than-light travel and Fermi is said to have asked Teller, "Edward, what do you believe the odds are for something material achieving faster-than-light travel within the next ten years?" Teller replied, "One in a million." Fermi countered, "I think it's much lower, perhaps one in ten." The debate continued as they walked on to lunch.

Later over lunch, and out of the blue, Fermi asked, "Where are they?" Everyone laughed because they knew that he was asking about extraterrestrial life. The conversation continued on, discussing that the closest living beings may be very far away indeed since planet Earth is in the boondocks of our galaxy, far, far away from its teeming galactic center.

York remembers that Fermi, known for his ability to make accurate calculations from minimal data, began to make calculations on the probability of earthlike planets, the probability of life on these planets, the number of suns, and so on.[3] His conclusion was that "we ought to have been visited long ago and many times over."

Fermi had another trait that enters into this discussion, especially with his students. He would pose questions to promote thought. Now, it's important to remember that the conversation and Fermi's comments, now referred to as the Fermi Paradox, started with the discussions of what was then called the flying saucer phenomenon so prevalent in New Mexico at that time. There have been a number of interpretations of what he was asking and skeptics say he meant that since none are here, they don't exist. I think that view is incorrect and stems from not looking at the facts, a practice not uncommon to many scientists when addressing this subject.

It seems odd to me as a nonscientist but merely a researcher that Fermi's statement is in many cases not viewed in the context it was made. When the dots are connected, after discussing flying saucers, then asking the Fermi Paradox followed by his calculations and resulting statement that "we ought to have been visited long ago and many times over," I believe he was saying that in all probability they are here and have been here from the beginning of the written word. The facts are present to make the case if one only takes the time to look. From biblical times we have the story of Ezekiel's Wheel, the pyramids, Easter Island, or perhaps the greatest ancient mystery of all, Puma Punku in Bolivia. The list is long and compelling and it has its skeptics and debunkers, the Galileoites. Of course, Galileo was really very lucky: he was confined to his home for believing the Earth revolved around the sun. Giordano Bruno not only believed the Earth revolved around the sun but wrote that there were other planets throughout the universe where life existed. He was burned at the stake.

Were we seeded on this young planet at the direction of the deity by ancient astronauts? If so, it doesn't run counter to religious beliefs but supports most religious teachings. Perhaps that thinking is a little over the top for some so I'll let that rest for now.

We again look at the debunkers who want a saucer to land on the White House lawn or in the Kremlin in order to believe. They, and many in science, expect our visiting neighbors to act as we do. If these visitors are thousands or even a million or more years advanced than *Homo sapiens* they understand the consequences of initial contact. This would be a turning point in history and their seemingly bizarre actions may be a conditioning phase before contact is made. Sixty years ago the White House lawn landing would have caused panic and bedlam. Today polls show that well over half of the population accepts the existence of ETs as fact and the proverbial White House lawn landing, although unsettling, would not cause the panic of sixty years ago.

If Fermi believed as I believe he did—they are here and have been coming here according to Fermi's calculations—there is no paradox and never has been. We are being conditioned to accept the reality of advanced extraterrestrial life and a whole new understanding of the physical world.

Third, we must discuss who or what they are, where they come from, and most important, what are their intentions. Unfortunately we don't have the answers to these questions, only speculation. The extraterrestrial hypothesis remains for many the most likely explanation for the phenomena. Well-known and highly respected nuclear physicist Stanton T. Friedman flatly states that after over fifty years of studying and lecturing on the subject, he is convinced we are being visited by an extraterrestrial presence.

To address the question of where they come from, Friedman believes that the research done by Kathleen Marden and himself on the Betty (Marden's aunt) and Barney Hill abduction case indicates the alien abductors were from the Zeta Reticuli star system. If all of this sounds like pure science fiction, it must be realized that this case was studied in great detail and the Zeta Reticuli system is well within our galactic neighborhood, only a little over thirty-nine light-years from Earth. Also, the Hills went through many hypnotic sessions with the highly respected Dr. Benjamin Simon of Boston. Betty Hill's hypnotic recount of a star map she was shown during her abduction by her alien abductor, and its years of recreation by the late Marjorie Fish, points to the Zeta Reticuli binary star system. It is a fascinating story that is told in detail by Kathleen Marden and coauthor Stanton Friedman in *Captured! The Betty and Barney Hill UFO Experience.*

There are a number of other theories to explain flying saucers, UFOs, or UAP (unidentified aerial phenomena). Time travel from the future is often mentioned, and string theory and the idea of a multidimensional universe is gaining support in the scientific community. Not being a scientist, I personally still embrace Occam's razor, which directs me to the ETH. This is a belief that I've held for many years and, as the evidence continues to mount, I have become more open with my belief in my writings and talks.

I'm often asked how I can justify that extraterrestrial visitors, maybe thousands or millions of years more advanced than humans, can fly across the vastness of space only to crash their craft when they reach Earth and then leave their dead to be recovered and examined. A very reasonable question, and my answer is based on observations of others and simple logic: These extraterrestrial craft are very advanced probes, much like our probes sent to Mars, and come from the huge motherships so often reported. The occupants are living engineered entities that are simply part of the crafts' operating systems; they are robots or androids and they are expendable. Again, this is speculation, but I believe the best evidence we now have points in that direction.

The question of why they are here is the least speculative. As we humans advance in our technological knowledge, so does their interest in us and the possibility of our own destruction or perhaps harm to others beyond our planet. The explosion of UFO sightings after the development of atomic weapons and the interest UFOs seem to have in our nuclear development goes to reinforce this belief. The interest this phenomenon has shown in our nuclear arms and nuclear power plants has been documented throughout this book. Also, many abductees, or experiencers as they are known in UFOlogy, state that their alien abductors have expressed a concern about our stewardship of the planet, as shown in Dr. John Mack's interview with the children in Zimbabwe. More chilling, of course, are the stories of the medical procedures, many sexual in nature, that have been performed on experiencers. On the surface at least this seems less than a benevolent presence.

Fourth, we have the question of the government of the United States and its involvement in a cover-up of knowledge of an extra-terrestrial presence. On this subject, volumes could be written. What appears certain: There was or is a control group buried within CIA counterintelligence or a part of CIA counterintelligence that has operational control over UFO issues. In researching this subject I have become acquainted with several former CIA personnel who retired to the Chesapeake Bay area where I live. I've asked each about their knowledge of two former intelligence operatives discussed in chapter 3, Art Lundahl and James Jesus Angleton. All were very familiar with Lundahl, who was considered the guru of photo interpretation. However, none had heard of Angleton, although he had a long and distinguished career at the CIA, eventually becoming deputy director and head of counterintelligence under Allen Dulles. He remained in that position until 1974 and, at the peak of his power, had an enormous budget and as many as three hundred employees working for him. As head of counterintelligence, he answered only to the DCI, had great autonomy, and was virtually unknown to most in the intelligence community. If there was/is a control group, Angleton, if not a member, would certainly have had some level of operational authority at the discretion of the group.

When we consider the high-security code word classification and compartmentalization of secrets covering the entire UFO/ETH/crash retrieval subject, it has made any definitive proof of what the government knows of this subject almost impossible to uncover. We have many tantalizing bits of evidence, such as Canadian Wilbert Smith's papers. Smith was a Canadian radio engineer who was highly thought of within the Canadian government. Smith, among other things, was a high-level UFO researcher for the Canadian government. In a meeting in the U.S. with high-level military officers, he was told that UFO issues were the most highly classified subject in the United States, even higher than the hydrogen bomb. Smith made the following statement in a Department of Transportation memo on geo-magnetics in 1950:

> The matter is the most highly classified subject in the United States Government, rating higher even than the H bomb. Flying saucers exist. Their modus operandi is unknown but a concentrated effort is being made by a small group headed by Dr. Vannevar Bush. The entire matter is considered by the United States authorities to be of tremendous significance.[4]

UFOS AND THE SCIENTIFIC COMMUNITY

Many late evenings I've sat alone with my thoughts, pondering at length in the dark and quiet of the night, just what I wanted this book to achieve. I thought of how I wanted to express what I've learned on my personal journey and research into what will be the greatest story in the history of mankind. I contemplated what the discovery of highly advanced intelligent life in the universe will mean to humanity and how to cover so many complicated issues in one book.

In those quiet hours I often lamented my lack of scientific education, a youth squandered on frivolous things instead of applying myself to the study of things that I now want so desperately to understand. But always I would end up pondering the thought that higher education to some can be a box that prevents free thinking.

Perhaps the reason that many in the scientific community reject the ETH is that they are afraid of it; they fear that a higher intelligence with unknown laws of physics will invalidate all they have studied, all the papers and theses they have written, and all they have taught for so many years. Unfortunately there is a historical basis and reality to this thought. To paraphrase the great German physicist Max Planck, "Science advances one funeral at a time."

Of course there are many scientists, many Ph.D.s, who are deeply involved in UFO research and understand that the UFO phenomenon is a true scientific subject. It's so many of those on the outside of UFOlogy that reject scientific examination or even rational discussion of the phenomenon that is so puzzling to those who have made an effort to study the subject. One notable exception is the highly respected theoretical physicist, Dr. Michio Kaku. Although Dr. Kaku states that he has no solid evidence that any UFOs are extraterrestrial in origin, he admonishes all to keep an open mind and not rule out that possibility. He has also stated that there is no acceptable explanation for many UFO events such as the Japan Air Lines Flight 1628 incident, the Tehran UFO incident, or the Belgian Wave of UFO sightings. All of these events involved visual sightings, radar contact, and electronic interference. The views of one of the most highly respected and brilliant scientists of our time are in sharp contrast to the debunkers mentioned earlier. Dr. Kaku thinks outside the box and is perfectly willing to admit where he has been wrong and where others, including Einstein, have been wrong. It seems that brilliance and an open mind are the signs of genius.

Throughout human history there have been landmark events that changed the course of human civilization: fire, the wheel, the written word, electricity, and so on. Each of these in their time could be considered the greatest event in the history of mankind. It is said that the discovery, or the disclosure of extraterrestrial life, will be the next greatest event in the history of mankind. It most certainly will change all of us forever. That is a fact, but it will also be temporary. As we move well into the twenty-first century and expand on our infantile exploration of our solar system, the galaxy, and the universe we will discover unimagined wonders and physical laws beyond comprehension. The existence of extraterrestrial life throughout the universe will be accepted and soon overshadowed by wonders beyond imagination.

FINAL THOUGHTS

This book represents over fifty years of personal study into what I consider the most fascinating story of all mankind. Most of the time it has been a rewarding effort mixed with great frustration, but I would, and will, continue my work as there is much more to be learned and said.

Do we have recovered alien craft and are those secrets being withheld from the public? If we reflect back on what President Roosevelt said in 1942 on the recovery of alien intelligence, "The information is vital to the nation's superiority and must remain within the confines of state secrets," we can appreciate that this was a different time, a time of war and, in some respects, a time of innocence. What President Roosevelt started and what President

Truman initiated post–World War II was a necessary and right thing to do. But emerging from the war as the world's leader, we lost our innocence in the atomic age, the doctrine of mutual assured destruction, and the amassed power of the military-industrial complex. President Eisenhower recognized the shift in power and saw the potential for great abuse to the public's interest. He warned us of this problem, but his warning went unheeded. As our scientific knowledge and achievements grew exponentially so did the potential for great wealth, and more importantly great power. In many cases it was used wisely, but in some cases it was not.

I suppose the argument can be made that if we are in possession of secrets of advanced physics obtained from a highly advanced race of extraterrestrials, they should remain secrets of the state, as Roosevelt said. That's a compelling argument if one wants to continue to move on as a country in a world of warring combatants. Perhaps Ronald Reagan, who many elitists feel was below their intellectual level, was far ahead of his time when he said "wouldn't the world unite as one to repel and attack from outside our world." In reality it would not have to be a threat of attack from outside our world, but a desire by a benevolent advanced intelligence from outside our world, intelligence more closely tied to our human development than we understand, to see all mankind on this planet living in harmony as one people. That may be a pipe dream, as all sovereign states wish to retain their independence, a feeling I also embrace, but one that I think may be necessary for the survival of the human race.

My great disappointment is in the realization that my government, or rather a small group that consists of high-level government bureaucrats and a select few in industry, have taken control of this scientific phenomenon and have been successful in concealing it from the public with disinformation, threats, and lies. If anyone still doubts this conclusion, I suggest they study in depth the work of the Robertson Panel of 1953 and the Colorado Project and resulting Condon Report of 1969. These two projects, or more specifically the project reports, form the core of biased and unscientific research for the government. Research initiated by certain elements within the military to take a subject of serious scientific value, that they were incapable of understanding and afraid to face, and turning it into a farce. This farce caused most in the scientific community to shun it and the population in general to view it as a subject only embraced by fools, imbeciles, and fringe radicals.

There is one other possibility for concealment of the phenomenon, and that is that the truth is simply too frightening to be revealed to the public, or the revelations would be destructive to the world order as we know it. I don't believe that to be the case as the facts don't point in that direction, but I have an open mind to any possibility.

I don't have the answers to this phenomenon, but I do know that the handling of the issue by our government and elements of the military continues to be a despicable disgrace to the people of the United States and the world population in general. It is time, past time, for our government to at least open its files in a controlled manner. If the information on the UFO issue is being tightly held and controlled by a very small group buried deep within the government, then the government should remove the security restrictions on all participants in UFO research and UFO encounters and let them tell their stories. An extraterrestrial presence is a matter of nature and the citizens have a right to know.

I'm not advocating a blanket disclosure of all the knowledge we possess, as I am sure that there is advanced technological information important to national defense that should remain highly classified. I am advocating that our government disclose the existence of an extraterrestrial presence because, as stated above, it is a fact of nature. We disclosed we had atomic weapons when they were used to end the war in Japan, but we did not disclose technical details except on a very limited basis. Almost seventy years later, we are still learning the details of the development of this weapon. Unfortunately we are still a world of warring nations, and the security of national secrets is important to our national defense.

There are people who do know some parts of the secret, people who have been involved as members of the military or the scientific community who have stories to tell, but because of their security agreements have remained quiet, but so desperately want to tell their stories. People like Dr. Milton Torres discussed in chapter 2. I am personally available to anyone who wishes to come forward with their involvement in the UFO issue.

To any who wish to do so, either openly or anonymously, I can be contacted through my Web site or e-mail at larryhol combe1@gmail.com.

List of Terms

AFB—Air Force base

ATIC—Air Technical Intelligence Center at Wright-Patterson Air Force Base

DoD—Department of Defense

EBD—Eisenhower Briefing Document

EBE—extraterrestrial biological entity

ET—extraterrestrial

ETH—extraterrestrial hypothesis

flying saucer—a true UFO believed by many to be extraterrestrial

NICAP—National Investigations Committee on Aerial Phenomenon

SOM 1-01—Majestic 12 group Special Operations Manual

UAP—unidentified aerial phenomenon

UFO—unidentified flying object

UFOB—early Air Force designation for UFO

Appendices

TOP SECRET
EYES ONLY
THE WHITE HOUSE
WASHINGTON

September 24, 1947.

MEMORANDUM FOR THE SECRETARY OF DEFENSE

Dear Secretary Forrestal:

As per our recent conversation on this matter, you are hereby authorized to proceed with all due speed and caution upon your undertaking. Hereafter this matter shall be referred to only as Operation Majestic Twelve.

It continues to be my feeling that any future considerations relative to the ultimate disposition of this matter should rest solely with the Office of the President following appropriate discussions with yourself, Dr. Bush and the Director of Central Intelligence.

TOP SECRET
EYES ONLY

(Courtesy of Dr. Robert Wood and Ryan Wood, www.majesticdocuments.com.)

TOP SECRET / MAJIC

EYES ONLY

NATIONAL SECURITY INFORMATION

****
* TOP SECRET *
****

EYES ONLY   COPY <u>ONE</u> OF <u>ONE</u>.

BRIEFING DOCUMENT: OPERATION MAJESTIC 12

PREPARED FOR PRESIDENT-ELECT DWIGHT D. EISENHOWER: (EYES ONLY)

18 NOVEMBER, 1952

<u>WARNING</u>: This is a TOP SECRET - EYES ONLY document containing compartmentalized information essential to the national security of the United States. EYES ONLY ACCESS to the material herein is strictly limited to those possessing Majestic-12 clearance level. Reproduction in any form or the taking of written or mechanically transcribed notes is strictly forbidden.

****
* TOP SECRET *

TOP SECRET / MAJIC   T52-EXEMPT (E)

EYES ONLY   EYES ONLY   00

EYES ONLY

COPY <u>ONE</u> OF <u>ONE</u>.

SUBJECT: OPERATION MAJESTIC-12 PRELIMINARY BRIEFING FOR
   PRESIDENT-ELECT EISENHOWER.

DOCUMENT PREPARED 18 NOVEMBER, 1952.

BRIEFING OFFICER: ADM. ROSCOE H. HILLENKOETTER (MJ-1)

NOTE: This document has been prepared as a preliminary briefing
only. It should be regarded as introductory to a full operations
briefing intended to follow.

    * * * * * *

OPERATION MAJESTIC-12 is a TOP SECRET Research and Development/
Intelligence operation responsible directly and only to the
President of the United States. Operations of the project are
carried out under control of the Majestic-12 (Majic-12) Group
which was established by special classified executive order of
President Truman on 24 September, 1947, upon recommendation by
Dr. Vannevar Bush and Secretary James Forrestal. (See Attachment
"A".) Members of the Majestic-12 Group were designated as follows:

        Adm. Roscoe H. Hillenkoetter
        Dr. Vannevar Bush
        Secy. James V. Forrestal*
        Gen. Nathan F. Twining
        Gen. Hoyt S. Vandenberg
        Dr. Detlev Bronk
        Dr. Jerome Hunsaker
        Mr. Sidney W. Souers
        Mr. Gordon Gray
        Dr. Donald Menzel
        Gen. Robert M. Montague
        Dr. Lloyd V. Berkner

The death of Secretary Forrestal on 22 May, 1949, created
a vacancy which remained unfilled until 01 August, 1950, upon
which date Gen. Walter B. Smith was designated as permanent
replacement.

****
* TOP SECRET *
****

TOP SECRET / MAJIC
EYES ONLY

EYES ONLY

T52-EXEMPT (E)

002

```
* TOP SECRET *
**************
```

COPY ONE OF ONE.

On 24 June, 1947, a civilian pilot flying over the Cascade
Mountains in the State of Washington observed nine flying
disc-shaped aircraft traveling in formation at a high rate
of speed. Although this was not the first known sighting
of such objects, it was the first to gain widespread attention
in the public media. Hundreds of reports of sightings of
similar objects followed. Many of these came from highly
credible military and civilian sources. These reports resulted in independent efforts by several different elements
of the military to ascertain the nature and purpose of these
objects in the interests of national defense. A number of
witnesses were interviewed and there were several unsuccessful
attempts to utilize aircraft in efforts to pursue reported
discs in flight. Public reaction bordered on near hysteria
at times.

In spite of these efforts, little of substance was learned
about the objects until a local rancher reported that one
had crashed in a remote region of New Mexico located approximately seventy-five miles northwest of Roswell Army Air
Base (now Walker Field).

On 07 July, 1947, a secret operation was begun to assure
recovery of the wreckage of this object for scientific study.
During the course of this operation, aerial reconnaissance
discovered that four small human-like beings had apparently
ejected from the craft at some point before it exploded.
These had fallen to earth about two miles east of the wreckage
site. All four were dead and badly decomposed due to action
by predators and exposure to the elements during the approximately one week time period which had elapsed before their
discovery. A special scientific team took charge of removing
these bodies for study. (See Attachment "C".) The wreckage
of the craft was also removed to several different locations.
(See Attachment "B".) Civilian and military witnesses in
the area were debriefed, and news reporters were given the
effective cover story that the object had been a misguided
weather research balloon.

```
**************
* TOP SECRET *
**************
```

* TOP SECRET *

COPY ONE OF ONE.

A covert analytical effort organized by Gen. Twining and
Dr. Bush acting on the direct orders of the President, resulted in a preliminary concensus (19 September, 1947) that
the disc was most likely a short range reconnaissance craft.
This conclusion was based for the most part on the craft's
size and the apparent lack of any identifiable provisioning.
(See Attachment "D".) A similar analysis of the four dead
occupants was arranged by Dr. Bronk. It was the tentative
conclusion of this group (30 November, 1947) that although
these creatures are human-like in appearance, the biological
and evolutionary processes responsible for their development
has apparently been quite different from those observed or
postulated in homo-sapiens. Dr. Bronk's team has suggested
the term "Extra-terrestrial Biological Entities", or "EBEs",
he adopted as the standard term of reference for these
creatures until such time as a more definitive designation
can be agreed upon.

Since it is virtually certain that these craft do not originate in any country on earth, considerable speculation has
centered around what their point of origin might be and how
they get here. Mars was and remains a possibility, although
some scientists, most notably Dr. Menzel, consider it more
likely that we are dealing with beings from another solar
system entirely.

Numerous examples of what appear to be a form of writing
were found in the wreckage. Efforts to decipher these have
remained largely unsuccessful. (See Attachment "E".)
Equally unsuccessful have been efforts to determine the
method of propulsion or the nature or method of transmission
of the power source involved. Research along these lines
has been complicated by the complete absence of identifiable
wings, propellers, jets, or other conventional methods of
propulsion and guidance, as well as a total lack of metallic
wiring, vacuum tubes, or similar recognizable electronic
components. (See Attachment "F".) It is assumed that the
propulsion unit was completely destroyed by the explosion
which caused the crash.

* TOP SECRET *

```
**************
* TOP SECRET *
**************
```

EYES ONLY   COPY ONE OF ONE.

A need for as much additional information as possible about
these craft, their performance characteristics and their
purpose led to the undertaking known as U.S. Air Force Project
SIGN in December, 1947. In order to preserve security, liason
between SIGN and Majestic-12 was limited to two individuals
within the Intelligence Division of Air Materiel Command whose
role was to pass along certain types of information through
channels. SIGN evolved into Project GRUDGE in December, 1948.
The operation is currently being conducted under the code name
BLUE BOOK, with liason maintained through the Air Force officer
who is head of the project.

On 06 December, 1950, a second object, probably of similar
origin, impacted the earth at high speed in the El Indio -
Guerrero area of the Texas - Mexican boder after following
a long trajectory through the atmosphere. By the time a
search team arrived, what remained of the object had been almost
totally incinerated. Such material as could be recovered was
transported to the A.E.C. facility at Sandia, New Mexico, for
study.

Implications for the National Security are of continuing importance in that the motives and ultimate intentions of these
visitors remain completely unknown. In addition, a significant
upsurge in the surveillance activity of these craft beginning
in May and continuing through the autumn of this year has caused
considerable concern that new developments may be imminent.
It is for these reasons, as well as the obvious international
and technological considerations and the ultimate need to
avoid a public panic at all costs, that the Majestic-12 Group
remains of the unanimous opinion that imposition of the
strictest security precautions should continue without inter-
ruption into the new administration. At the same time, contingency plan MJ-1949-04P/78 (Top Secret - Eyes Only) should
be held in continued readiness should the need to make a
public announcement present itself. (See Attachment "G".)


```
**************
* TOP SECRET *
```

TOP SECRET / MAJIC
EYES ONLY

EYES ONLY

T52-EXEMPT (E)

* * * * * * * * * * * * *
* TOP SECRET *
* * * * * * * * * * * * *

EYES ONLY   COPY ONE OF ONE.

ENUMERATION OF ATTACHMENTS:

*ATTACHMENT "A".......Special Classified Executive
                Order #092447. (TS/EO)

*ATTACHMENT "B".......Operation Majestic-12 Status
                Report #1, Part A. 30 NOV '47.
                (TS-MAJIC/EO)

*ATTACHMENT "C".......Operation Majestic-12 Status
                Report #1, Part B. 30 NOV '47.
                (TS-MAJIC/EO)

*ATTACHMENT "D".......Operation Majestic-12 Preliminary
                Analytical Report. 19 SEP '47.
                (TS-MAJIC/EO)

*ATTACHMENT "E".......Operation Majestic-12 Blue Team
                Report #5. 30 JUN '52.
                (TS-MAJIC/EO)

*ATTACHMENT "F".......Operation Majestic-12 Status
                Report #2. 31 JAN '48.
                (TS-MAJIC/EO)

*ATTACHMENT "G".......Operation Majestic-12 Contingency
                Plan MJ-1949-04P/78: 31 JAN '49.
                (TS-MAJIC/EO)

*ATTACHMENT "H".......Operation Majestic-12, Maps and
                Photographs Folio (Extractions).
                (TS-MAJIC/EO)

*From
Twining Files
Lib. of Congress
SFriedman*

THE WHITE HOUSE
WASHINGTON

July 13, 1953

TOP SECRET
Security Information

MEMORANDUM FOR GENERAL TWINING

The President expects you to attend the Extraordinary
Meeting of the National Security Council in the Broadcast
Room of the White House, Thursday, July 16, at 9:00 A.M.
The program will be explained in detail at the meeting.
It is advisable not to plan any other engagements before
6:00 P.M. on that day.

Due to the nature of the Meeting, it is necessary to
take special security precautions and to maintain absolute
secrecy regarding participation in, as well as the substance
of, the Meeting. It is requested that you enter the White
House grounds via the Southeast Entrance not later than
8:45 A.M. and descend from your car at the South (Diplomatic)
Entrance of the Mansion. Your car should be discharged and
not wait anywhere in the vicinity of the White House.

The President expects you to lunch with him at the
White House at 12:30 P.M.

*Note:
STF*

In order to avoid communication on this subject, it is
understood that in the absence of contrary word your concur-
rence in the above arrangements is assumed.

ROBERT CUTLER
Special Assistant
to the President

EYES ONLY

TOP SECRET
Security Information

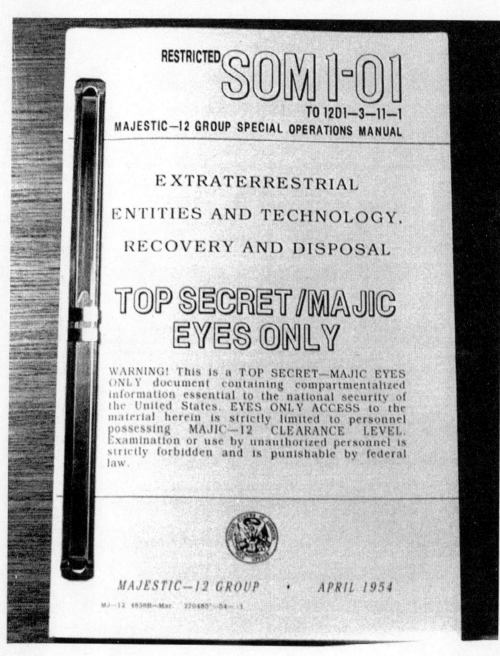

RESTRICTED

SOM 1-01

TO 12D1—3—11—1

MAJESTIC—12 GROUP SPECIAL OPERATIONS MANUAL

EXTRATERRESTRIAL

ENTITIES AND TECHNOLOGY,

RECOVERY AND DISPOSAL

TOP SECRET/MAJIC
EYES ONLY

WARNING! This is a TOP SECRET—MAJIC EYES ONLY document containing compartmentalized information essential to the national security of the United States. EYES ONLY ACCESS to the material herein is strictly limited to personnel possessing MAJIC—12 CLEARANCE LEVEL. Examination or use by unauthorized personnel is strictly forbidden and is punishable by federal law.

MAJESTIC—12 GROUP • *APRIL 1954*

MJ—12 4838B—Mar. 270460°—04—:1

Envelope to Tim Cooper mailed from FOIA Office, Fort Meade, Maryland, containing the declassified Bowen manuscript.

(Courtesy of Dr. Robert Wood and Ryan Wood, www.majesticdocuments.com.)

Vernon Bowen
51 Keofferam Road   1947-1955
Old Greenwich, Conn

120 Woodside Drive
Milbrook   1955-1959
Greenwich, Conn.

26 Shore Acre Drive   1959-
Old Greenwich, Conn. Present

AN ENCYCLOPAEDIA
OF FLYING SAUCERS

AN ENCYCLOPAEDIA
OF FLYING SAUCERS

THE HIGHEST CLASSIFICATION FOR THIS DOCUMENT
IS TOP SECRET/MAJIC NOFORN DISSEM. FOR US
"EYES ONLY". EXEMPT FROM DECLASSIFICATION
ORADA. "SPECIAL HANDLING REQUIRED—NOT
RELEASABLE TO FOREIGN NATIONALS"

by VERNON BOWEN

By

VERNON BOWEN

Other writings by
Vernon Bowen

<u>Children's Books</u>

THE LAZY BEAVER
THE WONDERFUL ADVENTURES OF TING LING
SNOW FOR CHRISTMAS
THE EMPEROR'S WHITE HORSES
(All published by David McKay Co.)
<u>Records</u> (Collaborations)

THE LITTLE TUNE THAT RAN AWAY (DECCA)
LITTLE TOMMY TINKLE (SIMON & SCHUSTER GIANT GOLDEN RECORD)

Interpretive material added by Dr. Robert M. Wood

Cover sheet from the Bowen manuscript with a top-secret Majic stamp

an orb twice the size of the **TOP SECRET/MAJIC** in the sky, a
strange blip on a radarscope, a cone-shaped object, a vague glow
in the sky, a cigar-shaped figure, or a splash of light like a
comet's tail. These dissimilar objects are converted, with the
flick of a typewriter, into saucers."

In considering all of the writing on saucers, it would
be interesting to know how many of the writers—or, for that matter,
how many of the sighters of so-called saucers—have read Charles Fort.

Is it conceivable that their writing—or their eyesight—
might have been affected by their reading of him?

But such a question is obviously absurd. The idea of
a hoax, started and continued by readers of Charles Fort, or by
members of the Fortean Society, is untenable. Too many people,
people who could only have heard of, or read the writings of Charles
Fort by the wildest of coincidences, especially among the European
peasantry, have reported seeing unknown objects, both in the skies,
and landed on earth. And thousands of people have seen these objects—
at least, the ones in the sky—at one time.

Such reasoning might lead to the asking of another question:
Are Major Keyhoe, Ray Palmer, Kenneth Arnold, George Adamski, Harold T.
Wilkinson, Donald E. Menzel, Frank Scully—and all other writers on the
subject of saucers—counter espionage agents for the U.S.Government?
Are all of them, by official directive, muddying-up the greatest
cover-up job of modern times?

Such a question is equally absurd in the light of the record,
in the light of the fact that saucers—or of things with the same
attributes of saucers—**TOP SECRET/MAJIC** centuries, if not for
milennia.

A page from the manuscript with a mention of Donald Menzel and a handwritten note in the border about hoping he keeps his mouth shut

Inconceivable is the possibility of hoax when you read such items as this: In The New York Herald Tribune for December 3, 1954, there appeared an editorial about a meteorite that ripped through the roof of the house of Mrs. ~~Howard~~ Hewlett Hodges of Sylacauga, Alabama, striking her on the ~~left/left~~ hip and hand. ~~The~~ USAF reportedly requested the meteorite for study. The World Telegram & Sun, in an article the same day, said that the rock was being studied at Wright-Patterson Air Force Base, Dayton, Ohio. That's headquarters for saucer investigations. Later, in the February 13, 1955, issue of American Weekly, Mrs. Hodges, writing as Ann Elizabeth Hodges, stated that one of the policeman who called at her house following Mrs. Hodges' call to them "explained that all police departments throughout the country were under orders to turn over to the Air Force any object that fell from the skies~~//~~ ." It is hardly conceivable that USAF would issue such an order--unless it expected something could fall from the skies.

        And here's another one: At least twice in 1954, Dorothy Kilgallen, in her column in The New York Journal American, had cryptic remarks. One: " Is it possible that new peeps through the telescope on Mt. Palomar indicate that many a scientist--and textbook--could have been wrong about the universe? " And again, in her column Broadway Bulletin Board, on November 15, 1954, Miss Kilgallen stated that "a Harvard professor is telling his classes that he can prove that there are people on other planets."

        These things don't sound much like hoax.

        Nor does this one:

TOP SECRET/MAJIC

[Handwritten marginal notes: "Highly dubious source information"; "What is DM doing?"]

A page from the manuscript referencing Dorothy Kilgallen with border notes asking, "What is DM doing?"

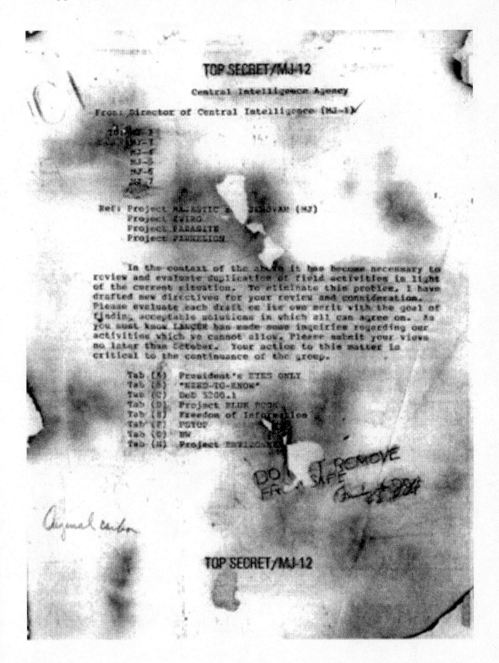

Note that the memo was sent to MJ-2 through MJ-7, indicating not all MJ-12 members were in agreement.

(Courtesy Dr. Robert Wood and Ryan Wood, www.majesticdocuments.com.)

Appendix G—The most chilling of the Burned Memo documents

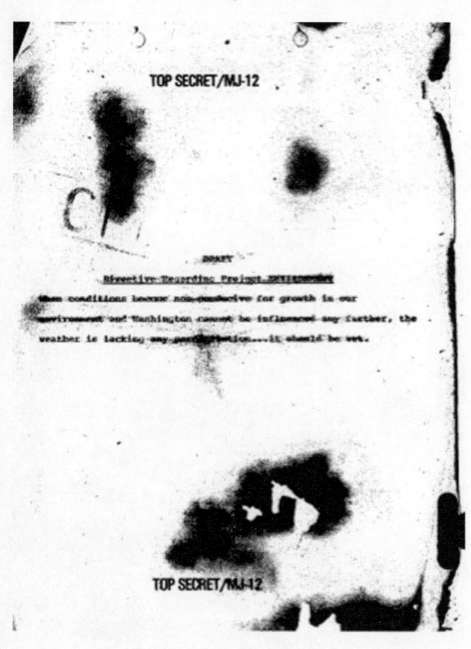

The reference to "wet" is a code name for assassination.

(Courtesy of Dr. Robert Wood, and Ryan Wood. www.majesticdocuments.com.)

NATIONAL INVESTIGATIONS COMMITTEE
ON AERIAL PHENOMENA
WASHINGTON, D. C. 20036

MAJOR DONALD E. KEYHOE
USMC (RET.) DIRECTOR

GORDON I. R. LORE, JR.
ASSISTANT DIRECTOR

ADMINISTRATIVE OFFICES
1536 CONNECTICUT AVE., N.W.

30 April 1968

TELEPHONE: (202) 667-9434

The Honorable Lyndon B. Johnson
President of the United States
The White House
Washington, D.C.

Dear Mr. President:

We believe it our duty to submit to you the enclosed evidence of
grave deficiencies in the University of Colorado UFO investigation,
financed by the Air Force with $523,000 of taxpayers' money, which
was publicly and officially announced as a totally objective scientific study.

Our knowledge is based on 17 months of close cooperation, at the
Colorado Project's request. During this time we briefed and fre-
quently conferred with Dr. E.U. Condon, project head, Mr. Robert J.
Low, project coordinator, and the project scientists. Our investigating subcommittees, located throughout the country, aided in the
training and operations of Project field teams. From our thousands
of UFO reports, we released hundreds of cases at the project's request, many of them verified reports by scientists, veteran pilots,
aerospace engineers, tower and radar operators and other competent
observers. To help the project weed out hoaxes and unfounded claims
of meetings with extraterrestrial beings, we privately briefed its
members. Project scientists frequently visited and examined information at NICAP, which is the world's largest UFO fact-finding organization, with over 300 scientific, military and technical advisers.

In the Air Force-Colorado University contract (copy enclosed), Dr.
Condon was named as the first principal investigator. Despite this,
Dr. Condon has not made a single field investigation. He has not
interviewed any of the pilots, scientists, aerospace engineers or
other competent witnesses in the hundreds of cases supplied to the
project. This was personally confirmed to me and to NICAP Assistant
Director Gordon Lore by Coordinator Low and several times by Dr.
David Saunders, project scientist in charge of the computer section.

In a number of press interviews with Dr. Condon (copies enclosed),
it appeared that he was strongly biased and was rejecting evidence
of UFO reality. Some of the quoted statements included: "My attitude right now is that there's nothing to it... but I'm not supposed to reach a conclusion for another year." Elmira N.Y. Star
Gazette, January 26, 1967. "This is like being chief of a fire department that only answers false alarms... The whole business is
crazy." Sydney, Australia, Sun-Herald, November 26, 1967. "...There
would be no sense in our checking into routine reports." Rocky
Mountain News, October 8, 1966. "It is highly improbable that they

A privately-supported fact-finding body serving the national public interest COPY LBJ LIBRARY

COPY LBJ LIBRARY

A four-page letter from Donald Keyhoe to President Johnson expressing his grave concern
over the Colorado Projects' handling of their UFO investigation. (Courtesy Lyndon Baines
Johnson Presidential Library)

(UFOs) exist." Denver Post, October 8, 1966.

In September, 1967, NICAP ceased transmitting UFO reports to the Project after we learned there was a split, with Dr. Condon and Mr. Low evidently preparing for a negative conclusion, and the majority of the scientists, including Dr. David Saunders and Dr. Norman Levine, strongly opposed. In a visit to NICAP headquarters, Mr. Low admitted the project split. In the presence of Assistant Director Lore and myself, he also confirmed that Dr. Condon had made no field investigations or questioned witnesses and added, "If he were to write a report today, the conclusion would be negative."

On November 14, I sent a list of questions to Dr. Condon and Mr. Low, stating we would resume transmissions if the answers were satisfactory. The questions (copies enclosed) asked if Dr. Condon intended to make any investigations, if he had examined any of the hundreds of NICAP submitted reports, and if the project was actually objective and impartial, as stated by university officials, the Air Force and Dr. Condon himself.

Both Dr. Condon and Coordinator Low refused to answer the questions.

Shortly after this, I was privately given a copy of proposals made by Mr. Low to University Vice President Thurston Manning and other university faculty members, discussing whether to accept the Air Force offer and if so how to handle the investigation.

In this proposal memorandum by Mr. Low (copy enclosed), he summed up some of the faculty members' views as follows:

"In order to undertake such a project one has to approach it objectively. That is, one has to admit the possibility that such things as UFOs exist. It is not respectable to give serious consideration to such a possibility. Believers, in other words, remain outcasts.... Our study would be conducted almost exclusively by nonbelievers, who, although they couldn't possibly prove a negative result, could and probably would add an impressive body of evidence that there is no reality to the observations. The trick would be, I think, to describe the project so that, to the public, it would appear a totally objective study but, to the scientific community, would present the image of a group of nonbelievers trying their best to be objective but having an almost zero expectation of finding a saucer. One way to do this would be to stress investigation, not of the physical phenomena, but rather of the people who do the observing.... If the emphasis were put here... I think the scientific community would quickly get the message."

In the Air Force contract, signed by Vice President Manning and Dr. Condon, an entirely different set of Colorado University proposals was incorporated, including this statement:

"The work will be conducted under conditions of strictest objectivity by investigators who, as carefully as can be determined, have
no predilections or preconceived positions on the UFO question.
This is essential if the public, the Congress, the Executive and
the scientific community are to have confidence in the study..."

At the request of Dr. David Saunders, we permitted our subcommittees
to continue field-team cooperation, though we transmitted no further
reports. Dr. Saunders explained that a majority group of project
scientists still hoped to persuade Dr. Condon to take a different
approach and examine all the serious evidence.

Some time later, a copy of the Low proposals was given to Dr. James
E. McDonald, a University of Arizona atmospheric physicist who has
carried out an extensive single-handed UFO investigation under a
university grant.

Early in February, 1968, Dr. Condon and Mr. Low learned of this.
Dr. Condon summarily discharged Drs. Saunders and Levine, who were
chiefly involved in giving McDonald the document. In a press release, Dr. Condon stated the cause was "incompetence." The project
administrative secretary, Mrs. Mary Louise Armstrong, resigned in
disapproval of the firings and the handling of the project. Dr.
Condon wrote McDonald and the President of the University of Arizona and
demanded return of what he called "stolen" papers, but McDonald
refused.

Shortly afterward, information about the firings, NICAP'S role, and
the Low proposals was given to author John Fuller for an article in
LOOK Magazine (copy enclosed). The article includes a box statement
by me as to our long cooperation and the reasons for our final break
with the Project.

We sincerely regret the failure of the project, to which so many
people looked for a fully impartial UFO evaluation, if not final
answers. We fear that public loss of confidence may make the
project's report, being prepared by Mr. Low, of little value.

The most serious effect, we believe, is that Congress, the press
and public may refuse belief in any further investigation arranged
by the Defense Department, although we know of no evidence that
the Air Force was aware of the negative proposals.

We respectfully suggest, Mr. President, that the void resulting
from the Colorado fiasco be filled as soon as possible by the
creation of a commission of carefully selected scientists, selected
by you but completely independent of any military or civilian agency
of the Government. From reactions to the Colorado situation, stated
to us by NICAP advisers and outside scientists, we feel sure that
scientists of high stature are available, with neither negative nor
positive conclusions but convinced that the UFO situation is a problem serious enough to require total investigation.

We suggest that all major decisions of such a commission be by majority vote, that the chosen men be recognized authorities on astronomy, aerospace operations and planning, electronics, and other fields related to UFO investigations.

More detailed suggestions will be forwarded to you as soon as we study the opinions of our Board of Governors, advisers and outside scientists. Meantime, NICAP offers any such created commission its full cooperation, including our massive evidence, and the assistance of our field investigators.

Sincerely yours,

Maj. Donald E. Keyhoe, USMC, Ret.
Director of NICAP

Office Memorandum • UNITED STATES GOVERNMENT

TO : DIRECTOR, FBI   DATE: 8/2/54

FROM : SAC, WFO (62-0)

SUBJECT: Mrs. FRANCES SWAN
MISCELLANEOUS - INFORMATION CONCERNING

This interview is predicated upon a telephone call received by
SAC L. L. LAUGHLIN on 7/29/54 from ████████████████████ Bureau of
Aeronautics, U. S. Navy Department.

On the same date ███████████ was interviewed in Room 2912, Main
Navy Building. Also present during the interview was ███████████████
███████████████████ and ███████████ furnished the following information:

They advised that the Office of Naval Intelligence had forwarded
a file to the Bureau of Aeronautics with enclosures which had been received
from ██. According to ████████ and ████████████████████ resided near ███████████████ who
had been receiving messages through thought transmission. ████████ approached
████████ and advised him that "flying saucers" were here to help mankind.
Information received by ████████ indicated that ████████ became interested
in the messages received by ████████ and felt that the matter should be
investigated by the Government.

████████ advised that ████████ wrote to Admiral ESPEY, Director
of Naval Intelligence, on 6/1/54 enclosing some of the messages received
by ████████ Receiving no reply to his original communication, ████████
again wrote ONI on 6/7/54. ████████ advised that the first letter that
████████ wrote to ONI contained information that ████████ was receiving
messages through thought control from "outer space" and wrote them down
as she received them. The letter, according to ████████, stated that ████████
would write without any effort on her part and would write continuously
for four or five hours at a time without getting tired. He stated that ONI
had in their possession the transmissions or messages that had been received
by ████████

████████ stated that ONI had advised that in the absence of any
definite evidence of conversations, they would do nothing in the matter.
He also stated that the Bureau of Aeronautics took no official action in

CAG:jfs

REGORDED - 150

INDEXED - 150

2 - Boston

EX - 109

12 AUG 1954

63- 85,894- 346

8-70

(Courtesy U.S. Government)

in the matter. ▓▓▓▓ was questioned concerning the position that the Bureau of Aeronautics had taken and he remarked that he did not believe that this was pertinent. After further questioning, he subsequently stated that the Bureau of Aeronautics was of the belief that this was a matter for ONI. **b7C**

▓▓▓▓ stated that he "unofficially" became interested in the matter and at the invitation of ▓▓▓▓▓▓ he went to ▓▓▓▓▓▓ where he spent 7/24,25,26/54 in the residence of ▓▓▓▓▓▓ **b7C** ▓▓▓▓ stated that he informed Admiral SAUCER, his superior in the Bureau of Aeronautics, that he was going to visit ▓▓▓▓▓▓

▓▓▓▓ stated that inasmuch as ▓▓▓▓ had received no response from the Government concerning this matter, he began reading books on flying saucers. ▓▓▓▓ advised that during the time that he was a house **b7C** guest of ▓▓▓▓▓▓ there was also present ▓▓▓▓▓▓ who was also interested in flying saucers. ▓▓▓▓ stated that ▓▓▓ was at ▓▓▓▓ residence with his family and was there in an unofficial capacity.

▓▓▓▓ advised that during his stay, he and ▓▓▓ had various interviews with ▓▓▓▓ and had had contact with the "outer space" through ▓▓▓▓. During the interview with ▓▓▓▓ and the contact with "outer space," ▓▓▓▓ stated that they sat in a group and he observed ▓▓▓ writing messages that she was receiving from someone in "outer space." According to ▓▓▓▓ informed him that the people from "outer space" could use her eyes and ears to see and hear. According to ▓▓▓ this is **b7C** accomplished by the use of a mechanical device and all conversations are recorded by the people in "outer space." ▓▓▓▓ indicated as an example as to how messages were relayed, he stated that he asked ▓▓▓▓ a question which she was to relay to the people in "outer space" and before she had time to relay the question, she began writing the answer down to his question on paper.

▓▓▓▓ stated that ▓▓▓ informed him that whenever she was to have contact with the people in "outer space," she would get a buzzing sound in her left ear to indicate that they were "on the line." ▓▓▓▓ stated that ▓▓▓▓ complained to the people in "outer space" that this buzzing sound gets very annoying and painful to her ear. She also **b7C** stated that the messages had been coming since May 27, 1954, and would come at all times of the night and consequently she was losing a great deal of sleep. According to ▓▓▓▓▓▓ arranged a schedule with the people in "outer space" so that the messages would not interfere with her sleep. ▓▓▓▓ advised that a schedule was arranged between ▓▓▓ and the people in "outer space" that she would receive messages on the following schedule: 8:00 in the morning, 12 noon, 6:00 in the evening, every day of the week.

       stated that ▓▓▓▓▓▓▓▓▓▓▓▓▓▓▓, and ▓▓▓▓
▓▓▓▓▓, had also heard the buzzing sound in their ears, but have
not been able to receive transmissions or messages. ▓▓▓▓ stated that the **b7c**
transmissions related to flying saucers, location and why they were here,
life on other planets, and life in the hereafter, and prophesies in the Bible.
▓▓▓▓ advised that ▓▓▓▓▓ could contact people in "outer space" by mental
thought control.

      According to ▓▓▓▓▓▓▓▓ stated that there were two space
ships from which she had been receiving messages. They were described as
150 miles wide, 200 miles in length, and 100 miles in depth. ▓▓▓▓ stated
that these ships are designated as M-4 and L-11 and they also contain mother
ships which measure approximately 150 to 200 feet in length. ▓▓▓▓ related
that ▓▓▓ had informed him that there were approximately 5,000 of these
mother ships. He stated that "AFFA" is the Manager or the Commander of the
ship M-4 which is from the planet Uranus and "PONNAR" is the Manager or the
Commander of the ship L-11 which is from the planet Hatann. ▓▓▓▓ related **b7c**
that ▓▓▓▓ stated that these contacts with "AFFA" and "PONNAR" were for
the purpose of protecting our own earth from destruction caused by the
explosion of the atom bomb, hydrogen bomb, and wars of various kinds which
they, "AFFA" and "PONNAR," say disrupt the magnetic field of force which
surrounds the earth. ▓▓▓▓ stated that ▓▓▓▓ also related that contact
was made for the purpose of protecting the whole universe because if the
"fault lines" break or go to pieces, it would effect the entire universe.
According to ▓▓▓▓▓▓▓▓▓stated, "AFFA" and "PONNAR" are presently
working in the area of the Pacific Ocean repairing "fault lines" which are
in danger of breaking.

      ▓▓▓▓ stated that both he and ▓▓▓▓ were looking for proof and
they wanted to know whether they could contact the man from "outer space."
According to ▓▓▓▓▓ advised that he and ▓▓▓▓ could make contact in
"outer space" on any frequency provided they informed her first of the
frequency that they were to use so that she could advise the people in
"outer space." ▓▓▓▓ stated that in connection with his contacting **b7c**
"outer space," he could make no commitment as he did not know how far
the Navy would go. He advised, however, that ▓▓▓▓ stated that he would
try to make contact with "outer space" on Sunday, August 1, 1954, and was
going to use a high frequency. ▓▓▓▓ stated that to make sure that contact was made, ▓▓▓▓ advised that the ship from "outer space" would
come within 100 miles of ▓▓▓▓▓▓▓, so that ▓▓▓▓ would have no
difficulty in making his contact.

      ▓▓▓▓ stated that ▓▓▓▓▓▓▓ wanted to know if physical **b7c**
contact could be had with the people in "outer space." ▓▓▓▓ advised ▓▓▓▓
and ▓▓▓▓ that the people in "outer space" wanted to know if they could
provide them protection and that if physical contact were to be made, they
would appear in a force which would consist of 5,000 "bells" or "flying saucers."

According to ████████ these "bells" or "flying saucers" would appear
over many nations of the world during the latter part of August 1954, and
would come close enough to the earth so that they could be seen by man   b7c
and that they in turn would be able to see people on the street.

████████ stated that ████████████ wrote a letter to MARGARET
CHASE SMITH, Senator from Maine, concerning this information, who forwarded
the information to the Secretary of Defense and copies were sent to the   b7c
Army, Navy, and Air Force. According to ████████████ also wrote a
letter to the President of the United States.

████████ stated that none of the persons involved in this matter were
interested in publicity. He stated that he would be willing to assist the   b7c
Bureau in the investigation of this matter if the Bureau desired, inasmuch
as he believed ████████ and ████████████ had confidence in him.

████ described ████████████ as being of middle-class circumstances, having a very modest home with furniture below middle-class. He
stated that she has ████████████████████████████████   b7c
He considered her to be a ████████████████████ person, ██████████████████
██████████, and one who has studied ████████████

The above information is being made available to the Office of
Special Investigations, United States Air Force, and no further action is
being taken by this office.

DEPARTMENT OF DEFENSE
OFFICE OF PUBLIC INFORMATION
WASHINGTON 25, D. C.

26 January 1953

Henry Holt & Company
383 Madison Avenue
New York 17, N.Y.

Dear Sirs:

This will acknowledge your letter of recent date regarding a proposed book on "flying saucers" by Major Donald E. Keyhoe, U. S. Marine Corps, retired.

We in the Air Force recognize Major Keyhoe as a responsible, accurate reporter. His long association and cooperation with the Air Force, in our study of unidentified flying objects, qualifies him as a leading civilian authority on this investigation.

All the sighting reports and other information he listed have been cleared and made available to Major Keyhoe from Air Technical Intelligence records, at his request.

The Air Force, and its investigating agency, "Project Bluebook," are aware of Major Keyhoe's conclusion that the "Flying Saucers" are from another planet. The Air Force has never denied that this possibility exists. Some of the personnel believe that there may be some strange natural phenomena completely unknown to us, but that if the apparently controlled maneuvers reported by many competent observers are correct, then the only remaining explanation is the interplanetary answer.

Very Truly Yours

Albert N. Chop
Air Force Press Desk

Notes

INTRODUCTION

1. The Robertson Panel will be covered in chapter 1.

2. The relationship between Nixon and Gleason and their mutual UFO interest will be discussed in chapter 5.

3. Taken from a Wikipedia note under the heading of "Estimate of the Situation."

4. There is a description with the dates *The Estimate of the Situation* was written. Col. William Coleman states it was 1949, and in the McDonald-Hynek exchange, Hynek said it was 1947. 1949 is most certainly the proper date since Project Sign did not start operations until January 1948.

5. The remake of *UFOs: Past, Present, and Future* was released in 1976 as *It Has Begun*. The remake included the AFFA story and a lengthy piece on cattle mutilations.

6. The number of individuals doing legitimate research into this subject is large and growing. In writing this book, I have cited the work of a limited number of individuals whom I feel are eminently qualified because of their education, background, and the hours they have spent in dedicated research into this

phenomenon. The exclusion of citing the work of others should not be interpreted as a lack of confidence in their respective work. I have also noted a number of documents that I feel are worthy of inclusion. Many of these documents are official and have been obtained through archival searches or through the FOIA. However, there are some documents that have been leaked from unofficial sources and thus have created various levels of controversy. Of this group I have only included documents that carry a high level of authenticity rating by those researching these documents. These include the Eisenhower Briefing Document, the Truman-Forrestal Memo, the Cutler-Twining Memo, SOM1-01, and the so-called Burned Memo.

CHAPTER 1: THE BEGINNING

1. UFO debunkers often invoke Occam's razor in their debates. This principle in essence says that the simplest answer is usually the correct answer. With the current exploration of space and the number of new suns increasing exponentially, even the most conservative of scientists now believe intelligent life is abundant in the universe. Since the Earth is a very young planet even in our own galactic neighborhood, it is unreasonable to think that there are civilizations thousands, millions, or even a billion years more advanced than the inhabitants of Earth. Civilizations that have laws of physics beyond our comprehension, civilizations that want to observe and study life on this emerging young planet. Thus, using Occam's razor to explain a strange sighting that defies known physics, an extraterrestrial presence would be the simple explanation.

2. Throughout this work various documents will be referenced or cited and in some cases shown in the Appendix. In all

cases, these documents are part of the authenticating efforts of Dr. Robert Wood and Ryan Wood and are taken from their Web site www.majesticdocuments.com. An in-depth study of the MJ-12 documents is available in the well-researched book *Top Secret/Majic* written by nuclear physicist Stanton T. Friedman. The MJ-12 documents will be outlined in chapter 2 of this book.

3. The Truman signature on the Truman-Forrestal Memo has created great controversy. It appears to be a cut-and-paste of a Truman signature from another document, and in fact after much research that appears to be the case. This has led critics of the document and other MJ-12 documents (discussed in chapter 2) to claim the document was bogus. The facts are that this document was a five-year-old copy, no doubt from CIA files that were included with a briefing document on the Roswell UFO incident given to President-elect Eisenhower before he took office. At that time, Walter Bedell Smith was director of the CIA. Having served as Eisenhower's chief of staff, he knew Eisenhower well and knew that he would want to see a presidential signature on the document. It is most likely that the cut-and-paste was actually done by the CIA to assure Eisenhower that the document was authored by Truman.

4. It is widely believed that two saucers crashed in the same event; the remains from the Foster ranch at Corona were primarily debris. Another craft discussed later in the chapter appears to have crashed on the Plains of San Agustin and was relatively intact. In their research, Don Schmitt and Tom Carey believe there was only one saucer that exploded over the Foster ranch, then a pod or core of the craft flew on and crashed much closer to Roswell, and this was where the bodies were located. Although there is disagreement on the

number of craft, there is no disagreement that the craft were extraterrestrial in origin.

5. Jesse Marcel had been an amateur (ham) radio operator since his early years and, as a child, built a radio receiver in his home. With his knowledge of radio equipment, it's ridiculous to think he didn't recognize radio equipment, equipment that still used vacuum tubes, and was used in Project Mogul.

6. General Dubose passed away prior to the 1994 Air Force report on Roswell. However, before his death, he signed an affidavit confirming the call from General McMullen. He also videotaped an interview describing the incident.

7. It is important to consider that in the precomputer military, historically nothing happened until paperwork was generated. If the project was classified, the paperwork would also be classified at the proper classification level. Once the project or event is declassified, the paperwork is also declassified. If the Roswell incident was in fact a Project Mogul matter, there would be paperwork authorizing the cleanup. Since the project is now declassified, the paperwork would also be declassified. One official document stating that cleanup of Project Mogul debris from the Corona, New Mexico, ranch was authorized would put an end to the controversy, but none exists, even in the over thousand-page official Air Force report on the Roswell incident. UFO debunkers like to say that "absence of evidence is evidence of absence." In cases where the government/military take a position that seems at odds with the facts as they are known, and they offer no official documentation that directly supports their position, one must assume that *absence of evidence is evidence of a cover-up.*

8. Using the planet Venus to explain so many UFO sightings has been grossly overused for years. Venus, as well as other planets, can be very bright at various times and from time to time can, no doubt, cause a single individual to be so startled as to think they are seeing something strange. In this case there are multiple witnesses and their accounts don't favor Venus as an explanation.

9. In rereading Keyhoe's book, I was struck with how advanced his thinking was from his 1949 research as noted in his summary. He felt that Earth had been under extraterrestrial observation for at least two centuries. He also attributed the increase in saucer sightings in the late 1940s to our atomic explosions and our rocket tests. This is a theory that is widely accepted by today's UFOlogists.

10. In the 2012 book, *UFOs and Government*, Dr. Possony, an intelligence adviser to the Air Force, is said to have run a "special study group" inside General Stamford's (Air Force Director of Intelligence) office and was involved with UFO study. Possony felt that UFOs were real and very solid craft that had been developed by the Soviets to carry their yet-to-be-developed atomic weapons. Possony requested permission for him and his staff to travel to Europe to investigate his theory. He returned convinced that UFOs had no connection to Soviet development and began to embrace the ET hypothesis.

11. On July 24, 1948, Eastern Airlines Flight 576 was near Montgomery, Alabama. At the controls were two pilots that Eastern considered their best, Capt. C. S. Chiles and John B. Whitted. At a little before 3:00 A.M. they spotted an object coming at them. As it got closer it appeared to be cigar- or rocket-shaped with no wings or tail. It appeared to

be about a hundred feet long with a body diameter about the size of three B-29s. As it streaked past, both pilots reported windows or portholes along the fuselage. When they landed the shaken men filed a report and within short order were interviewed separately by Air Force investigators from Project Sign. The drawings they each made are remarkably similar.

12. *UFOs and Government: An Historical Inquiry,* page 81.

13. Credit for information on the disarray in the Pentagon and the feelings of the New Mexico scientists goes to Swords and Powell's excellent work, *UFOs and Government.*

CHAPTER 2: FIRST CONTACT?

1. Overlord was the Battle of Normandy and the invasion of Western Europe.

2. BBC News on released UFO files, September 5, 2010.

3. Dr. Bush was a world-renowned scientist who is considered by many to be responsible for developing the compartmentalization of classified data that is still the backbone of government security today. The term "need to know" in classified work means that no matter what security classification you may possess, top secret and above, if you don't have the need to know you don't have access to that information. This includes the president of the United States.

4. Adm. Roscoe Hillenkoetter, early director of the CIA, presents a problem to the Majestic 12 issue since he is shown as an original member. If we are to believe that MJ-12 was a real group authorized by President Truman to study the UFO issue (as I do), Hillenkoetter's actions in the 1950s, his friendship with Donald Keyhoe, his public advocating for the Air Force to release UFO-related information, and his work with NICAP all conflict with his inclusion in the original MJ-12

group. One possible hypothesis is that he was a maverick within the group who advocated disclosure of an alien presence and was removed from the group. His security clearance wouldn't allow him to divulge what he knew, but he became active in the support of Keyhoe and NICAP's efforts to gain release of this information. This, of course, is conjecture and needs more research.

5. The letter from Truman to Twining directing him to go to New Mexico is an emulation of a letter to Gen. Albert C. Wedemeyer directing him to go to China. (See *Flying Saucers and Science*, by Stanton Friedman, page 277.)

6. I am in concert with Dr. Alexander on many of his views. My major disagreement is his disbelief in a highly classified control group handling the UFO issue. In the past few weeks it has been rumored that he has new information that such a group does exist. That is being researched at present.

7. Information on Dr. Milton Torres's 1957 UFO encounter was taken from his address at the 2009 X-Conference held at the National Press Club in Washington, D.C.

8. Today the government's direct and indirect involvement in scientific research has expanded exponentially.

CHAPTER 3: THE GREAT CONSPIRACY THEORY

1. This information was gained in 1986 after UFO researcher Stanton Friedman received approval from Menzel's wife to review his unpublished autobiography. Friedman had to get written permission from the chairman of the astronomy department and head of the Smithsonian Observatory to access his files.

CHAPTER 4: LEADER FOR SPACE

1. Information on Lyndon Johnson and the space race was taken from an article by Alan Wasser published in *The Space Review*, June 20, 2005.

2. *Firestorm: Dr. James E. McDonald's Fight for UFO Science*, Wild Flower Press, P.O. Box 1429, Columbus, NC 28722. www.5thworld.com/Firestorm or Ann Druffel at anndruffel@aol.com.

3. From Dr. Jacques Vallée's foreword in *Firestorm: Dr. James E. McDonald's Fight for UFO Science*.

4. In Swords and Powell's *UFOs and Government*, page 215, note 50, states that the Center for UFO Studies in the early 2000s received letters and a draft manuscript from Hubert Humphrey's science adviser, Frank Rand, describing a "private" study done for President Johnson. Rand, along with Lockheed Skunk Works's Kelly Johnson and other noted scientists wrote the study. Rand stated Kelly Johnson and one other noted scientist were absolutely convinced the UFOs existed as technological devices.

5. There are some exceptions to this, such as the Childs-Whitted Eastern Airlines 1948 sighting.

6. The Lunar Lander is used as an example only and is not a reasonable candidate as an explanation for the event.

7. The subject of abductions is not the focus of this book but it is such an important component of the phenomenon that it will be discussed in the last chapter.

8. The recount of events at Vandenberg is an edited version of Dr. Jacobs's own words taken from his essay posted on the Web site wikia.com.

9. Johnson's letter to the chairman of the Federal Power Commission is a matter of public record and is noted in a number

of books and publications so no single source is cited in this book.

10. Information for this incident was taken from the book *Faded Giant*, by Robert Salas and James Klotz, as well as the author's discussions with Robert Salas.

11. The Rendlesham Forrest–Bentwaters AFB UFO incident is one of the most important UFO events in modern history and on the level of Roswell because it happened in 1980. It is well documented and so many witnesses are still living. I chose not to go into great detail about the event in this book for three main reasons. First, it has been, and continues to be, well documented in books and videos. Second, as far as we know it didn't involve President Carter, and third, it is simply too long and complicated to have this book do it justice. This in no way is meant to belittle it, and I highly recommend anyone not knowledgeable of this important event to study it. Former MoD officer Nick Pope, who contributed to this book, has a new book out, *Encounter in Rendlesham Forest*, with coauthors Jo Burroughs and Jim Penniston, two MPs involved in the event.

12. I received notification from the Johnson library in Austin, Texas, dated August 28, 2013, stating that my requests would be "nonresponsive."

CHAPTER 5: PLAN FOR DISCLOSURE

1. The Robertson Panel was a group of scientists established by the CIA to study the UFO problem and find ways to reduce public concern. The panel is covered in chapter 1.

2. The Colorado Project and the resulting Condon Report will be discussed in detail in chapter 7.

CHAPTER 6: SWAMP GAS

1. This statement and other information on the sightings were taken from the *Detroit News* story "The Great Michigan UFO Chase," by Vivian M. Baulch.

2. Projects Sign, Grudge, and Blue Book were Air Force official investigations into the UFO phenomenon and evolved into a public-relations program to steer public interest in the phenomenon away from the subject rather than an investigative program. They were run by midlevel officers who were being given guidance from their superiors. By all accounts, these people were not in the small loop of inside knowledge about what a very few insiders knew about the issue, information that was never in jeopardy of being exposed.

3. When Condon was first announced to head the Colorado Project, it received great media coverage. At that point Condon made a number of remarks to indicate his total objectivity with the subject. He stated that he did not exclude the possibility that some UFOs contained outer-space visitors but would need incontrovertible evidence to hold such a position. He went on to say that he did not consider ETH proponents nuts. We now know that such remarks at the very beginning of the project were merely to soothe the number of noted people like Dr. James E. McDonald who were concerned about his objectivity.

4. Consideration should be given to this statement on the number of extraterrestrial races visiting Earth in the Air Force textbook and Kathleen Marden's discussion of the number of races of aliens involved in abductions in chapter 13, The Abduction Phenomenon.

5. Wood unfortunately had to drop out late, as his superiors

thought it unwise to get involved in any form of congressional hearings or even a symposium.

6. The Low memorandum written by Robert Low, Condon's assistant, to the dean of the University of Colorado, James Archer, stated that the Condon Committee was to pretend to research the UFO question with an anticipated negative outcome.

7. This quote and much of the data in this segment are taken from a thesis written by Paul E. McCarthy for his doctoral degree at the University of Hawaii and published by the Sign Historical Group. Other information was from the Project 1947/Sign Historical Group Web site.

8. Gerald R. Ford Presidential Library, collection title: White House Central Files, subject file, box number 2, folder title: OS 5 General.

9. After receiving these documents from the Ford library and including them in my manuscript, I contacted Mr. Rumsfeld through his foundation's Web site to ask for clarification on these letters and his general view of the UFO issue. His secretary responded that Mr. Rumsfeld would consider my request if I would forward the chapter in question. I sent the chapter along with a cover letter. His secretary responded that she printed the e-mailed documents and put them on Mr. Rumsfeld's desk. I have not received a reply.

10. When campaigning for president, George W. Bush was asked about UFOs and his reply was "Go ask Cheney."

11. Unfortunately the tower radar was down for repair.

12. This was most likely Lt. Col. Olin Mooy who filed a confidential report to Washington.

CHAPTER 7: PRESIDENTIAL SIGHTING AND NASA

1. The CRS Web site states that it serves only Congress; there is no mention that it serves any other branch of government.

2. These pictures sound remarkably like the Russian film footage of a crashed disc with Russian military looking over the craft. The film is on many YouTube sites and is probably a hoax.

3. Project Moondust. USAF operation to locate and recover foreign space material.

4. If these collection facilities exist, as Marchetti says they do, then they certainly don't have to limit their operation to the recovery of UFOs but also top-secret military hardware. As such, one of the units could very well account for the CH-47 Chinooks in the Cash-Landrum incident.

CHAPTER 8: JAL FLIGHT 1628–THE HUDSON VALLEY SIGHTINGS

1. Information on then Governor Reagan's UFO sighting was condensed from a number of Internet reports (including www.openminds.tv) that the author feels are creditable sources of information.

2. The O'Hare UFO sighting is a prime example of this unorthodox FAA position and will be discussed in chapter 13.

3. The most complete report on this spectacular UFO event was researched and written by Dr. Bruce Maccabee and originally published in the *International UFO Reporter,* March/April 1987, and published by the Center for UFO Studies. The title of the report is *The Fantastic Flight of JAL 1628.*

4. A legitimate argument could be made that alien abductions are less than benign, but apart from the mental anguish imposed on the experiencers, in many cases the abductors have

shown some level of compassion toward the abductees. There are also reports of pilots being lost in pursuit of UFOs while the Air Force orders were to "shoot them down" in the 1950s that was quickly rescinded.

5. To be discussed in a later chapter.

CHAPTER 9: THE BELGIAN WAVE AND STS-48

1. Many of General de Brouwer's comments and recollections are taken from investigative journalist Leslie Kean's excellent book *UFOs: Generals, Pilots, and Government Officials Go on the Record*. It is a well-researched book that is highly recommended by this author.

2. I assume General de Brouwer is referring to the large cooling towers at nuclear power plants.

CHAPTER 10: THE ROCKEFELLER INITIATIVE

1. Various YouTube sites of Bill Clinton's visit to Belfast, Northern Ireland, November 1995.

2. At the time of the Rockefeller Initiative, both Rockefeller and Bigelow were outside the loop of inside knowledge of UFO issues. More recently, Bigelow has become more deeply involved in UFO issues and may have been brought into the loop of UFO insiders, although that is speculation. Bigelow will be discussed in more detail in chapter 12.

3. See discussion of this case in chapter 7.

CHAPTER 11: STEPHENVILLE UFO AND THE CRAWFORD WHITE HOUSE

1. On the date this event occurred I, along with my wife, was spending the winter in a rented property in New Braunfels, Texas, about two hours south of Stephenville. We have children and grandchildren in New Braunfels, and spend most

winters there. I considered driving to Stephenville when the story broke because the idea for this book was just forming. I made the decision not to go for several reasons; it's a decision that I regret.

2. In the MUFON summarization the authors state that "Twice radar picked up an object flying at 1,900 to 2,100 mph. Admittedly, it could have been a coincidental radar hit . . . but in both cases the coincidence occurred when a witness saw a fast moving object in the same direction as the target painted by the radar."

3. AWACS, or E-3 Sentry, is a radar system on a Boeing 707 platform designed to detect aircraft, ships, and other vehicles, and perform communication to other platforms such as fighter aircraft. It is an assumption on the part of the researchers based on the radar data they studied that the return in question was an AWACS.

4. According to the JTCG/ME manual for flare effectiveness, the optimum deployment height is two thousand feet. With a minimum seven thousand feet air operation altitude flare deployment doesn't seem reasonable.

CHAPTER 12: THE PODESTA FACTOR

1. Taken from the FBI Web site www.fbi.gov.

CHAPTER 13: THE ABDUCTION PHENOMENON

1. Bret Oldham is an abductee who tells his story in *Children of the Greys.*

CHAPTER 14: FINAL THOUGHTS

1. Wobbling while hovering is a characteristic noted in almost all flying saucer sightings.

2. His calculations were based on 1950s science without help or knowledge from our modern space observatories.

3. Interview of Admiral Lord Hill-Norton by James Fox www .siriusdisclosure.com.

4. *Above Top Secret*, p. 183.

Bibliography

Ambrose, Stephen E. *Above Top Secret*. New York: William Morrow and Company, 1988.

—— *Eisenhower: Soldier, General of the Army, President-Elect*. New York: Simon & Schuster, 1983.

Dolan, Richard M. *UFOs and the National Security State*. Charlottesville, VA: Hampton Roads, 2002.

Druffel, Ann. *Firestorm*. Columbus, NC: Wild Flower Press, 2003.

Friedman, Stanton T. *Flying Saucers and Science*. Franklin Lakes, NJ: New Page Books, 2008.

—— *Top Secret/Majic*. New York: Marlowe, 1996.

—— *Top Secret/Majic*. New York: Da Capo Press, 2005.

Good, Timothy. *Need to Know: UFOs, the Military, and Intelligence*. New York: Pegasus Books, 2007.

Heaphey, James J. *Legerdemain*. New York: History Publishing Co, 2008.

Hellyer, P. (2005). University of Toronto. Speech, Sept. 25, 2005.

Hylton, Wil S. "The Gospel According to Jimmy." *GQ*, January 2006.

Kean, Leslie. *UFOs: Generals, Pilots, and Government Officials Go on the Record*. New York: Three Rivers Press, 2011.

Manchester, William. *American Caesar*. New York: Dell, 1979.

Marcel, Jesse. *The Roswell Legacy*. Pompton Plains, NJ: New Page Books, 2008.

Marchetti, Victor. "How the CIA" Views the UFO Phenomenon. *Second Look*, May 1997.

Marden, Kathleen, and Denise Stoner. *The Alien Abduction Files*. Pompton Plains, NJ: New Page Books, 2013.

Newman, John. *Oswald and the CIA*. New York: Carroll & Graf, 1995.

Reader's Digest. Illustrated History of WWII. New York: Reader's Digest, 1969.

Sagan, Carl. *Unidentified Flying Objects*. New York: Rand McNally, 1963.

Salas, Robert. *Faded Giant*. Charleston, SC: BookSurge Publishing, 2005.

Sturrock, Peter A. *The UFO Enigma*. New York: Warner Books, 1999.

Swords, Michael, and Robert Powell. *UFOs and Government: An Historical Inquiry*. San Antonio: Anomalist Books, 2012.

Yeager, Chuck, and Leo Janos. *Yeager*. New York: Bantam Books, 2008.

Index